MEL LAB: Experiments in Perception, Cognition, Social Psychology & Human Factors

James D. St. James
Millikin University

Walter Schneider
University of Pittsburgh

Kimberly Hinds
Psychology Software Tools

Table of Contents

Acknowledgements

The MEL Lab represents the efforts of many individuals. We, the authors, appreciate their efforts. Most of the specific experiments were written by Tom Yates and Lance Kennelty. The major system programmers on the project were Anthony Zuccolotto and Nick Bethmann (who developed the MEL system) and Jim Sueker (who developed the disk installation and editing features). Leslie Kuntz and Jim Sueker edited several versions of the task. Sue Schneider did the copy lay out. Barb and Louis Frey produced the figures. Colin McLeod provided the text, initial program, and data analysis for the Stroop experiment. The University of Pittsburgh and Millikin University have provided support and an excellent environment to develop and test these tools. We thank the undergraduate students who have dealt with early versions of the system and provided us with suggestions for improvement. We are also appreciative of the original researchers whose procedures have provided the basis for all of the enclosed experiments and in some cases for the specific material that they provided us.

0 General Information

What distinguishes the sciences from other approaches to understanding the world is a reliance on empirical research. Scientific ideas must be tested against the world to determine their value. The science of psychology seeks to understand many aspects of human and animal behavior, including the mechanisms of perception, cognition, and social interaction that underlie those behaviors. The application of that knowledge to improve the conduct of human affairs is also a goal of psychology. The MEL Lab was developed to acquaint you firsthand with many of the empirical methods used to test scientific ideas in psychology.

In support of that goal, the MEL Lab offers to you a set of experiments in many areas of psychology. Many are rightly regarded as "classics." These are experiments that have in many ways defined the field of experimental psychology, providing its general methods of research as well as interpretation of data. In this Workbook we detail the many considerations that go into the designs of these experiments, including discussions of experimental control. The logic of how to interpret the results of experiments is also stressed.

We hope that you will gain from the MEL Lab a wide base of knowledge about empirical procedures in psychology, and can use that base to develop and extend psychological knowledge. The experiments included in the MEL Lab were chosen not only for their contributions to our knowledge of psychology, but also because they have provided the field with new approaches to gaining knowledge. We hope that you will consider, as you do the experiments and read about them, how you might extend the techniques you are learning to the study of other aspects of psychology.

Additionally, we feel that you cannot truly understand an experiment unless you know what the subjects in that experiment actually experienced. The MEL Lab will give you the opportunity to participate as a subject in many of the most important experiments from the last several decades in psychology.

Because graphic presentation of data is such an important part of the reporting of experimental results, and because knowing how to interpret such graphs is a necessary tool in understanding research, this manual contains worksheets including blank graphs and data tables for most experiments. The worksheets permit you to graph both your individual data and the class averages. At the end of any experiments for which blank graphs are provided, you will see a display of your data (e.g., mean reaction time or proportion correct). Please take a few minutes to copy down those data in the data table provided and plot the points on the graph. You will also see a graph of your data on the computer screen.

We suggest that you plot your data on the blank graph provided (the one labeled "Individual Data") and compare it to the graph you will see on the screen. While it may seem unnecessary to graph the data by hand when the computer will display the graph, we have found that students become good at interpreting graphs far more quickly if they have practice in graphing data, rather than just looking at computer-generated graphs. Your instructor may require that you turn in your data graphs. If so, spread the workbook flat on the page you want to remove and gently remove the page.

The MEL Lab deliberately contains more experiments than your instructor is likely to have you complete. This was done to permit some choice and flexibility, since each instructor will take a somewhat different approach to teaching experimental methodology. Please feel free to explore the other experiments, which may provide the basis for your own research project.

Along with this workbook, you will have either two 5.25" disks or one 3.5" disk for running these experiments on IBM™ compatible personal computers, or one 3.5" disk for the Apple Macintosh™ computers. Section 0.1 shows you how to initialize the disks and Section 0.2 shows you how to run the experiments. We recommend you do not use the enclosed disks until your laboratory section has met and you have discussed how to initialize disks. At the end of the initialization process (see Section 0.1) you will be asked to make working copies of your disks. At that point you can copy the information to other format disks (e.g., 3.5") or to a hard disk. The disks you received with this Workbook contain the program to run experiments, the files that store the information for each experiment, and the files that store data when you run the experiments. Be sure to keep these disks safely stored. The 5.25" disks are especially fragile. If they are bent or the surface of the disk is dirty or scratched, the computer may not be able to read information from them. The disks are also subject to damage by magnetic fields and heat. Do not leave them in a closed car in the sunshine, or in other places where the temperature is uncontrolled. Instructions are given below for making back-up copies of the disks, so that you will have replacements if these are damaged.

The MEL Lab contains an experiment generator that permits you to implement many experiments in psychology, and to easily modify the five base paradigms outlined in Section 0.6. In addition, if your Department has a copy of the full MEL experimental authoring system, you can take advantage of its power to implement an even wider variety of experiments. The MEL system is in use by over a thousand psychological research laboratories in over twenty countries. With the MEL Lab you have access to many of the powerful research tools used in advanced psychological research. The implementing of experiments is an advanced function used late in the course with the assistance of the teaching assistant (see Section 0.6). When reading the experiments consider how you might modify the procedures for psychological research projects.

0.1 Getting started - initializing disks and making working copies

This section describes how to use the MEL Lab, and the information you will need to enter *the first time you use it*. **Read this entire section (0.1)** *before* **you run the STARTUP program.** Before you run any of the experiments you must initialize the disks and make backup copies.

The first time that you use the MEL Lab you will have to "initialize" your disks, recording some data to them for later use. This will only have to be done once. **You will need the following information, and cannot begin without it:** The *course number*, your *section number*, the *zip code of your college or university*, and your *subject number*. Your instructor will assign a random subject number to each student. Be sure you make a note of it. This number will serve to identify your data and make it possible for the instructor to keep records of which students have completed the assignments. A random number is assigned so other students will not be able to identify your data unless you tell them your number. **You will also need to have blank disk(s) for making backup copies of your disks.** Your instructor will give you information about the kind of disks needed. If you are working on the IBM, you will need either two 5.25", double-sided, double density (360K) floppy disks, one 3.5" disk, or one 5.25" high-density (1.2 megabyte) floppy disk. If you are working on the Apple Macintosh, you will need either one 3.5", double-sided, double-density (800K) disk, or one 3.5", double-sided, high-density (1.4 megabyte) disk. Most book stores will sell these. **THESE DISKS MUST BE BLANK AND ALREADY FORMATTED** (see your DOS Manual or Macintosh Owner's Guide).

To begin, "boot" the computer. If you are working on the IBM, set the drive designation to drive A: or drive B: (this depends on the configuration of the computer). Your instructor will show you how to complete these steps. Once the computer is booted and the correct disk drive chosen, simply insert Disk 1 into that drive and type **STARTUP**. (This does not have to be in capital letters.) On the Macintosh computers, insert Disk #1 and double-click on the **STARTUP** icon. A few seconds later, you will see a 'Welcome' screen followed by two screens of instructions. Next, you will see a screen like the one illustrated in Figure 0.1.1. This is the diskette initialization screen. It contains information about how to initialize your diskette. Simply follow the instructions, answering each of the questions you are asked. We recommend that you fill in the information in Figure 0.1.1 before you try to initialize your disks.

If during initialization you make a mistake as you are entering this information, you can use the backarrow and DELete keys to correct mistakes until you press <Enter> to record the information. If you discover a mistake after hitting <Enter>, you will have a chance later to correct it. When all of the information is entered, you will be

Figure 0.1.1 Diskette initialization screen

Initializing Student Disk

Please answer each of the following questions as they appear.

   Use the [Backspace] and [Delete] keys to edit an answer. Press the
[Enter] key after typing in your answer. You will have a chance to correct
any mistakes after all questions have been answered.
   You can press the [Esc] key at any time to quit the program without
saving your information.

Please enter the following information:
       Your first name: _____
       Your last name: _____
       Your sex (M/F): _
       Your age: ___
       The course number (digits only): ___
       The section number (digits only). Hit <Enter> if only 1 section: ____
       The zip code of your college or university: _____
       Your subject number (digits only, provided by your instructor): ___

                 Confirm information as correct? (Y/N):

---

asked to confirm the information as correct. If you answer "Y" the program will initialize your disk. If you answer
"N" you will be asked to re-enter the information. When the information is correct, you will see the screen shown
in Figure 0.1.2, indicating that initialization is complete. If you discover an error after this point, ask your instructor
for information on how to re-initialize the disk. (Re-initialization can only be done once.)

Figure 0.1.2 Screen when initialization is complete

YOUR DISK IS NOW INITIALIZED

Your disk is now initialized. You should not initialize it
again unless the information you have entered is incorrect.

You have 1 more chance to change your initialization information.

To run an experiment in the MEL Experiment Library, type
"EXPERIMENT" at the DOS prompt and press the [Enter] key.

Press the [Esc] key to continue.

Once disk initialization is complete, will be asked to make backup copies of the disks. It is best to make working copies and save the originals. Instructions for doing so will be displayed on the screen. You can make working copies at this point or later. You will need blank disks in order to make working copies. **After you have completed making the disks be sure that you write your name both on the distributional disks and the working copies.** This will facilitate getting the disks back to you if you turn them in to the instructor or leave them in a public computer laboratory.

0.2 Starting MEL Lab

After the installation is complete you can run the MEL Lab exercises. For the IBM, insert disk 1 into the disk drive (e.g., A for the first floppy). Then type:

A:EXPERIMENT<Enter>

For the Macintosh, insert Disk #1 and **double-click on the EXPERIMENT icon.**

First you will see the opening display. Next, you will see the screen shown in Figure 0.2.1. This is the topic selection screen, and allows you to tell the computer the topic area of the experiment you wish to perform. The index to the workbook shows you which topic area is relevant for each experiment. Simply hit the up- and down-arrow keys (to the right of the letters on the keyboard) to select the topic area of your experiment, then hit <Enter>. On the Macintosh, you can also use the mouse to select the topic.

Once you have selected a topic area, an experiment selection screen (illustrated in Figure 0.2.2) will appear, with a list of the experiments in that topic area. Again, use the arrow keys to select an experiment, then hit <Enter>. Note that the list of experiments includes an approximate running time for each experiment. The times needed to complete the experiments varies, so be sure you have enough time to complete your assignment before beginning. You can stop before you finish, but you will then have to do the entire experiment over. After you finish each experiment, a check-mark will be displayed beside that experiment name the next time you start the program, to help you keep track of which ones you have completed. When you have finished all of the experiments in a topic area, the topic selection screen will show a check-mark by that topic.

After you have selected an experiment, you will be given instructions about changing diskettes (if you are using 5.25" diskettes). Insert a different disk as instructed. Next you will see the "mode selection" screen shown in Figure 0.2.3.

Figure 0.2.1 Topic selection screen

MEL EXPERIMENT LIBRARY
Use the arrow keys to move to an item, ◄─┘ to select, or [Esc] to exit

1.0 Experiments in Perception
2.0 Experiments in Cognition
3.0 Experiments in Social Psychology
4.0 Experiments in Human Factors
5.0 Appendix/Other

You may run experiments in the MEL Lab in either of two modes--*normal* or *demonstration*. Use Normal mode for all class assignments, unless you are instructed otherwise. In this mode, you will serve as a subject in the entire experiment, and the data will be stored on the disk. The estimated running times displayed on the experiment selection screen refer to the time to complete experiments in this mode. Demonstration mode should be used only to review an experiment (for example, to refresh your memory for the details when writing it up for class) or to preview experiments. In this mode the experiment lasts only about 5 minutes, and no data are collected.

Figure 0.2.2 Experiment selection screen

1.0 EXPERIMENTS IN PERCEPTION
Use the arrow keys to move to an item, ←⏎ to select, or [Esc] to exit

1.1 **The Blind Spot in Vision (20 min.)**
1.2 **The Duration of the Icon (20 min.)**
1.3 **Signal Detection (45 min.)**
1.4 **Perceptual Matching (12 min.)**
1.5 **Selective Attention and Response Competition (16 min.)**
1.6 **Mental Rotation of Images (12 min.)**

Figure 0.2.3 Screen for selecting experimental mode

1.1 The Blind Spot in Vision

Select the mode for running this experiment.

To select **NORMAL** mode type "N".
  This runs the full experiment and collects data. Use this mode for class assignments.

To select **DEMONSTRATION** mode type "D".
  This runs a short version of the experiment. Use this mode to preview or review an experiment. No data are collected and not all experiment conditions will occur.

To return to the main menu press the [Esc] key.

You may run an experiment as often as you like in demonstration mode. You may also re-run an experiment in normal mode, but be cautious! The space for data storage is limited, and indiscriminate re-running of experiments may use up that space, making it impossible to run other experiments. We recommend that you *not* run an experiment more than twice in normal mode.

After you select the mode for the experiment, hit the space bar and the experiment will begin. You will first see a title screen like that shown in Figure 0.2.4. When you hit the space bar as instructed, you will see the instructions for the particular experiment you are running. Carefully read those instructions, then follow the instructions on the screen to begin the experiment itself.

At the end of the experiment, the computer will display tables of your data and, for most of the experiments, a graph of the results. Record the indicated numbers in your workbook and plot your data points on the graph provided in the workbook.

Figure 0.2.4 Example Title Screen in Normal Mode

```
1.0 EXPERIMENTS IN PERCEPTION


1.1 The Blind Spot in Vision


NORMAL MODE

Approximate duration: 22 minutes

The full experiment will be run and data will be collected.



Press the [Spacebar] to begin the experiment.

Press the [Esc] key to return to the main menu.
```

When you have finished you may need to turn in a disk to the instructor, who will merge the data from all subjects and then report the group averages to the class. If you are using two 5.25" disks, always turn in Disk 2.

After the first time you use the MEL Lab you will *not* have to enter the initialization information again. On the IBM, boot the computer if necessary, then select the disk drive. Then simply insert Disk 1 in the appropriate disk drive and type **A: EXPERIMENT** (*not STARTUP*). If you are running on the B floppy, type **B: EXPERIMENT**. If you are on a hard disk, move to the directory on which the file resides (e.g., type "CD\lab" then "EXPERIMENT"). On the Macintosh, insert Disk #1 and double click on the **EXPERIMENT** icon (not *the STARTUP icon*). From now on, the first screen you see will be the title screen, followed by the topic, experiment, and mode selection screens.

When a new experiment is assigned you should first read the section in that chapter of this workbook on *Instructions for Running the Experiment*. This will tell you if any special materials are needed, and give any other special instructions.

How to end an experiment early. If you find yourself in the middle of an experiment and suddenly realize you have a class to get to in two minutes, or some other emergency arises, you can end any experiment early. On the IBM, hit Ctrl/Shift/Alt; that is, hold all three keys at once. Use the left shift and control keys. On the Macintosh, press cmd-shift-> (the cmd key is the one that is marked with a cloverleaf or propeller looking symbol; the '>' is the 'greater-than' key). You will then be asked if you want to quit. (You may have to continue to the end of a trial before this occurs.) Answering "yes" will end the experiment at that point. **No data will be recorded,** and you will have to rerun the experiment from the beginning.

0.3 General Instructions for Running Experiments

Most of the experiments in this series involve the measure of either *reaction time* or *accuracy* as the dependent variable. General instructions are given below for both types of experiments. You will be referred back to this section when appropriate. In the **Instructions for Running the Experiment** section of each chapter, and at the beginning of each experiment, you will be told whether the experiment involves accuracy or reaction time.

0.3.1 Experiments Measuring Accuracy

Accuracy as a dependent variable is usually measured by determining the number of trials of an experiment on which you made a correct response, and then dividing by the total number of trials to yield the *proportion correct*. Multiplying the proportion correct by 100 yields percent correct. By comparing accuracy under varying conditions of an experiment, we can gain information about the processes involved in the task.

Please note that **experiments that involve accuracy usually are designed so that you will have fairly high error rates.** After all, if you were almost always correct in each condition, then there would be little difference in accuracy on which to base an analysis. Note also that in experiments that involve accuracy you should **not** try to make fast responses. If you attempt to respond as quickly as possible to these tasks you will probably have extremely low accuracy.

0.3.2 Experiments Measuring Reaction Time

RT is a measure of the time elapsed between onset of a stimulus and completion of a response (key-press). That measure of RT is then used to try to infer something about the nature of the underlying psychological processes involved, by comparing the RT's under different conditions. An example (from the exercise "Perceptual Matching") is that it is harder (longer RT) to decide that two letters seen at the same time have the same name (like Aa) than to decide that two letters are physically the same (AA or aa). But if you see one letter two seconds before the other this effect disappears. This is one piece of evidence that verbal items in short-term memory are stored by sound code, rather than visual imagery, and that it takes about 2 seconds to produce that sound code. Thus the advantage of physical sameness is lost when you must match the second letter against a memory of the sound of the first letter.

RT is an important measure in psychology, and a powerful one. But as with experiments using any other methodology, you have to be careful. A number of factors affect RT, aside from the experimental ones in which we are interested, and some consideration must be given to those.

The first and foremost concern in RT research is that you *respond as quickly as you can while keeping errors to a minimum*. You are to try to react as soon as you can without being sloppy. For most experiments, this means that you should have no more than 10% errors, and you should usually have far fewer. Again, the stress is on speed, but without sacrificing accuracy. Remember, these are not guessing games. Wait until you see the stimulus before you respond!

Do not try to produce the "correct" result. Any effort to be faster in one condition than another will lead to slow, sloppy responding in all conditions. Just do the task as instructed. If your performance is not just like the "average," do not worry. There are large individual differences in overall RT, though most people will show the same general *pattern* of RT's across various conditions of the experiment.

There are a few things you can do to help maintain good speed and accuracy. For most experiments you must push a designated key to start each trial. Be sure that you are paying close attention to the task when you press the key to start the next trial. If there is a fixation mark (typically a "+") on the screen that tells you where to look during the trial, make sure that you have that mark in good, clear focus when you start a trial.

You can sit and run trial after trial and finish a little sooner, but at the cost of eye-strain and decreased accuracy. For the sake of both your comfort and the accuracy of the data, plan to stop for a few seconds after every few trials (the number will depend a lot on the type of task). It is possible to sit and stare at the screen for a long time, but you may have difficulty maintaining concentration and your performance will deteriorate. So take a break every 5-10 minutes. Stand up and stretch. Relax your eyes. Not only will you feel better, but your performance will also be better!

While you may not have complete control over your surroundings during testing, you can probably at least avoid some of the worst problems. If you have control over the brightness and contrast of the CRT screen, make sure that the stimuli are clear and sharp. A dim screen will make your RT's both slower and less accurate. Also be sure to eliminate any glare on the screen, since this may partially mask (cover up) the stimuli.

For experiments measuring RT, the computer will report your mean (average) RT for each condition, and this is the dependent variable. The reason that the mean is used is that your RT will vary from trial to trial as a result of many things other than the type of stimulus, although that is the only variable we are interested in. Momentary changes in degree of attentiveness, clarity of focus, interest or boredom, or many other factors can affect RT. By testing you in many trials of each type, and using the mean of those trials as your score, we can control for all of those variables, since poor attentiveness (or other factors) will occur about equally often for each trial type, and thus the effect will be canceled out.

0.4 Printing Tables of Your Data

At the end of most experiments you will see a table displaying your data (usually percent correct or mean correct RT for each condition of the experiment). You should copy those numbers to the corresponding table in the workbook. If for some reason you do not, but you wish to look at the table again later, you can easily print a copy of the table, which is stored on your disk (Disk #2, if you have a two-disk set). On the IBM, simply insert the disk in the appropriate drive and type **PRINT GRAF1.PRN**. On the Macintosh, use your favorite word processor to print the text file **GRAF1.PRN**. Note, though that the same file name is used for every experiment, so you must print out this file before you run the next experiment.

0.5 Graphing data

Most chapters of this Manual have blank graphs for you to use in practicing the graphic presentation of the data. One graph is for your own, individual data, which are displayed for you at the end of each experiment. The other graph is for the group data averaged across all subjects. Those data will be given to you by your instructor, after the individual data are merged and averaged.

You will notice in looking at the blank graphs in each chapter that the Individual Data graph for experiments that concern *accuracy* is labelled along the Y axis from 0 to 100 percent. On the other hand, the Individual Data graph for experiments that concern *reaction time* has none of the points along the Y axis labelled. This is deliberate, so that you can scale the graph appropriately for your own data. Each subject will need to scale these somewhat differently, depending on their own fastest and slowest reaction times. (For experiments concerning accuracy, the percent correct across conditions often covers nearly the full range from 0 to 100 percent, so these are labelled for you.)

You will also notice that the Y axis is labelled for the Group Data graphs. We were able to specify these labels based on experience with many samples of subjects, because the group means do not typically differ very much from one group of subjects to another. In this section, we discuss general principles of graphing, including the selection of the range of scores to use.

We are typically interested in presenting our data graphically so that they can be easily interpreted by the reader. Note that we could present the data in a table, instead of a graph. A table of the data would actually convey more accurate information, since it would contain the exact value of the dependent variable for each level of the independent variable. However, a table of data is often more difficult to interpret than is a graph. In many instances, ease of interpretation is sufficiently important that the slight loss of accuracy is quite acceptable.

The Main Rule of Graphing

Make the graph as easy as possible for the reader to understand. The goal of graphical presentation is to convey information to the reader as quickly and easily as possible. The guidelines below are designed to help make your graphs readable and clear, while avoiding distortions. *To deliberately distort or misrepresent data is a violation of scientific ethics.*

Graphs with One Independent Variable.

A simple graph is shown in Figure 0.5.1, along with the same data in table form. The data here are from the experiment on Mental Rotation of Images in Chapter 1.6. The dependent variable is the time required to decide whether two figures are identical or mirror images, and the independent variable is the degree of rotation of one figure relative to another. The typical finding is that reaction time increases with increases in the degree of rotation. Note the relationship between the table and the graph.

There are several issues to be addressed in constructing a graph like the one above, and those are now considered in some detail. One thing to note is that it is the common convention to **always graph the dependent variable on the Y axis.**

Choosing the range of values on the Y axis. One of the first decisions that must be made about a graph is how to scale the Y axis. You can choose the minimum and maximum values of the dependent variable to include on the graph, along with the number of divisions, and the number of points labelled. Consider the graphs in Figure 0.5.2, which each present the same data. In Graph A, the Y axis begins at 0 msec and goes to 4000 msec. Note the result: the changes in reaction time with increases in rotation appear to be rather small, and it is difficult to read off exact values of the dependent variable without being very careful and using a ruler. This is not very satisfactory.

Figure 0.5.1 Table versus Graph presentation

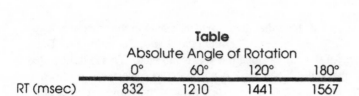

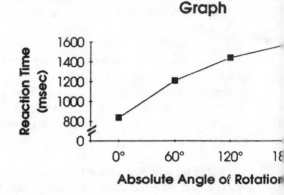

A better result is shown in Graph B, in which the minimum value of the Y axis is set to 800 and the maximum to 1600, which just encompasses the range of the data. In this case, the values can easily be read, and differences between means are clear.

Figure 0.5.2 Choosing the range of values on the Y axis

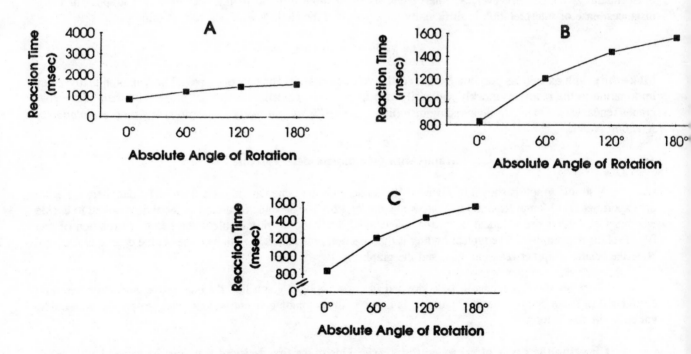

There is, however, a potential problem. A reader who did not carefully examine the labelling of the Y axis might assume that it begins at zero, and thus interpret the graph as showing reaction time at 180° as 10 times what it is at 0° (it has actually not quite doubled). In this sense, then, this is a misleading graph.

The preferred way to handle this problem is shown in Graph C. Note that the Y axis is the same, except that it now begins at 0 msec, with a "cut" in the line to signal the discontinuity. In the final analysis, of course, it is up to the reader to be alert to the scaling of the axes, and we recommend that you *cultivate the habit of always checking the labelling of the Y axis.*

In general, then, we recommend that you choose a minimum value for the Y axis that is slightly below the minimum value of the dependent variable, and a maximum that is slightly above the maximum value of the dependent variable. As discussed in more detail below, it is a good idea to choose values of the minimum and maximum that make it easy to divide and label the Y axis. You would not, for example, want to use values of 750 and 1625 for the minimum and maximum values in Graphs B and C!

Labelling the Y axis. In addition to determining the range of values to display, you must also determine the number of divisions and how they are to be labelled. Figure 0.5.3 illustrates several possibilities.

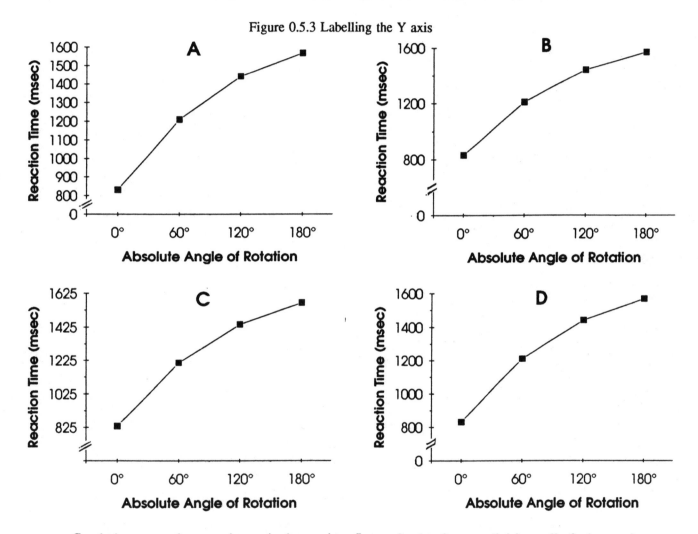

Figure 0.5.3 Labelling the Y axis

Graph A presents the same data as in the previous figures, but has frequent divisions, all of whose points are labelled. This results in a rather "messy" graph.

Graph B has the opposite problem from graph A: now there are very few hashmarks, and only three are labelled. The result is that the reader must carefully calculate the intermediate values. While that may not be terribly difficult, the reader just wants the information. He or she is unlikely to want an exercise in arithmetic.

Graph C was produced using a computer graphics package that automatically chose the scaling of the dependent variable. Note the result: The number of divisions and labels is appropriate, and the differences between levels of the independent variable are clear. But the labelling of the points along the Y axis is strange. The reader would again have to be very careful indeed to read the values of the dependent variable. (Most computer graphics packages will choose the minimum and maximum for you by "default." They also permit you to choose the labels, and we recommend highly that anyone using such a package learn choose their own labels.)

Graph D provides the best result--there are enough divisions and labels to make interpolation reasonably accurate, but not so many as to produce a cluttered appearance.

Choosing a histogram or a line graph.

Figure 0.5.4 Choosing a histogram or a line graph

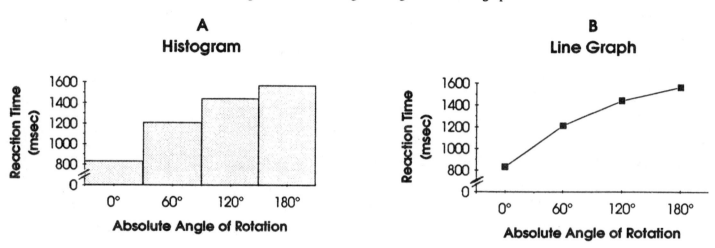

Compare the two graphs in Figure 0.5.4, which again present the same data. Graph A uses a *histogram* or bar-graph, indicating the value of the dependent variable (reaction time) by the height of the bar corresponding to each level of the independent variable (degree of rotation). Graph B is a line *graph*, and indicates the value of the dependent variable for each level of the dependent variable by a dot (or some other symbol), with the dots connected by lines. These modes of presenting the data are sometimes interchangeable, but the following are suggested as guidelines.

Use a line graph if the function relating the dependent and independent variables is continuous. In the case of data presented here, it is clear that we could have tested any values of the independent variable in between those actually used. That is, we can reasonably assume that there is a "true" function relating reaction time to angle of rotation that includes all points between 0° and 180°, and not just the points we happened to measure.

If there is a single independent variable, with discrete levels, use a histogram. Suppose that this experiment compared your ability to mentally rotate different shapes, but they were always rotated the same amount. The X axis would now be labelled "Shape of Stimulus," and the levels of the variable might be "oval," "circle," and "square." Note, though, that the order in which we graph the three levels of Shape is arbitrary, as indicated in the three graphs of Figure 0.5.5, that differ only in the order in which the three shapes are presented on the graph. These represent levels of a *discrete* variable. Any variable measured at a nominal scale is discrete. (The case of multiple independent variables offers some complications, and is discussed below.)

Figure 0.5.5 Varying the order of levels on a histogram

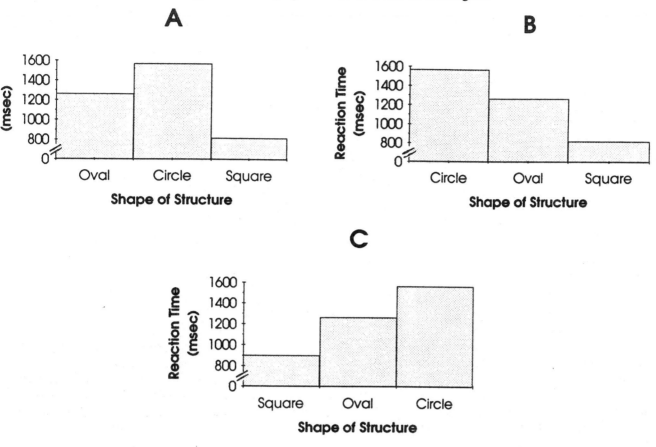

Always use straight lines to connect the dots or other symbols of a line graph. While you may be tempted to "smooth" the graph by using curved lines, that is not recommended, since it implies that you know something about the values of the dependent variables for levels of the independent variable that are in between those actually tested. You certainly might want to assume that the function is continuous between the points actually tested, but the graph is intended to convey the *actual* data. The lines are not there to indicate exact intermediate values, but rather to aid the eye in moving from one dot to another.

Graphs with Two Independent Variables

In this section we offer some suggestions for graphing the data from experiments with two independent variables. The standard approach is to indicate the levels of one IV along the X axis, and then use separate lines on the graph for each level of the other IV. As an example, consider Figure 0.5.6, based on the same data as those above, except that there are now three lines, to represent the results of rotating images which differ in their complexity (either 4, 8 or 12 sides).

Note that there are now three lines, and that different symbols are used for the points along each. In this case, a square is used for 4-sided figures, a diamond is used for 8-sided figures, and an asterisk for 12-sided figures. Of course, we now must label the three lines to indicate how they differ. That is sometimes done on the graph itself, but a more frequent approach is to use a *legend* to indicate what each symbol stands for. In this case, the legend appears in the upper right-hand corner of the graph, but it may be placed elsewhere if there is a large blank space on the graph. The symbols typically used include •, o, ■, □, *, +, and x.

Figure 0.5.6 Graph with two independent variables

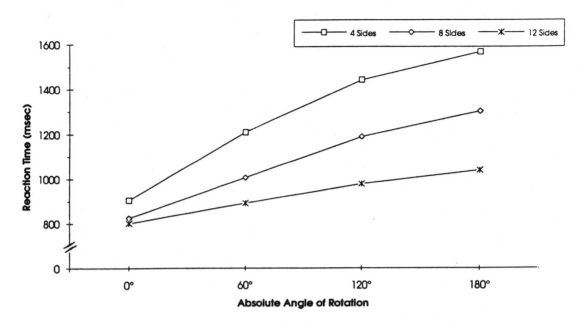

We suggested above that when there is only a single, *discrete* IV, you should use a histogram. However, when there are two IV's a histogram often becomes rather difficult to read, as illustrated in Figure 0.5.7, which graphs the same data as Figure 0.5.6. Note that these are *not* discrete variables, but still illustrate the greater difficulty of interpreting a histogram with two IV's. Just as with a line graph, the level of one IV is graphed along the X axis. Levels of the other are indicated by separate bars at each X-axis division, with the bars shaded differently to indicate the different levels of the second IV.

Figure 0.5.7 Histogram with two independent variables

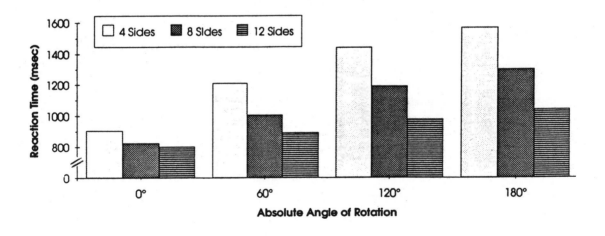

Which variable goes on the X axis? When there are two independent variables, you have a choice as to which is to be graphed on the X axis, and which is to be indicated by separate lines. **If one IV has more levels than the other, put that variable on the X axis.** That is, you should usually keep the number of lines to a minimum.

If both IV's have the same number of levels, you can put either variable on the X axis, with the levels of the other indicated by separate lines. You should probably try it both ways, then choose whichever of the graphs seems to most clearly convey the information you wish your reader to have.

Graphs With More Than Two Independent Variables

When there are three (or more) IV's there are several strategies you can adopt:

[1] Indicate the levels of the third IV by using a separate graph (each with two IV's) for each level of the third. Thus, if there are two levels of the third IV, you would have two graphs (labelled identically, shown side by side.

[2] Indicate the levels of one IV on the X axis, the second by different symbols (e.g. •, O, ■, □, *, +, x), and the third by different types of lines (solid, dotted, dashed).

[3] Indicate the levels of one IV on the X axis, the second by different symbols (e.g. •, ■, ♦, and the third (if it has two levels) by open versus filled symbols (e.g. ◊ vs. ♦).

0.6 Implementing Your Own Experiments

One major feature of the MEL Lab is an experiment generator that allows you to set up your own experiments. You may use this feature for your semester research project or for independent or honors research. In this section, we present an overview of the five basic research paradigms available to you. To set up an experiment of your own, you will actually modify one of these base programs to suit your needs. Your instructor has received, as part of the Instructor's Guide, a detailed description of each of the paradigms, as well as the programs that make up the experiment generator. If you are interested in using these materials, the instructor may copy them for you.

In setting up an experiment using the experiment generator, you actually start with the existing experiment for the paradigm and then make modifications to the instructions, stimuli, and parameters such as timing to change that experiment into the one you want to implement. This approach makes it far easier to set up experiments than with any existing software, including the professional version of MEL. Of course, that ease of use means that there are some limitations. For example, the experiment generator does not permit you to use graphics mode. However, most of the experiments in the MEL Lab could be set up using the experiment generator.

We hope that you will take advantage of this feature for your semester research project or independent research. There are suggestions in most chapters of this workbook for variations on the experiments in the MEL Lab that might be of interest, and many of these could be implemented using the experiment generator. Of course, you may also come up with your own ideas for interesting research projects. There is no better way to solidify your knowledge of the research process than to be actively engaged in research. The next section of this workbook details the MEL Lab Undergraduate Competition, to which you can submit experiments that you have set up.

The paradigms

Five research paradigms are included to provide a wide range of experiments that can be quickly implemented. Each paradigm can be adapted to implement a wide range of procedures. The paradigms can implement experiments that present primarily textual material to subjects. Procedures that involve specialized graphics (e.g., the Mental Rotation, Section 1.6) or computer subroutines to vary the display (e.g., the Blind Spot experiment, Section 1.1) cannot be implemented with the experiment generator. To implement experiments such as these requires developing experiments in the full MEL Professional system. However, most of the other experiments in the MEL Lab could be implemented with the experiment generator. All of the paradigms outlined below begin with general instructions to the subject, followed by (optional) instructions for each block of the experiment, and end-of-session feedback.

Reaction Time. The general reaction-time paradigm consists of a block of practice trials followed by one or more blocks of actual trials. Each trial consists of a get-ready message (that can also permit the subject to decide when to begin the trial), a study stimulus (optional), a fixation stimulus to show the subject where the probe stimulus will appear on the screen, the critical probe stimulus, an optional masking stimulus, and feedback about accuracy and reaction time.

List Learning Procedures. The general list-learning paradigm presents lists of words (or other items) to the subject, then tests either recall or recognition. The study list is presented for a specified length of time. Following that, subjects must either recognize the items (indicate which of several stimuli were on the study list), recall the items by entering them via the keyboard, or do a paper-and-pencil recall, then check that against the original list displayed on the computer and enter the number of items correctly recalled.

Questionnaires. The general questionnaire paradigm permits you to ask multiple choice, true/false, or bipolar (scaling) questions, and score them for accuracy.

Social Bargaining. The social bargaining paradigm runs the Prisoner's Dilemma Game (see Chapter 3.l), but permits you to enter your own strategies for the computer to play against the human subjects.

Human Factors. The general human factors paradigm consists of presenting instructions in varying formats and then testing subjects' use of those instructions. This can implement experiments such as the comparison of phone systems used in Chapter 4.1, as well as variants such as different methods for programming a VCR, or simulations of other complex functions.

Before using the experiment generator:

The steps that you need to complete before beginning to implement your experiment or modification of an existing experiment involve many of the issues of research design that you will study in your research methods course. The points raised here are treated in more detail in Section 5.1 on Reaction Time Procedures.

What will happen on each trial? Since the individual trial (presentation of a stimulus and collection of a response) is the basic unit of an experiment, you should begin by considering the general events that will take place on each trial. What will the stimulus be like? What sort of warning should be given? What sort of feedback should be given? How should the start of each trial be controlled? A number of different issues in regard to the events within a single trial are considered in the Appendix chapter on Reaction Time Procedures.

What will change from trial to trial? Carefully consider what aspects of the stimuli you are manipulating. These are the independent variables, and you should be certain that you know what variables you want to manipulate and how. Independent variables may also differ from one block of trials to the next. You may want to test different subjects for the various conditions (between-subjects design), or you may want to test each subject under all conditions (within-subjects design). Each of these points should be considered. You should also make a detailed listing of the trials to be run in each block: What is the stimulus? What is the correct response? How many times should this trial be repeated? We recommend that you list all of the single trials on paper to be sure that you have completely specified them.

How should I control for extraneous factors? Some factors (control variables) that cannot be manipulated must nevertheless be carefully controlled so that they do not invalidate the results. Randomization and counterbalancing are two techniques often used to avoid having the results of an experiment contaminated by extraneous factors.

What sort of instructions will be needed? Your subjects will have to be told what will be happening during the experiment, and what sorts of responses to make. While the experiments in the MEL Lab have to use written instructions, it may be preferable to *read* the instructions to the subjects when you are testing only one (or a few) at a time. This gives the subjects the opportunity to ask questions, as well as establishing a human context of social interaction, which most subjects find more motivating that computer-presented instructions. You also need to consider the type of debriefing that will be given after each subject completes the experiment.

Using the Experiment Generator

After you complete the planning of your experiment, you will need to become familiar with the operations of the experiment generator itself. In order to accomplish that, we recommend that you work through the detailed example for the paradigm you are using that was provided to your instructor (who should copy those materials for you). Analyses of the data from your experiment can be performed by using the SANALYZE program that your instructor has.

0.7 The MEL Lab Undergraduate and Graduate Competition

You are invited to submit experiments that you have written or modified to the MEL Lab Undergraduate Competition. Each semester, Psychology Software Tools, Inc., publishers of MEL and the MEL Lab, will award six cash prizes, along with certificates of participation, to students who submit their course projects or independent/honors research projects for judging. We hope that you will share the fruits of your labor with us, and through us with others. Cash prizes to be awarded *each semester* are $100 for first place, $50 for second place, and three prizes of $25 each for third place winners. Certificates of participation will be awarded to all students submitting completed projects that come through the initial review stage. We, the authors of MEL Lab, would like you to share well developed experimental projects so other students can learn from your work. Add your contribution to a worldwide development effort. MEL is now in use in over 1000 institutions and twenty countries. A well developed project can strengthen your application to graduate school. Further, your efforts may advance our knowledge of psychological processes.

Who can submit?

Undergraduate Competition. Any undergraduate student at a college or university using the MEL Lab to implement or modify experiments for course projects, independent studies, or honors research may enter their experiment in the MEL Lab Undergraduate Competition. You are not competing against graduate students.

Graduate Student Competition. Any university graduate student using MEL Lab to implement or modify experiments for courses or research may enter their experiment in the MEL Lab Graduate Competition.

Why should I?

Implementing an experiment, either from scratch or by modifying an existing experiment, is a tough process. You have to think about all the aspects of experimental design that you learn in your Research Methods/Experimental Psychology course. You have to test subjects and then analyze the data. After all that work, it is a shame to just forget the whole thing! There are at least three reasons to consider submitting your experiment:

1. Recognition.

2. This will make a very nice addition to applications to graduate school. Your certificate establishes that you have completed a formal research project, which is a major "plus" in the eyes of graduate admissions committees (even in clinical psychology).

3. Your experiment will become part of a public-domain library of experiments maintained by Psychology Software Tools. Along with other experiments contributed by students and professionals, your experiment will be made available to users of the MEL Lab throughout the world. Your authorship of the experiment will be explicitly recognized.

How and when do I submit materials?

We realize that most semester projects are not completed until near the end of a semester, and that you are then faced with exams, etc. We strongly suggest, therefore, that you make your submission during the semester *after* the one in which the project was completed. That will provide you with more time in which to prepare your materials for submission.

The MEL Lab Undergraduate and Graduate Competitions will be held each semester (Fall and Spring), with judging of submissions beginning November 1 (for Fall submissions) or April 1 (for Spring submissions).

Your entry should contain the following:

1. A written description of the experiment, including references to relevant literature. If you are replicating an existing experiment, please indicate that. If your experiment is a modification of an experiment in the MEL Lab, please indicate that as well. Include a brief introduction, detailing the nature of the problem being studied, and how this experiment addresses that problem. Also, describe the experiment as you would for the Methods and Results sections of a formal report. If you have written a report of the experiment for your class which contains this information, you may submit it.

2. The following MEL files on disk (with the name of your files in place of "expname"): expname.INS, expname.ANL, and expname.DAT.

3. A detailed description of the names of the variables, as well as the coding of their values. Please see "Variable Names and Coding" in any chapter of the Instructor's Manual.

4. Your name, address, and telephone number, the name of your college or university, and the name of your instructor/advisor and the course for which the project was designed.

Send those materials to:

MEL Lab Undergraduate Competition
OR
MEL Lab Graduate Competition
Psychology Software Tools, Inc.
511 Bevington Road
Pittsburgh, PA 15221

Deadlines for submission are **October 15** for Fall and **March 15** for Spring. Submissions received after those dates will be considered in the next semester's competition. All entrants will be notified of the winners by approximately December 1 for Fall and May 1 for Spring.

1 Experiments in Perception

A basic issue for psychology, as well as for philosophers down through the ages, is how we come to gain knowledge of the world. Knowledge comes through experience with the world, and that experience is what the study of perception seeks to understand. What we know about the world and the things in it is learned through looking, hearing, touching, smelling, and even tasting the world. (Babies seem so inordinately fond of tasting the world because their sense of taste and sense of touch in their mouths are better developed than their other senses.) The act of perception begins with our sense organs such as the eye, the ear, and the vestibular system that helps us balance. Those organs are sensitive to different aspects of the external world (and of our own bodies), and translate experience into signals to the brain to indicate what is currently being sensed.

But perception is more than just a passive receiving and interpreting of sensory signals. Perception is also an *activity* that we engage in. Not only do we actively move our eyes to gain new information, but we also move our bodies in order to use our senses most effectively. We move so that we can look around things when we want to know what is behind them, and climb hills to see what is on the other side. Perception is thus an activity that we control (though imperfectly). We can select what parts of the world we perceive by moving in the world, but we can also restrict attention to only part of what we could currently perceive (for example, paying the most attention to a single instrument while listening to an orchestra). And perceiving things also involves knowing what they are--in short, recognizing them. So memory plays a role in perception, as well.

Various aspects of perception, how we actively use perception, and how memory and perception are related are explored in the experiments and exercises that follow.

1.1 The Blind Spot in Vision

Abstract

Where the optic nerve and blood supply for the retina enter the eye, there is a fairly large area with no receptors for light, and thus no vision. This exercise examines how it comes about that we only notice the blind spot under special conditions, and how it is that the blind spot is "filled in" to resemble the general pattern of the background. In this exercise the blind spot is first demonstrated, and its anatomical nature described. Next, a retinocortical mapping theory of why the blind spot isn't usually apparent is tested, followed by a series of demonstrations of how the blind spot is filled in. Finally, the blind spot is mapped, to determine its size and location.

The first recorded description of the blind spot came in 1668, when Mariotte showed that by looking off to the side of an object in monocular (one-eyed) vision, the object can be made to disappear. The existence of this blind spot soon became known to King Charles II, who amused himself by "beheading" members of his court with it (Walls, 1954). The blind spot occurs where the optic nerve and the blood vessels serving the retina enter the eye, as shown in Figure 1.1.1. Because there are no receptor cells present in this area, no vision can occur there. Why do we not notice this blank patch in the visual field? One reason is that the part of the retina in the other eye corresponding to that location in space *does* see that area in normal binocular vision. Figure 1.1.2 illustrates the approximate size and location of the blind spot for each eye. Note that the blind spot is typically centered about 15 degrees from the fovea, and subtends an area of approximately 6 degrees of visual angle. But try covering one eye. You probably still can't find the blind spot. One reason for this is that the area is "filled in" by the visual system. This exercise is in part concerned with the nature of the filling in process.

Figure 1.1.1 Cross-section of the human eye

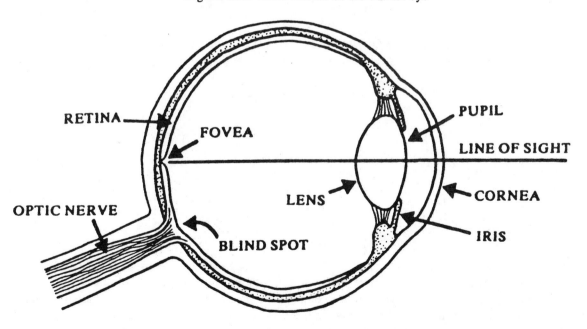

The first part of this exercise is designed to demonstrate the blind spot, and get you used to finding it. The next part is concerned with testing a theory about how the blind spot is filled in. This theory will be outlined below. The exercises testing it were suggested by E. B. Titchener (1901) in the *Instructor's Manual* of his *Experimental*

Figure 1.1.2 Projection of visual blind spot image

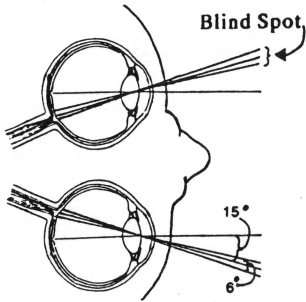

Psychology. Following that, and another brief demonstration of the filling-in process not in Titchener's demonstration, you will measure the size and shape of your blind spot for one eye. No *Method* section accompanies this demonstration, since the instructions you will need are given step-by-step as you do the exercise.

One possible explanation of why the blind spot is so difficult to see is that information from receptors close to it project onto the cortex in a distorted way, so that no part of the cortical map(s) are left blank. This is illustrated schematically in Figure 1.1.3, where each X represents a receptor in the retina, and each + represents its cortical projection. This retinocortical mapping theory was the one Titchener set out to test.

Figure 1.1.3 Diagram of the retinocortical mapping theory

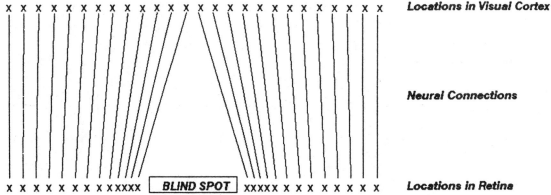

Titchener noted that this theory suggests that there should be a systematic distortion of vision around the blind spot. The second part of this exercise tests for such distortions in various ways. On the basis of these types of demonstrations, Titchener rejected the distortion of space-values as an explanation of our usual inability to see the blind spot. This means that the blind spot is being filled in somehow by "seeing" stuff that isn't there. The third part of this exercise will examine what we see in the blind spot against various backgrounds.

Instructions for Running the Experiment

To run this experiment, insert Disk 1 into your computer and enter the MEL Lab as instructed in Section 0.2. Select **Perception** from the topic menu and **The Blind Spot in Vision** from the specific experiment menu. Instructions on the computer screen will then explain the experiment and what keys to use for your responses. This experiment does not call for quick responses, but rather asks you to make a series of observations about how the blind spot affects vision. *Materials needed*: Pencil and laboratory workbook to trace the map of the blind spot at the end of the experiment, and a ruler (see the last page of this chapter) to measure the screen. *Please note*: This exercise requires that you keep your eyes very still. We typically move our eyes often, so this may be a strain. Feel free to take frequent breaks between the parts of the exercise. It is especially important for mapping the blind spot that you be looking *directly* at the fixation mark when you start each trial of the mapping. *Remember*: this experiment works best if you maintain the same position relative to the computer, so try to move as little as possible during each demonstration.

Expected Running Time = 20 minutes

Questions

1. What is the size of your blind spot in degrees of visual angle? Where is it located, relative to straight ahead? What is the shape? (For information on how to calculate the size of the blind spot in *degrees of visual angle*, see the laboratory workbook for the Selective Attention experiment, Section 1.5).

2. Do your observations agree with the retinocortical mapping theory of how the blind spot is filled? That is, were there the sorts of distortions in perception around the blind spot that the theory predicts?

3. How, then, is the blind spot filled in? For a recent review of research on the filling in of the blind spot, see Kawabata (1984). What role might visual acuity play in filling in the blind spot? That is, how well can you see in peripheral vision around the blind spot?

4. What did you perceive when you moved the line through your blind spot? What does this tell us about the nature of the filling-in process?

5. This experiment involves introspective report of your experience. How do you compare such data across subjects? How do you deal with disagreements in introspection?

6. Assume you are driving and you can only see out of your left eye. At a distance of 20 meters (or 65 feet) where is the blind spot located and how large is it?

References

Kawabata, N. (1984). Perception at the blind spot and similarity grouping. *Perception and Psychophysics, 36,* 151-158.

Titchener, E. B. (1901). *Experimental Psychology, Qualitative.* *Instructor's Manual.* New York: Macmillan.

Walls, G. L. (1954). The filling-in process. *American Journal of Optometry. 31* 329-341.

The Blind Spot in Vision

Individual Data

Measurements of the Blind Spot

Distance from eye to screen = _____ mm

Inner Measure of the Blind Spot
(based on point of disappearance)

Height (mm): _____

Width (mm): _____

Height (degrees): _____

Width (degrees): _____

Area (mm^2): _____

Outer Measure of the Blind Spot
(based on point of reappearance)

Height (mm): _____

Width (mm): _____

Height (degrees): _____

Width (degrees): _____

Area (mm^2): _____

Student Name:_____

Section/Lab:_____

The Blind Spot in Vision

Individual Data

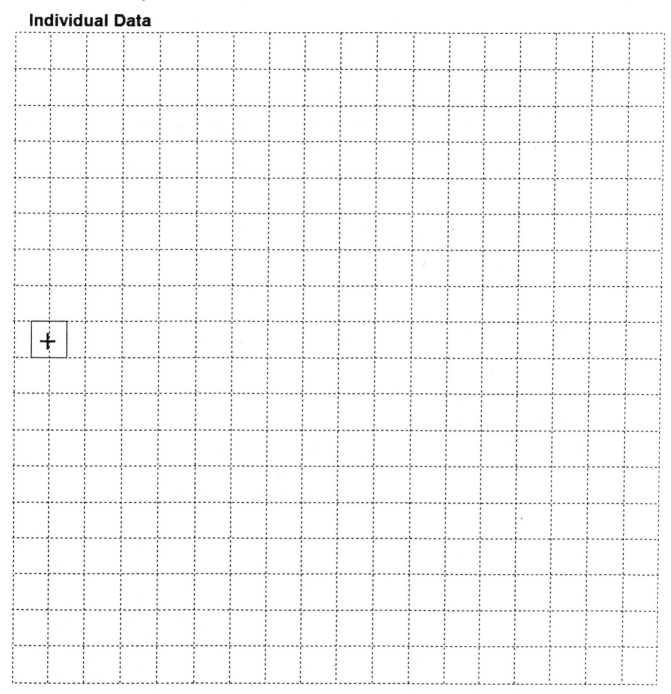

Draw thin or dotted lines for inner portion (points of disappearance)
Draw thick or solid lines for outer portion (points of reappearance)

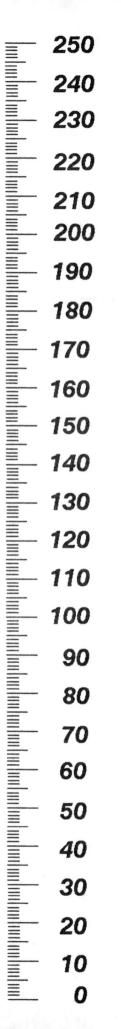

Millimeter ruler for blind spot measurements

```
250
240
230
220
210
200
190
180
170
160
150
140
130
120
110
100
 90
 80
 70
 60
 50
 40
 30
 20
 10
  0
```

Use this ruler to measure the distance from your eye to the screen. If you are sitting more than 250 millimeters from the screen, you can use an 8 1/2 by 11 inch page along with this ruler to make the measurement. The long side of the paper (11 inches) is equal to 280 millimeters. Attach this ruler to the first page and make your measurement.

Example of distance from screen:

Computer Display

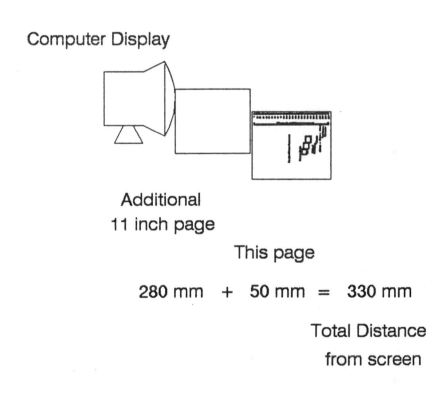

Additional
11 inch page

This page

280 mm + 50 mm = 330 mm

Total Distance
from screen

1.2 The Duration of the Icon

Abstract

Visual information no longer present in the environment "persists" briefly in the "sensory register" or icon following its disappearance. One limitation to the study of the icon is its very brief duration. As people begin reporting the contents of the icon, it is already disappearing. Sperling (1960) invented the partial-report technique to overcome this difficulty, and was able to show that the icon has a large capacity and measure its duration. This classic experiment is repeated in this exercise.

The term "icon" was introduced by Neisser (1967) to refer to the brief persistence of information from a visual display after the display is no longer present. (Other terms used for the same phenomenon are the precategorical visual store, preperceptual visual store, the visual sensory register, and iconic memory.) Early work on reading (e.g., Erdman and Dodge, 1898) had been concerned with this phenomenon and asked how much information could be acquired at a single fixation in reading. The typical finding from briefly presenting a set of letters and having the subject report as many letters as possible was that the perceptual span was 4 to 5 letters. This set the apparent limit of the size of the icon (as it came to be known).

One problem with these findings, claimed to indicate a very limited perceptual span, was that it is possible that the information in a brief display *decays* rapidly, and that the 4 to 5 letters reported was not the limit of how much was *perceived*, but rather was the limit of how much could be *reported* before the perceptual impression vanished. If this were the case, the icon might be capable of holding a larger amount of information which is available only briefly. To get a feeling for this sort of visual display, think of when you have seen a nearby lightening flash on a dark night. Such a flash gives you a very brief exposure to a visual stimulus. If you were asked to describe what you had seen (assuming you weren't familiar with the scene, and just recalling from memory), you probably would omit many objects and details. But we certainly have the feeling of having seen a very rich visual display during the lightening flash. Such is the topic of the experiment on the icon--how much can you see in a brief visual display, and how long does that visual information last after the display is turned off?

How can we get around the problem of the older studies of perceptual span--that subjects' reports might be limited by a rapid decay of the visual persistence rather than by a severe limit to its size? Sperling (1960) devised a method. He reasoned that the visual persistence (later called the icon) decayed too rapidly for subjects to report all they had seen. But suppose we tell them after they see the display to report only a part of it? If a person could report most of a randomly selected part of the display on one trial, and most of another part on another trial, this would suggest that they had seen much more than they could report.

Sperling's test was much like the older studies--he presented a 3 x 3 matrix of letters, flashed for 50 msec. But rather than just using the *whole-report* method of previous studies (report as much as you can of the whole display), he used a new *partial-report* method. In his study, subjects saw the display of letters, then heard a tone that was either high-pitched, low-pitched, or in between. The high-pitched tone indicated "report the top line of the display," with the medium and low tones signalling the report of the middle and bottom lines, respectively.

What Sperling found was that subjects could report about 80% of the letters on a line, if the tone was sounded just before the letters were presented. That drops only slightly, to about 75%, when the tone immediately follows the letters. However, if the tone is delayed by only a half second, subjects can only report about 50% of each line, which corresponds to the 4 to 5 letters previously estimated as the span of a visual impression. Sperling's experiment showed quite conclusively that the limit in report of letters from a brief visual display was due to a rapid decay of the visual trace or icon, rather than to a severe limit on the size of the icon itself.

Later investigators, such as Averbach and Coriell (1961) and Eriksen and Collins (1967) have studied the icon further, and have shown that it has a duration of about 250 msec and a storage capacity of at least 9 items. There are many problems with estimating the upper limit to iconic capacity, and it is probably much greater than 9 items.

Method

Because the task involved is a difficult one, a large amount of practice (120 trials) will be given before you begin the 120 trials of the actual experiment. All practice trials will involve partial report with no delay between presentation of the letters and the tone to indicate which line to report. After the practice trials, each subject will be tested in four blocks of 30 trials each. On each trial, there will be a 100 msec presentation of a matrix of letters consisting of three rows of four letters each, with the 12 letters randomly chosen from the 21 consonants. One block of trials will require whole report--there will be no tone, and you must try to report as many letters as you can from anywhere in the display. The other three blocks of trials will differ in the delay between the letters and the onset of the tone indicating the line to be recalled. Delays will be 0, 150, and 500 msec. The order of the four blocks will be counterbalanced across subjects. A high-pitched tone will signal report of the top line of the display, with medium- and low-pitched tones signalling reports of the middle and bottom lines, respectively. Before the experimental trials begin, you will be given some practice trials so you can become familiar with the tones.

After each trial, you will be cued to enter as many of the letters from the appropriate row as you can. If you are not familiar with the typewriter keyboard, you might want to write the letters down immediately after each trial. You can then take your time entering them when cued. If possible, execute this experiment in a dimly lighted room (not as bright as a normal classroom, but enough light to see by).

Instructions for Running the Experiment

To run this experiment, insert Disk 1 into your computer and enter the MEL Lab as instructed in Section 0.2. Select **Perception** from the topic menu and **The Duration of the Icon** from the specific experiment menu. Instructions on the computer screen will then explain the experiment and what keys to use for your responses. The displays used in this experiment are only visible for 1/10th of a second, so be sure you are looking right at the focus cross when you start each trial. Also be sure that the room lighting is dim, and that the screen is free of reflections. *Materials needed*: Pencil and paper, if no printer is available, to copy down the results reported in the table at the end of the experiment. *Things to notice*: Do you feel that you can see the entire display of 12 letters clearly?

Expected Running Time = 60 minutes

Questions

1. What is the dependent variable in this experiment? *% recalled*

2. What is the independent variable? *Recall Condition*

3. What are some important control variables? What sort of counterbalancing is used in this experiment?

4. According to your data, what is the duration of the icon? *500 ms* Does the capacity seem to be greater than the 4 to 5 letters (33 - 42% recall) usually found in whole-report procedures? *no* Do your results agree with Sperling's?

5. What was the technique used by Eriksen and Collins (1967) to measure the duration of the icon? Do their results agree with Sperling's?

Advanced Questions

1. Suppose you wanted to determine the upper limit of capacity of the icon. Could you simply extend this experiment to a 4 x 4 or 5 x 5 matrix of letters? What procedural problems might you encounter in doing so? (Hint: Miller (1956) discusses the issue of absolute judgement and the number of distinguishable tones. See his Figure 1 and discussion on page 84.)

2. If the icon is a visual persistence of information after the actual objects being perceived are no longer present, can we extract usable information from the icon? That is, do we actually *use* the icon in normal perception? Loftus, Johnson, and Shimamura (1985) attempted to measure how much an icon is "worth."

3. Are there phenomena equivalent to the icon for other sensory modalities? Describe their characteristics.

4. How would you test for a tactile or auditory icon?

Extension Experiments

1. This experiment employed different delays before the signal of which line to report. Does it matter whether the delays are the same for a whole block of trials (*blocked*), or change from trial to trial (*random*)?

2. Sperling found that the icon's duration was partly dependent on the adaptive state of the subjects' eyes. Does the icon last longer if the eye is dark-adapted?

3. Is iconic memory different for pictures than letters?

References

Averbach, E., & Coriell, A. S. (1961). Short-term memory in vision. *Bell System Technical Journal, 40,* 309-328.

Eriksen, C. W., & Collins, J. F. (1967). Some temporal characteristics of visual pattern perception. *Journal of Experimental Psychology, 74,* 476-484.

Erdman, B., & Dodge, R. (Psychological studies on reading.) Cited in R. Woodworth & H. Schlossberg *Experimental Psychology.* New York: Holt, 1958.

Loftus, G. R., Johnson, C. A. & Shimamura, A. P. (1985). How much is an icon worth? *Journal of Experimental Psychology: Human Perception and Performance, 11,* 1-13.

Miller, G. A. (1956). The magical number seven, plus or minus two: Some limits on our capacity for processing information. *Psychological Review, 63,* 81-97.

Neisser, U. (1967). *Cognitive Psychology.* New York: Appleton-Century-Crofts.

Sperling, G. (1960). The information available in brief visual presentations. *Psychological Monographs, 74* (Whole number 11).

Thought Questions

1. When you were asked to report all 12 letters, were you able to see more of the letters than you could report?

2. When you were asked to report only one line, was it harder if the tone was delayed?

3. Did you sometimes report the wrong line because you weren't sure whether you heard the high, medium, or low tone?

The Duration of the Icon

Individual Data

Recall Condition

	0 ms Delay	150 ms Delay	500 ms Delay	Full Report
In Order	32.50	20.00	21.67	16.57
Out of Order	39.17	24.17	25.00	30.70

Cell entries are MEAN PERCENTAGE RECALLED

The Duration of the Icon

Student Name: Ken Hill

Section/Lab: A

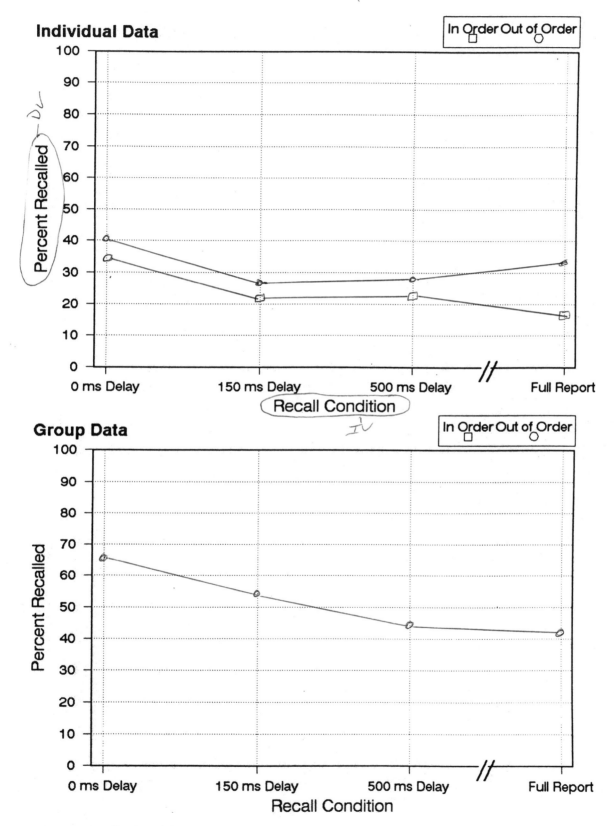

Individual Data

In Order ☐ Out of Order ○

Percent Recalled — DV

Recall Condition — IV

0 ms Delay · 150 ms Delay · 500 ms Delay · Full Report

Group Data

In Order ☐ Out of Order ○

Percent Recalled

0 ms Delay · 150 ms Delay · 500 ms Delay · Full Report

Recall Condition

Perception: The Duration of the Icon

35

1.3 Signal Detection

Abstract

Signal Detection Theory is concerned with solving a problem from classical psychophysics, namely that persons asked to detect a signal (e.g. a faulty part coming off an assembly line) are influenced by more than just how well they can see or hear (sensitivity). Their *willingness* to report a signal (bias) is also important. Traditional measures of sensory thresholds confound bias and sensitivity, while signal detection theory permits us to measure (or manipulate) them separately. In the four experiments in this exercise signal strength is shown to affect sensitivity, while the probability of a signal and the rewards and punishments associated with particular types of responses are shown to affect bias. The applicability of signal detection theory to a wide variety of human endeavors is also demonstrated. Graphing of data onto Receiver Operating Characteristic (ROC) curves is part of the exercise.

One of the earliest concerns for psychology was the measurement of *thresholds* for various senses. This is a very basic question for the study of perception--how intense must a light be before I can see it? And how much brighter must a light get before I can detect the change in brightness? The *absolute threshold* was defined as the smallest stimulus intensity that can be detected 50% of the time, while the *difference threshold* was the smallest change in stimulus intensity that can be detected 50% of the time.

One way to measure the absolute threshold for light is to present a very dim light, and then increase the intensity of the light gradually until the subject can just detect its presence. You could also start with a fairly bright light and decrease the intensity until the subject reported that it was no longer visible. By taking an average of these two intensities, you could arrive at a good estimate of the absolute threshold for that person. Of course, the same basic procedure could be used to measure how intense a sound must be before you can hear it, or to measure the acuity of any other sense.

An example of the use of absolute thresholds is the dark-adaptation curve, which is obtained by measuring a subject's absolute threshold for light every few minutes after they enter a totally darkened room. As you know from personal experience, your ability to see in a dark room improves considerably when you have been in the room for a while. A more familiar example is the common eye test, where you see letters of diminishing size and must try to read them. Your absolute threshold for letter recognition is being measured. If your threshold is higher than average, you will likely be buying some glasses or contact lenses.

There are some problems with this approach, which is called "classical" psychophysics. A major limitation to this approach is that it confounds sensitivity and bias. This means that the usual measure of a threshold is measuring both sensitivity and bias, and you cannot be sure how much each is influencing the score. Sensitivity refers to the actual functioning of your sense organs and nervous system, and this is what psychologists (and optometrists) are usually interested in measuring. Bias refers to how willing you are to report that you detect a stimulus. Bias can alter our measure of sensitivity using classical psychophysical procedures to measure thresholds, because these procedures measure both sensitivity and bias. The basic reason for this is that there is always some degree of "noise" present, either in the environment or in your nervous system.

Here is an example of noise in your nervous system. You have probably had the experience at some time of being in a totally dark place--a photographic darkroom or a cave with no lights. What do you see? You don't see total blackness, but rather you see occasional points of light, vague gray shapes, and the like. The basic reason for this is that neurons "fire" at some background rate even when they are not being stimulated at all. The "physiological gray" that you see in a totally darkened room is due to that occasional, random firing of neurons in

Of course, noise can occur in the environment as well. An example would be trying to find a traffic signal light at night on a street that has lots of bright, flashing neon signs. The same traffic signal would be easy to see at an intersection in a residential neighborhood, where there were few other lights, and thus less noise.

You can see, then, that you might occasionally "detect" a faint light in a totally darkened room even when it is not actually present, due to the background noise created by your own nervous system. Or you might not see a traffic light, because of visual noise in the environment. The consequences of the latter could range from a traffic ticket to a burial.

Signal detection theory is a psychophysical method of separating sensitivity and bias in any kind of task where a person must detect a signal against a background of noise. That signal might be the radar echo of a plane which an air traffic controller must be able to detect against the noise on the radar screen due to rain and other atmospheric "noise." It might involve detecting misprinted words in books--proofreading. Here, the noise is all the other words on the page. Detecting a tumor on an x-ray is another example of signal detection, where the noise is the x-ray shadows produced by various body organs. As you can see, signal detection theory deals with issues that directly affect our everyday lives.

Obviously, the sensitivity of your eye (or of a radar scope) has an effect on how well you can perform in a signal detection task. The level of the noise against which you are trying to detect the signal can also affect performance. Bias plays a part as well. Under some circumstances (discussed in more detail below) you are more *willing* to report detecting a signal--it depends upon the consequences of being right or wrong.

There are four versions of the signal detection task in the program. Your instructor will tell you which versions you are to complete. The four versions are intended to illustrate variables that affect bias but not sensitivity, and variables that affect sensitivity but not bias.

Method

In this experiment, you will perform the following task: You will start each trial by pressing the spacebar. On each trial you will see a number of letters presented briefly on the computer monitor. Most of the letters will be V's (Noise). On some of the trials, there will also be a U on the screen (Signal). Your task is to detect the U's, and indicate by pressing the appropriate keys whether there was a U present (Signal + Noise) or not (Noise only).

As usual, you will begin with some practice trials. You must have 70% or more correct before you can begin the main part of the experiment. Note that each display is presented for 500 msec. If you have fewer than 70% correct, the display duration will be increased by 100 msec. If you have 90% or more correct, it will be decreased by 100 msec.

In all versions of this experiment you will perform two blocks of 150 trials each, with the order of the blocks randomized. In one version the two blocks will differ in the probability of a signal (80% for one block, 20% for the other). In another version you will win "points" for correct responses and lose points for errors. Try to accumulate the highest score you can. The two blocks will differ in the "payoffs," or the number of points won and lost for various conditions. Another version of the experiment varies the "intensity" of the signal by presenting one block of trials where a single U is used as the target and another block where four U's appear when the signal is present. The remaining version manipulates the level of noise. One block of trials has five V's as noise, while the other block has 20 V's. Except for the version where the probability of the signal is manipulated directly, the signal will occur on half of the trials, in random order.

The Receiver Operating Characteristic and Calculation of d' and β

As noted above sensitivity and bias can be separately measured, using signal detection theory. What follows is a brief explanation of how these are calculated, and of how the data from signal-detection experiments are graphed

MEL Lab: Student Workbook v.1.6; © *PST - Do not reproduce*

in a Receiver Operating Characteristic curve.

There are four outcomes in signal detection: reporting a signal when it is present (a hit), failing to report a signal when it is present (a miss), reporting a signal when it is not present (a false alarm), and correctly reporting that no signal is present (a correct rejection). But note that if the number of trials on which a signal was present or not is known, the miss and correct rejection rates are completely redundant, since they can be determined if we know the hit rate and false alarm rate. For this reason, signal detection analysis is based on hits and false alarms only. These outcomes are presented graphically below.

Report of whether or not there was a signal

		"Yes"	"No"
State of the world	Noise only	False Alarm	Correct Rejection
	Signal + Noise	Hit	Miss

The measures of sensitivity and bias are symbolized as **d'** (pronounced dee-prime) and **β** (beta). The calculations of d' and β are quite straightforward, requiring only that you have a table of values of z (the unit normal distribution) with the area above and the ordinate of the distribution for each value of z. A table of selected values is shown below. The proportion of hits and false alarms for each condition is reported to you at the end of the experiment, along with the corresponding values of d' and β. Use the proportion of hits and false alarms to calculate d' and β, and check your calculation with the values displayed on the table. Your instructor may also give you the values for other members of the class who served as subjects in different versions of the experiment. Note that d' and β are calculated only for individual subjects. To get an average d' or β, they should first be calculated for each subject individually, and then averaged.

The ROC Curve

A graphical way of representing sensitivity and bias simultaneously is the Receiver Operating Characteristic "curve". This is constructed by plotting one point on the ROC graph for each condition of a manipulation. Suppose that for one condition your hit rate (proportion of hits) was 0.7 and your false alarm rate (proportion of false alarms) was 0.1. You would plot that point by finding where the lines for "Probability of a hit" of 0.7 and "Probability of a false alarm" of 0.1 intersect. The further a point is from the bold diagonal, the greater the sensitivity: many signals were correctly detected, but few false alarms occurred. In the case of the point just plotted, d'= 1.8, indicating good sensitivity. Note, however, that the point plotted is to the left of the thin diagonal line. This indicates a slight bias toward responding "No:" False alarms occurred somewhat less often than they would have if no bias were present. In fact the value of β is 1.98 (β = 1 indicates no bias). If we now varied some condition of the experiment (any of the four manipulations that make up the versions of this experiment), we could plot a series of points that make up an ROC curve. For example, if we varied the probability of a signal (which affects bias only), we would expect to find those points falling along a curve such as one in Figure 1.3.1, representing changes in bias while sensitivity remained constant. On the other hand, if we varied a condition like the intensity of the noise (which affects sensitivity but not bias) we would expect to find the points differing in their distance from the bold diagonal (varying sensitivity), but remaining about equidistant from the thin diagonal (no variation in bias).

You should plot the points representing probabilities of hits and false alarms for each of the two blocks of trials in the version of the task that you completed. A more complete experiment would of course map out more than just two points on the ROC curve, but the number of trials needed to do so is greater than can easily be accommodated. Do sensitivity and/or bias seem to differ between the two conditions? The Discussion section below presents expected outcomes for each version. You should then calculate values of d' and β to determine the actual levels of bias and sensitivity.

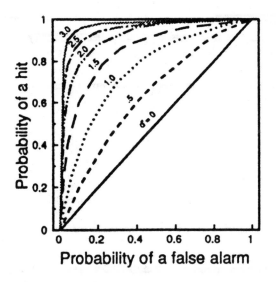

Figure 1.3.1 Typical ROC curves illustrating d'

Calculation of d'

The calculation of d' (the measure of sensitivity) requires that you look up the z-scores associated with the probability of a hit and the probability of a false alarm. The probability of hits and false alarms are the same as the proportion of hits and false alarms reported to you. The formula for d' is

d' = [z for p(false alarm)] - [z for p(hit)]

Table of values of z and ordinate
for selected values of "p."

p	z	ordinate	p	z	ordinate	p	z	ordinate	p	z	ordinate	p	z	ordinate
.99	-2.33	.0264	.89	-1.23	.1872	.79	-0.81	.2874	.69	-0.50	.3521	.59	-0.23	.3885
.98	-2.05	.0488	.88	-1.18	.1989	.78	-0.77	.2966	.68	-0.48	.3555	.58	-0.20	.3910
.97	-1.88	.0681	.87	-1.13	.2107	.77	-0.74	.3034	.67	-0.44	.3621	.57	-0.18	.3925
.96	-1.75	.0863	.86	-1.08	.2227	.76	-0.71	.3101	.66	-0.41	.3668	.56	-0.15	.3945
.95	-1.64	.1040	.85	-1.04	.2323	.75	-0.67	.3187	.65	-0.39	.3697	.55	-0.13	.3956
.94	-1.55	.1200	.84	-0.99	.2444	.74	-0.64	.3251	.64	-0.36	.3739	.54	-0.10	.3970
.93	-1.48	.1334	.83	-0.95	.2541	.73	-0.61	.3312	.63	-0.33	.3778	.53	-0.08	.3977
.92	-1.41	.1476	.82	-0.92	.2637	.72	-0.58	.3372	.62	-0.31	.3802	.52	-0.05	.3984
.91	-1.34	.1626	.81	-0.88	.2709	.71	-0.55	.3429	.61	-0.28	.3836	.51	-0.03	.3988
.90	-1.28	.1758	.80	-0.84	.2803	.70	-0.52	.3485	.60	-0.25	.3867	.50	0.0	.3989
.49	0.03	.3988	.39	0.28	.3836	.29	0.55	.3429	.19	0.88	.2709	.09	1.34	.1626
.48	0.05	.3984	.38	0.31	.3802	.28	0.58	.3372	.18	0.92	.2637	.08	1.41	.1476
.47	0.08	.3977	.37	0.33	.3778	.27	0.61	.3312	.17	0.95	.2541	.07	1.48	.1334
.46	0.10	.3970	.36	0.36	.3739	.26	0.64	.3251	.16	0.99	.2444	.06	1.55	.1200
.45	0.13	.3956	.35	0.39	.3697	.25	0.67	.3187	.15	1.04	.2323	.05	1.64	.1040
.44	0.15	.3945	.34	0.41	.3668	.24	0.71	.3101	.14	1.08	.2227	.04	1.75	.0863
.43	0.18	.3925	.33	0.44	.3621	.23	0.74	.3034	.13	1.13	.2107	.03	1.88	.0681
.42	0.20	.3910	.32	0.48	.3555	.22	0.77	.2966	.12	1.18	.1989	.02	2.05	.0488
.41	0.23	.3885	.31	0.50	.3521	.21	0.81	.2874	.11	1.23	.1872	.01	2.33	.0264
.40	0.25	.3867	.30	0.52	.3485	.20	0.84	.2803	.10	1.28	.1758			

To illustrate, suppose that for an individual subject the proportion of hits was 0.70 and the proportion of false alarms was 0.10. Looking up 0.70 (under "p") in the table, we find a corresponding value of $z = -0.52$. Looking up 0.10 in the table in the same way, we find $z = 1.28$. Applying the formula, we have

$$d' = Z_{(0.10)} - Z_{(0.70)}$$
$$= [1.28] - [-0.52]$$
$$= 1.80$$

Note that a positive d' indicates that sensitivity was at better than a chance level, and the higher the d', the greater the sensitivity. If the proportion of hits and false alarms are equal, however, d' will be zero, indicating that performance was at a chance level. D' can also be negative, though only when the proportion of false alarms exceeds the proportion of hits. In this case, sensitivity is at a level worse than merely guessing.

Calculation of β

The calculation of β (the measure of bias) requires that you find the ordinate, or height of the unit normal distribution, associated with the probability of a hit and the probability of a false alarm. These values are obtained the same way as for d', except that we use the column labelled "ordinate." The formula for β is

$$\beta = [\text{ordinate for } p(\text{hit})]/[\text{ordinate for } p(\text{false alarm})]$$

To illustrate, assume we have the same values as above of $p(\text{hit}) = 0.70$ and $p(\text{false alarm}) = 0.10$. Looking up "p" = 0.70 in the table gives a value of the ordinate of 0.349, while looking up "p" = 0.10 gives a value of the ordinate of 0.176. Applying the formula gives

$$\beta = [\text{Ordinate}_{(0.70)}]/[\text{Ordinate}_{(0.10)}]$$
$$\beta = [0.349]/[0.176] = 1.98$$

which indicates a bias toward responding "No," whether a signal is present or not. A value of $\beta > 1$ indicates a bias toward responding "No," whether a signal is present or not, while a value of $\beta < 1$ indicates a bias toward responding "Yes," whether a signal is present or not. If β is 1, then no bias is present.

The data illustrated thus would have come from a subject whose sensitivity was pretty good, but whose hit rate was lower than it might have been, partly due to a bias toward reporting that no signal was present.

Note that you will need to round the values of p(hit) and p(false alarm) in order to use this table. Your calculations based on this table may differ from those reported at the end of the experiment since those are not rounded. Most statistics textbooks contain more extensive tables that will allow you to make more accurate calculations.

Discussion

The four versions of this experiment were designed to illustrate four general types of variables that affect signal detection. Two of these (the probability of a signal and the payoffs) should affect bias but not sensitivity, while the others (intensity of the signal and intensity of the noise) should affect sensitivity but not bias.

Variables Affecting Bias

Version I: Manipulation of the probability of a signal. Note that for this part of the experiment on signal detection, there are values of both p(hit) and p(false alarm) for two different probabilities of a signal. The expected outcome is that bias (rather than sensitivity) will be affected, with a positive bias (β<1) occurring when the probability of a signal is 80%, and a negative bias (β>1) occurring when the probability of a signal is only 20%. When a signal occurs on most trials, subjects begin to expect it, providing a bias toward responding "Yes." On the other hand, when the signal is relatively rare, subjects begin to expect that there will not be a signal, resulting in a bias toward responding "No." Thus the value of β (bias) should differ between the two probability conditions, but d' (sensitivity) should not.

Version II: Manipulation of payoffs. In this version of the experiment, the probability of a signal is 50%, but the number of "points" won or lost by the subject is manipulated. In one block of trials the "payoff" is to win five points for each hit and lose only one for each false alarm. Ideally, this should result in a bias toward responding "yes" (β<1), since the payoff for a hit is large, but the penalty for a false alarm is low. Indeed, if the penalty for a false alarm is low enough, a strategy of just ignoring that penalty and always responding "Yes" might seem reasonable. In effect, you would not even have to bother to look! In the other block of this manipulation, the payoffs are reversed: win one point for a hit, but lose five points for a false alarm. With false alarms so costly, the subjects are expected to respond "yes" only when they are absolutely certain that the signal was present. This should result in a bias against responding "yes" (β>1). Again, the value of β (bias) should differ between the two payoff conditions, but d' (sensitivity) should not.

Variables Affecting Sensitivity

Version III: Manipulation of intensity of the signal. In this version of the experiment the intensity of the signal is manipulated by changing the number of times the target letter U occurs in the display: either once or four times. It is expected that it will be easier to spot a U if there are a lot of them present than if there is only one. Because this manipulation makes the signal easier to see, it should affect sensitivity, and not bias, with sensitivity being greater (larger d') when the more "intense" signal is present. Since the target appears on 50% of the trials and no explicit payoffs are presented, β should be near 1 for both blocks of trials. (Individual subjects may actually show a bias toward "Yes" or "No," based on implicit payoffs and their own expectations about what is "good" performance. In this case, β may be greater or less than 1, but the bias should still be about the same in each block of trials).

Version IV: Manipulation of the intensity of the noise. In this version, intensity of the noise is manipulated by varying the number of V's displayed on the screen: either five or twenty. When only five noise letters are on the screen it is expected that determining whether or not a U was present should be relatively easy. On the other hand, when there are twenty V's on the screen, a U will be more likely to "disappear" into the background of noise. This manipulation thus affects the ability of the subject to see the target and should thus affect sensitivity but not bias, with d' greater (reflecting greater sensitivity) when there is less noise. Since the target appears on 50% of the trials and no explicit payoffs are presented, β should be near 1 for both blocks of trials. (As in the manipulation of signal intensity, individual subjects may actually show a bias toward "Yes" or "No," based on implicit payoffs and their own expectations about what is "good" performance. In this case, β may be greater or less than 1, but the bias should still be about the same in each block of trials).

Instructions for Running the Experiment

To run this experiment, insert Disk 1 into your computer and enter the MEL Lab as instructed in Section 0.2. Select **Perception** from the topic menu and **Signal Detection** from the specific experiment menu. Before the experiment begins you will be asked to pick a version of the experiment to run. Your instructor will assign you to one of the four versions, or tell you to select option number 5, in which the computer will counterbalance the version based on your subject number. Instructions on the computer screen will then explain the experiment and what keys to use for your responses. Note that you must get 7 of the 10 practice trials right before you can begin the actual experiment. (If you miss more than 3 practice trials, you will have to repeat them.) The displays will be presented for only a very brief time, and your accuracy is important, not your reaction time. *Materials needed*: Pencil and paper, if no printer is available, to copy down the results reported in the table at the end of the experiment.

Expected Running Time = 45 minutes

Questions

1. What are the dependent variables in these experiments?

2. What are the independent variables in each experiment?

3. What are some important control variables?

4. What are the results? What effect does each independent variable have on bias and on sensitivity?

5. A real-world signal detection task is decision-making by a jury in a criminal case. What would be a hit? A false alarm? What might bias the jury in favor of a guilty verdict or in favor of acquittal? How might you improve the sensitivity of the jury?

Advanced Questions

1. Other real-world signal detection tasks that you could analyze in signal-detection terms include inspection of parts coming off an assembly line, airport security checks for weapons and explosives, detection of shoplifting, and detection of when the driver of a car in front of yours slams on the brakes. What bias might be appropriate for each and why?

2. What happens to the hit rate if the false alarm rate is zero? What are the implications of this for real-world tasks like jury decisions?

3. Can signal detection bias be a problem in intelligence testing of children?

4. How does forced choice responding reduce bias effects?

Extension Experiments

1. Devise other signal-detection tasks, along with ways to manipulate both sensitivity and bias. The search task used in the experiment on automaticity (Section 2.13) could be studied using signal-detection measures.

References

Gescheider, G. A. (1976). *Psychophysics: Method and theory.* Hillsdale (NJ), L. A. Erlbaum Associates.
Wickens, C. D. (1984). *Engineering psychology and Human Performance.* Columbus, OH: Charles E. Merrill.

Signal Detection

Copy the values presented at the end of the experiment into the appropriate spaces below. Fill out only the part of the table corresponding to the version of the experiment that you completed.

VERSION Condition	Proportion of		d'	ß
	Hits	False Alarms		
I. Probability of a Signal				
80% Signal, 20% Noise	___	___	___	___
20% Signal, 80% Noise	___	___	___	___
II. Payoffs				
Hit=+5, False Alarm=-1	___	___	___	___
Hit=+1, False Alarm=-5	___	___	___	___
III. Intensity of the Signal				
Low Intensity Block (1 U when target present)	___	___	___	___
High Intensity Block (4 U's when target present)	___	___	___	___
IV. Intensity of the Noise				
2 = Low Intensity Block (5 V's present)	.88	.05	2.78	1.84
1 = High Intensity Block (20 V's present)	.60	.28	.83	1.15

(handwritten margin notes: "4 variables", "Dh", "Bh", "Bl", "Dh", "Dl")

Signal Detection

Individual Data

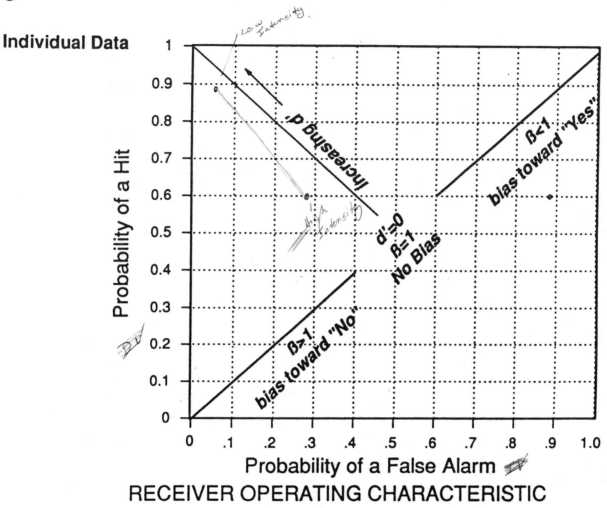

RECEIVER OPERATING CHARACTERISTIC

Condition

2

Version

3

4

1.4 Perceptual Matching

Abstract

In this exercise, letters are compared, and subjects must indicate whether they are the same or different. Two letters are the "same" if they have the same letter name but different physical appearance (Aa), or if they are physically the same (AA). Comparisons of interest concern name- vs. physical-match, and the time interval between presentation of the first and second letters. The experiment repeats one by Posner, Boies, Eichelman, and Taylor (1969) that suggests that visually presented letters are quickly recoded into a sound representation. The usual advantage in speed of reacting to physical matches over name matches disappears with an inter-stimulus interval (ISI) of 1.5 seconds, suggesting that the first stimulus is now represented only as a name code, wiping out any advantage to matching two visually coded letters.

A basic question concerning perception and memory is how we compare two stimuli to determine whether they are the same. If you are asked to compare two visual stimuli that are both visible at the same time, you need only examine them visually to determine whether they are the same or not--you don't need to name the stimuli in order to do this. On the other hand, if only one stimulus is visible at a time, the first must be remembered for comparison to the second. There is considerable evidence that, in most cases, short-term memory for visual stimuli is based on a sound or name code. For example, if shown the letter "b", we remember the sound "bee" rather than a visual representation of the letter "b." Evidence for the use of this name code in Short Term Memory (STM) comes from work by Sperling (1963), who found that errors in recall in a task involving brief visual presentation of sets of letters were usually acoustic confusions. That is, subjects who had seen an F were more likely to incorrectly recall an S (which sounds like *ef*) than an E (which looks like an F). This finding has been replicated and extended by Conrad (1964).

The experiment for this exercise replicates (with minor changes) Posner, Boies, Eichelman, and Taylor's (1969) Experiment 1, which examines whether information presented visually is encoded only in a name code in STM, or whether it might also be coded visually. The experiment also provides evidence about how quickly a visual stimulus can be converted to a name code in STM.

This experiment uses a letter-matching task in which subjects see two letters presented visually on the computer screen. They must decide, as quickly as possible, whether the two letters are the same (for example, AA or Bb) or different (AB or Ba). On some trials, both letters are presented at the same time. On other trials, one letter is presented either one or two seconds before the other.

What do we expect? If both letters are presented at the same time, and they are physically identical (AA), you should be able to respond "same" more quickly than if the letters are only identical in name (Aa). The physical match might involve comparing the decaying visual representation of the first letter to the second. In contrast, the name match requires that both letters be converted to a common form before they can be compared. For example, both visual forms must evoke a letter name that must be compared. The difference between "same" RT's for the physical identity and name identity matches will then be an indication of how long it takes to produce the name code of a letter in STM.

Another comparison of interest is to see whether the advantage of physical identity over name identity is a general one, or whether it disappears when you have more time to process the first stimulus. The disappearance of the physical identity advantage with more time would suggest that (at least for these materials) information in STM may remain in a visual code temporarily and then be remembered only on the basis of its name. Posner et al. (1969) found that a physical match (AA) is faster than a name match (Aa) for simultaneous presentation, but there is no difference between the conditions at an inter-stimulus interval (ISI) of 2 seconds, suggesting that the letters are now represented only by a name code in STM.

Method

Each subject performs three blocks of 64 trials each. On each trial of each block, the subject must make a decision about whether the two letters presented are the same (for example, AA or Bb) or different (for example, AB or bA). The three blocks of trials differ only in the time interval between the first and second letters (the inter-stimulus interval or ISI). This interval is 0, 1, or 2 seconds, and is the same for all trials of a block. The first letter remains on display after the second appears, and both remain in view until a response is made.

The 64 test trials of each block consist of 32 *same* pairs and 32 *different* pairs. The letters used are A, B, F, H, and K. Of the 32 pairs of each type, there are 8 each of Upper case followed by Upper case (AA), Upper followed by Lower (Aa or Ba), Lower followed by Upper (kK or hF), and Lower followed by Lower (aa or fb). Reaction time to classify the letters as same or different will be the dependent variable. Reaction time is measured from the onset of the second letter (this is, of course, the same as the onset of the first letter for ISI = 0). The 192 trials of the experiment are made up of 48 physically identical pairs, 48 name-identical pairs, and 96 different pairs.

Same pairs and *different* pairs occur equally often, in random order, as do the four combinations of case. Inter-stimulus interval (ISI) is blocked, with the order of the blocks randomized for each subject.

Instructions for Running the Experiment

To run this experiment, insert Disk 1 into your computer and enter the MEL Lab as instructed in Section 0.2. Select **Perception** from the topic menu and **Perceptual Matching** from the specific experiment menu. Instructions on the computer screen will then explain the experiment and what keys to use for your responses. Note that you must get 8 of the 10 practice trials right before you can begin the 192 trials of the actual experiment. (If you miss more than 2 practice trials, you will have to repeat them.) *Reaction time is important* for this experiment, so please respond as quickly and accurately as you can to each stimulus. *Materials needed*: Pencil and paper, if no printer is available, to copy down the results reported in the table at the end of the experiment. *Things to notice*: Are name matches (**A** same as **a**) harder than physical matches (**A** same as **A**)?

Expected Running Time = 24 minutes

Questions

1. What is the dependent variable for this experiment?

2. What are the independent variables?

3. What are some important control variables?

4. What are the results? Does the RT advantage for physical over name matches decrease with increasing ISI? If so, there should be a significant interaction between ISI and type of *same* match.

5. In what ways did this experiment differ from that of Posner et al.'s Experiment 1? Do these differences seem to have had any effect on the results?

Advanced Questions

1.   How long does it take to produce a name code in STM? That is, how long does it take to encode a visually-presented letter by its sound (name)? One approach to answering this question is Donders' *subtractive method* (Donders, 1868/1969, and see the further discussion in Section 2.3, "Additive Factors Methodology"). Donders proposed that you can determine the duration of a stage of mental processing by comparing the RT to a task that includes this stage to the RT for a task that is the same in all respects except one--it doesn't require that stage of processing. By this logic, we can subtract the RT for *same* judgments where the letters shared only the same name from RT for *same* judgments where the letters were physically identical, as well as having the same name. That difference should reflect the added time it takes to produce a name code for the letters, so that they can be compared. Of course, this subtractive method only works if these two conditions (physical + name identity and name identity only) really differ *only* in omitting the stage of encoding the name of the letter. Does this assumption seem warranted for this experiment?

2.   Another point that needs consideration is whether, for an ISI of zero, the advantage of a physical match over a name-only match for *same* judgments might simply be due to the two stimuli being present in the icon, or sensory register, so that the match doesn't require visual encoding in STM. If this point is valid, then the claim that these data support a visual encoding in STM (in addition to the well-documented name coding) is rather weak. What aspects of the data might lead you to conclude that the physical match is not just a match of percepts on the icon?

3.   There is another interesting issue to raise, though it doesn't directly address the questions concerning visual and name coding in STM. Were you faster for *same* judgments than for *different* judgments? Most researchers find just that result, in many different types of same/different tasks. Why might this be the case?

Extension Experiments

1.   What is the time-course of change in available attentional capacity during a task like the one used in this experiment? See Posner and Boies (1971, especially Experiment 2) for a discussion of a method for measuring available attentional capacity using a second task (RT to a probe sound) superimposed on the letter-matching task.

2. How would you test a picture/word match effect (e.g., line drawing of simple objects such as a car or plane)?

3. If the subject is told before the trial to expect to see an upper case letter, do you think he could image a visual stimulus that would allow a response as fast as a name match?

References

Conrad, R. (1964). Acoustic confusions in immediate memory. *British Journal of Psychology*, 1964, 75-84.
Donders, F. C. (1869/1969). On the speed of mental processes. In W. G. Koster (Ed. & Trans.) *Attention and Human Performance II. Acta Psychologica*, *30*, 412-431.
Posner, M. I., Boies, S. J., Eichelman, H. W., & Taylor, R. L. (1969). Retention of visual and name codes of single letters. *Journal of Experimental Psychology Monographs*, 79(1, Pt. 2).
Posner, M. I. & Boies, S. J. (1971). Components of attention. *Psychological Review*, *87*, 391-405.
Posner, M. I. & Keele, S. W. (1967). Decay of visual information from a single letter. *Science*, *158*, 137-139.
Sperling, G. (1963). A model for visual memory tasks. *Human Factors*, *5*, 19-31.

1. Did you sometimes feel that you could make the judgement of whether or not the letters were the same by simply comparing what they look like?

2. Did you sometimes feel that you could make the judgement of whether or not the letters were the same by simply comparing what the letter names sound like?

3. Did name matches (Aa) seem harder than physical matches (AA)?

Perceptual Matching

Individual Data

Condition	Inter-Stimulus Interval (sec)		
	0	1	
Identical	____	____	___
Same Name	____	____	___
Different	____	____	___

Cell entries are MEAN CORRECT REACTION TIME (msec)

Perceptual Matching

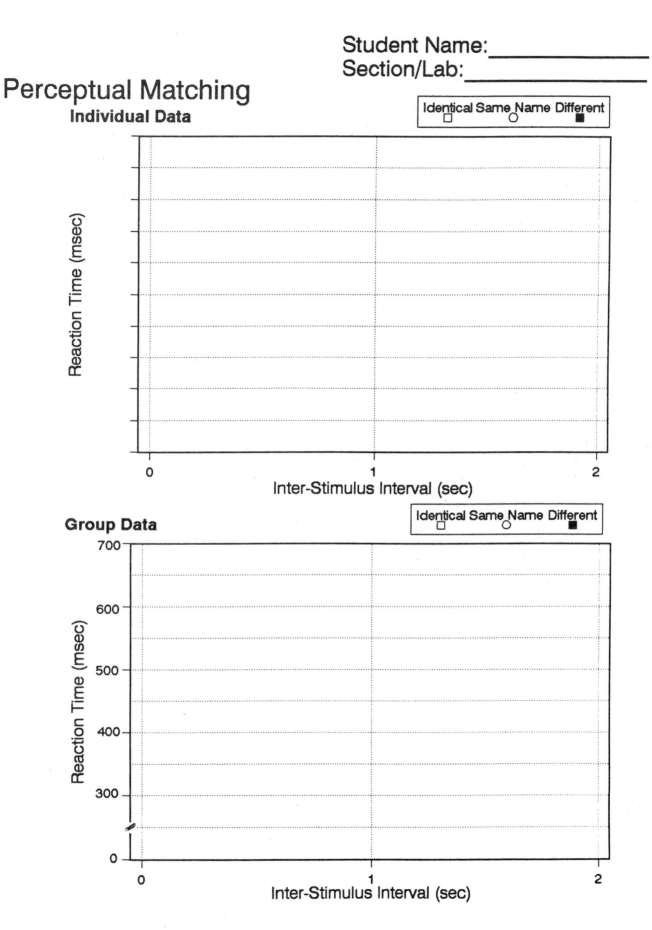

1.5 Selective Attention and Response Competition

Abstract

Selective attention involves focusing on one aspect of the environment while excluding other interfering stimuli. One way to measure the success of selective attention is through the use of experimental conditions that produce response competition--a slowing in the correct response due to "priming" of the incorrect response. As the conflicting stimuli are moved farther from the target, their influence should be diminished if subjects can successfully restrict attention solely to the target. This provides a measure of the area to which visual selective attention can be focused.

In this experiment, you will study selective attention. Selective attention refers to a focusing of attention on some perceptual inputs to the exclusion of others. Selective attention can operate in several ways. One is to select the perceptual modality attended to--when attending to visual material, you are less sensitive to auditory inputs. An example you are familiar with is being so intent upon a book you are reading or studying, that someone else has a hard time getting your attention by calling your name. You were selectively attending to the book. Another way that you can selectively attend is to try to attend to one dimension of a single stimulus, while trying to ignore other dimensions. An example would be reading a word while ignoring the color in which it was printed. This type of selective attention is the focus of Section 1.7 on Attentional Interference and the Stroop effect. Finally, you can selectively choose one physical location to attend to while trying not to attend to other locations. That type of selective attention is the focus of this experiment.

One way that we very easily attend selectively to one location in the visual environment is simply to change where our eyes are pointing. If we wish to attend to a page of print, rather than the images on a television screen, we point our eyes at the printed page instead of the television. Indeed, we do this sort of selective attention so easily that we are hardly aware of changing eye (or head) position. But can we focus attention selectively within a single fixation? That is, can we decide which part of the visual array to attend to *without moving our eyes*? And if so, how small an area can we choose to focus attention on?

B. A. Eriksen and C. W. Eriksen (1974) suggested a simple procedure for answering these questions. A single target letter appeared in a known location, and subjects had to press a lever either left or right to indicate which letter they saw. On some trials the target letter was flanked on the left and right by one of several types of noise letters. Sometimes there were compatible noise letters that were simply repetitions of the target letter. Sometimes there were "neutral" noise letters that never appeared as targets. Finally, sometimes the noise letters were letters that called for the opposite response as the target letter. This "incompatible" noise led to a marked increase in reaction time, since subjects did not seem to be able to ignore it if the noise letters were right next to the target letter. This slowing is referred to as *response competition*, since it seems that the target and noise letters are each priming a response, which slows the execution of the correct response. This shows a *failure* of selective attention--subjects could not focus their attention on the targets and ignore the noise letters. But what would happen as the noise letters are moved farther away from the target? Note that the target letter always occurred in the same location. If subjects can selectively attend to only part of the visual array, it is to their advantage to do so in this experiment, to try to avoid the slowing in reaction time caused by incompatible noise. Suppose that subjects could restrict their attention to an area of one degree of visual angle (see below for a discussion of visual angle). In that case, incompatible noise only a half degree from the target should produce a slowing in reaction time, while noise farther than a degree away should successfully be ignored, and hence should produce no change. Thus, Eriksen and Eriksen argued, we can use the degree of response competition to measure the size of the selective attentional focus--the area to which we can restrict attention. That area is determined by seeing how far away the flanking noise letters must be moved before they produce an increase in reaction time.

In this replication of Eriksen & Eriksen's experiment, we will make use of the *response competition* produced when two competing responses are both triggered. The task will involve identifying which of two letters appears above a fixation mark. On some trials, the opposite target letter will appear to the left and right of the target letter. By varying the distance from the target to the conflicting letters, we can determine how far away those letters must be before the response competition effect disappears. This will give us a measure of the degree to which visual attention can be voluntarily focused.

Method

In this experiment, you will perform a series of 192 trials of a reaction-time task. On each trial, an S or an H will appear directly above a fixation mark on the screen. The letter above the fixation will be the target, and you will respond to it by pressing the appropriate key to indicate whether the letter was an S or an H. The two target letters occur equally often, in random order. From trial to trial there will also be various types of noise in the display, with the noise consisting of other letters flanking the target. Note that the letter over the fixation is always the target--you should try to ignore the flanking letters. On some trials there will be no flanking letters. When the flanking letters occur, they will be one of three types--compatible noise (flanking letters the same as the target), incompatible noise (flanking letters are S if the target is an H, and vice versa), or neutral noise (flanking letters are letters other than S or H). Flanking letters will appear immediately beside the target or 3 or 8 spaces away from the target. The separation of the target and noise will vary randomly from trial to trial, with each spacing occurring equally often. The order of the four trial types will also vary randomly, with each occurring equally often. After you have finished this experiment, you will be able to call up examples of each of the three spacings in order to measure how far the noise letters were from the target. You will also need to measure the distance from which you viewed the letters, in order to calculate the size of the display in degrees of visual angle, as described below.

Measurement of Visual Angle

Since the main issue of this experiment is how far away the incompatible noise has to be before the response conflict effect disappears (indicating that you can selectively attend to the target, and ignore the noise), it is important to report that distance correctly in the write-up of the experiment. The size of a display, or the distance between elements in a display, is usually reported in *degrees of visual angle*. This measure assures that the size of the object and its distance from the viewer are taken into account--a 1-inch object at 2 feet subtends the same visual angle as a 2-inch object at 4 feet. Thus, comparisons across experiments are easier--they are all reported in degrees of visual angle.

How do you determine degrees of visual angle? To do so, you must know the size of the display, and the distance from the display to the viewer's eye. That presents a problem when using a computer screen, unless subjects use a chin-rest, or otherwise restrict their head placement. In doing this experiment, you should avoid shifting closer to and farther from the screen during the experiment. Measure the distance from your eyes to the center of the screen. (For most published experiments, care must be taken to insure that this distance is known within very close tolerances.) Also measure the distance of the flanking noise letter from the target for each of the three spacings. Measure this from the centers of the letters. At the end of the experiment you will be given the opportunity to make these measurements. You can use the ruler provided at the end of Chapter 1.1. Given the size of the display and the distance from the display to the viewer, you can solve for visual angle using the law of cosines. With a calculator with inverse trigonometric functions you can solve the equation: visual angle = inverse tangent ($^W/_D$). This can be approximated by:

Visual angle in degrees = 57.3W/D

where W = width of object
D = distance from object to viewer
and W and D are in the same units.

For example, a character that is 5mm millimeters high at a distance of 500 mm has a visual angle of inverse tangent (5/500) = .5719°. Note, if you use the approximation (5/500 x 57.3) you get .573°.

Instructions for Running the Experiment

To run this experiment, insert Disk 1 into your computer and enter the MEL Lab as instructed in Section 0.2. Select **Perception** from the topic menu and **Selective Attention and Response Competition** from the specific experiment menu. Instructions on the computer screen will then explain the experiment and what keys to use for your responses. Note that you must get 8 of the 10 practice trials right before you can begin the 192 trials of the actual experiment. (If you miss more than 2 practice trials, you will have to repeat them.) *Reaction time is important* for this experiment, so please respond as quickly and accurately as you can to each stimulus. *Materials needed*: Pencil and paper, if no printer is available, to copy down the results reported in the table at the end of the experiment; ruler to make millimeter measurements (one is provided at the end of Chapter 1.1). *Things to notice*: What effect do the flanking letters have on your reaction time?

Expected Running Time = 24 minutes

Questions

1. What are the dependent variable for this experiment?

2. What are the independent variables?

3. What are some important control variables?

4. What is your estimate of the width of the attentional field at its narrowest focus?

5. Does this estimate agree with that of Eriksen and Eriksen (1974)?

Advanced Questions

1. How far does response competition extend? That is, does it reach to the level of the responses themselves, or might it only influence response preparation? See Coles, Gratton, Bashore, Eriksen, and Donchin (1985) and Eriksen, Coles, Morrison, and O'Hara (1985).

Extension Experiments

1. You have estimated the size of the attentional field when the subjects are trying to restrict it to a minimum, and have all the time they need to do so (since the target was always in the same place). This operation of restricting attention can be assumed to take some time to occur. How might you estimate the time required to restrict attention? See Eriksen and St. James (1987). While their experiment was fairly complex, the basic idea is to vary the position of the target, with a precue appearing at various times before the target to indicate its location.

2. How would you measure how long this interference lasts as a function of the stimulus onset asynchrony (SOA) of the target and distractors?

3. What would the effect be of letters that are visually similar to the response stimulus but a different letter (Eriksen & Eriksen, 1974)?

References

Coles, M. G. H., Gratton, G., Bashore, T. R., Eriksen, C. W., & Donchin, E. (1985). A psychophysiological investigation of the continuous flow model of human information processing. *Journal of Experimental Psychology: Human Perception and Performance, 11*, 529-553.

Eriksen, B. A., & Eriksen, C. W. (1974). Effects of noise letters upon the identification of a target letter in a nonsearch task. *Perception and Psychophysics, 16*, 143-149.

Eriksen, C. W., Coles, M. G. H., Morris, L. R., & O'Hara, W. P. (1985). An electromyographic examination of response competition. *Bulletin of the Psychonomic Society, 23*, 165-168.

Eriksen, C. W. & St. James, J. D. (1986). Visual attention within and around the field of focal attention: A zoom lens model. *Perception and Psychophysics, 40*, 225-240.

Stroop, J. R. (1935). Studies of interference in serial verbal reactions. *Journal of Experimental Psychology, 18*, 643-662.

Thought Questions

1. When the target letter was surrounded by the opposite target (HSH or SHS), did you sometimes press the wrong key, but then press the correct key a fraction of a second later?

2. Did you ever make that same kind of "double response" when only the target letter (H or S) was present?

3. Did you seem to be able to ignore the flanking letters when they were farther away from the target letter?

Selective Attention and Response Competition

Individual Data

Record the measurements you made of the size of the displays below. Record
these to the nearest millimeter. The distance from the target (center letter)
to the noise letters (in either direction) should be measured from the center of
the target letter to the center of either of the noise letters.

SPACING   DISTANCE

1 space _____   3 spaces _____   8 spaces _____

Also record the distance from your eyes to the center of the screen. This may
have to be approximate, since you may have moved somewhat during the experiment,
but please measure this distance from your usual sitting posture during the
experiment.

Distance to screen _____

Noise Type

Spacing	No Noise*	Compatible	Neutral	Incompatible
1	_____	_____	_____	_____
3	_____	_____	_____	_____
8	_____	_____	_____	_____

Cell entries are MEAN CORRECT REACTION TIME (msec)

Noise Type

Spacing	No Noise*	Compatible	Neutral	Incompatible
1	_____	_____	_____	_____
3	_____	_____	_____	_____
8	_____	_____	_____	_____

Cell entries are MEAN PERCENT CORRECT

* Note that "spacing" has no meaning for the no noise condition. Thus, the
means for the three spacings for no noise should be nearly identical, since
these are really all the same condition.

Selective Attention and Response Competition

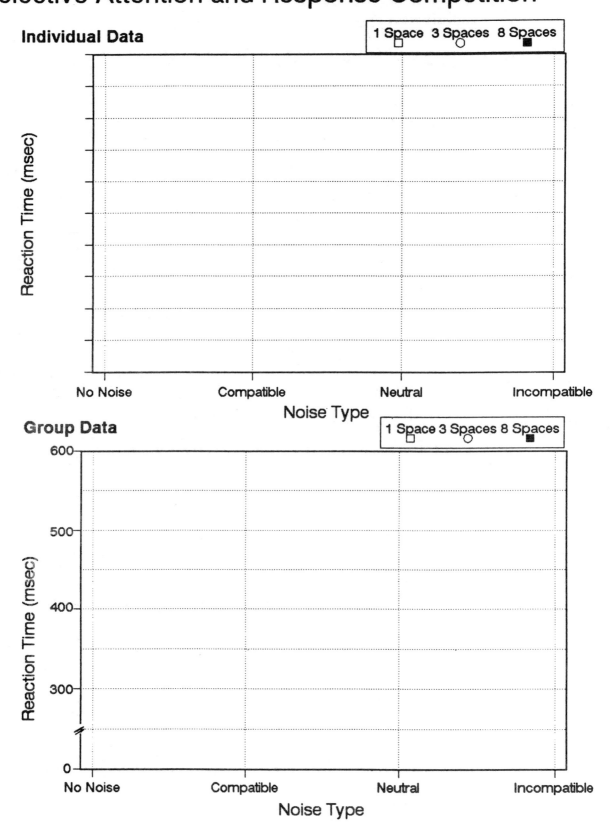

1.6 Mental Rotation of Images

Abstract

Psychology had an early concern for mental imagery, but problems with that research led to the virtual abandonment of the study of imagery. More recently, researchers have found ways to measure certain aspects of imagery. One successful technique uses "rotation" of mental images. A person is shown two shapes, and must decide if they are the same or not (regardless of rotation). One shape is sometimes rotated with respect to the other, and people report that they make the judgement by rotating their image of one shape to see if it matches the other. If peoples' reports are accurate, it should take longer to rotate the image if the stimulus is rotated farther from straight-up. Shepard and his colleagues have done a number of experiments of this type, and find that images do seem to be rotated, and at a steady, measurable speed. This exercise has students do this same task to measure the speed of rotation of mental images.

How many windows are in your family home? Take a moment to answer that question before you continue. In order to answer that question, you probably constructed an image of each room in your house, or of the outside of it viewed from various directions, and counted the number of windows you "saw." That's an example of a mental image. Other examples might be imagining a friend's face, or picturing to yourself which buildings you have to walk by to go to the library.

Research on mental imagery goes back to the very beginnings of psychology and the use of trained introspection as a way to explore the contents of consciousness. The introspective method fell on hard times early in this century, partly due to the rise of Behaviorism as the principal point of view in psychology (which in turn was partly due to problems with the method of introspection itself). For the behaviorists, psychology was to be restricted to studying the relations between stimuli and responses, defined as overt events in the physical world that could be measured in a physical way. Behaviorists banished the study of mental processes from their psychology, because they believed that such events are fundamentally private--they cannot be observed directly by anyone else, and so cannot be measured by independent observers. With the rejection of the study of the contents of consciousness came a rejection of the study of mental imagery.

The revival of interest in cognition, and the rise of cognitive psychology to a prominent place in experimental psychology, reflected a rejection of the strong claims of the behaviorists. However, the reliance on public events (stimuli and responses that can be observed by more than one person) and the rejection of introspection as a formal research tool remain. Cognitivists are willing to use those stimulus-response measurements to try to infer how cognitive processing works, including how mental images are manipulated. Many thorny problems remain in regard to mental images, but one approach to studying them has met with considerable success, that is the study of how people manipulate mental images. Specifically, these studies are concerned with the rotation of mental images.

If mental images are in some ways analogous to direct perceptions of objects, then images should follow some of the same rules that govern perception of physical objects. For example, if I showed you a picture of someone and asked you who it was, but I handed you the picture upside-down, you would probably have to turn the picture right-side up in order to recognize the face. That operation (rotating the picture) would require some time. Do mental images operate in a similar fashion?

A series of studies suggests that they do. Cooper and Shepard (1973) briefly presented subjects with pictures of letters that were rotated left or right in varying degrees between right-side up and up-side down. The letters also varied in that some were mirror images of actual letters. The subject's task was to report whether the letter was normal or mirror-image. The main question was whether subjects would take longer to make that judgement when the letters were rotated further from vertical. The result was that the farther the letter was rotated, the longer it took to make the judgement about whether it was normal or mirror-image.

Shepard and Metzler (1971) did a similar experiment, except that they presented *two* figures at once, and subjects had to decide whether the two figures were the same or not. The figures varied in that one was rotated with respect to the other. Again, the greater the rotation, the longer it took to identify two figures as the same or different. The experiment in which you will participate in this exercise is a replication of the Shepard and Metzler (1971) experiment.

Method

This experiment consists of a series of trials on each of which two shapes are presented above a central fixation point on the computer screen. The two shapes are either the same or mirror images, with each type occurring equally often, in random order. On each trial, one will be rotated with respect to the other, at rotations of 0, 60, 120, and 180 degrees, ignoring direction of rotation. The four rotations will occur equally often, in random order. Subjects must judge whether the two shapes are the same or mirror images (regardless of rotation), making a fast, accurate judgment.

There will be a total of 10 practice and 128 test trials.

Instructions for Running the Experiment

To run this experiment, insert Disk 1 into your computer and enter the MEL Lab as instructed in Section 0.2. Select **Perception** from the topic menu and **Mental Rotation of Images** from the specific experiment menu. Instructions on the computer screen will then explain the experiment and what keys to use for your responses. Note that you must get 8 of the 10 practice trials right before you can begin the 128 trials of the actual experiment. (If you miss more than 2 practice trials, you will have to repeat them.) *Reaction time is important* for this experiment, so please respond as quickly and accurately as you can to each stimulus. *Materials needed*: Pencil and paper, if no printer is available, to copy down the results reported in the table at the end of the experiment. *Things to notice*: How do you do this task? Be prepared to explain what you were doing mentally to decide whether the two figures you saw were the same or mirror images of each other.

Expected Running Time = 18 minutes

Questions

1. What is the dependent variable in this experiment?

2. What is the independent variable?

3. What other variables are controlled in this experiment? If they are not controlled, how might that affect the results?

4. Can we rotate images in more than the two dimensions used in this experiment? Shepard and Metzler (1971) performed such an experiment, and you might want to refer to their article.

5. What is the speed of rotation of the shapes? Calculate this in degrees per second. Was the speed constant? Compare your results to Shepard and Metzler's (1971) findings with "picture-plane" pairs. If there is a difference, how might it have been influenced by the nature of the shapes used?

6. Another task that has been used to study the manipulation of mental images has been mental paper-folding, in which a subject is shown a diagram of a box that has been unfolded into a flat surface. Two edges are marked, and the subject must decide whether those edges would meet if the object were folded into a box again. Here is an example: "B" marks the bottom of the box, and the task is to decide whether the two edges marked with the arrows would meet if the box were folded up.

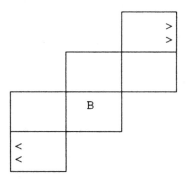

For this task, it seems that you must make a series of discrete manipulations of the mental image, rather than a continuous change such as rotation. Shepard and Feng (1972) did an experiment using this task. Are their results consistent with the studies on mental rotation? Are the differences between individuals in the ability to perform this task similar to the differences in your results?

7. How clear are your mental images? Discuss this with your classmates. You may find that some people claim that they "see" their images almost as clearly as if they were actually looking at the object. Others will report that they have only rather vague images. These reports are like the introspection used by early psychologists. What sorts of problems are there in interpreting these reports?

Advanced Questions

1. If you find that your results differ from those of Cooper and Shepard, for example by being slower overall, what aspects of the procedures used might account for that difference?

2. This experiment is on visual imagery. Can imagery occur for other senses? Recall that Beethoven composed his Ninth Symphony after he had become deaf. You might also want to look up an experiment by Carpenter and Eisenberg (1978). They report very similar findings to those of Cooper and Shepard (1973) with congenitally blind subjects, to whom the letters were presented haptically (by touch).

3. There have been some objections raised to the notion of mental images, especially to the notion that we store images in memory. Pylyshyn (1973) has argued that what we store in memory are abstract propositions, or descriptions, rather than images themselves. Are there aspects of images that you recall from memory that seem unlikely to be stored as propositions? In regard to this question, you might again consider the task faced by a deaf composer, or how you figured out how many windows there are in your home.

Extended Experiments

1. What are the results for non-visual presentation? Specifically, what happens if the shapes are presented haptically? See Carpenter and Eisenberg (1978).

2. Is the speed of rotation dependent on the specific shapes used? (Note that in this experiment, the data were averaged across shapes but the data as to what shape was used on each trial was stored by the computer, and could be subject to analysis.)

3. What is the effect of advanced information about the degree of rotation of the target shape? See Cooper and Shepard (1973).

4. What would happen if the images to be compared differed in other attributes (e.g., color and shape) as well as size (see Kosslyn, 1980)?

References

Carpenter, P. A. & Eisenberg, P. (1978). Mental rotation and the frame of reference in blind and sighted individuals. *Perception and Psychophysics*, *23*, 117-124.

Cooper, L. A. & Shepard, R. N. (1973). Chronometric studies of the rotation of mental images. In W. G. Chase (Ed.), *Visual information processing*. New York: Academic Press.

Kosslyn, S. (1980). *Image and mind*. Cambridge, MA: Harvard University Press.

Paivio, A. (1971). *Imagery and verbal processes*. New York: Holt, Rinehart & Winston, Inc.

Pylyshyn, Z. W. (1973). What the mind's eye tells the mind's brain: A critique of mental imagery. *Psychological Bulletin*, *80*, 1-24.

Shepard, R. N. & Feng, C. A. (1972). A chronometric study of mental paper folding. *Cognitive Psychology*, *3*, 228-243.

Shepard, R. N. & Metzler, J. (1971). Mental rotation of three-dimensional objects. *Science*, *171*, 701-703.

1. Please describe how you did this task. That is, what did you do in order to make the judgement about whether the figures matched?

2. In deciding whether there was a match, did you compare the overall figures, or did you try to compare single features of them that stood out?

3. Did you ever make mistakes because you "flipped" one figure over, rather than "rotating" it?

Mental Rotation of Images

Individual Data

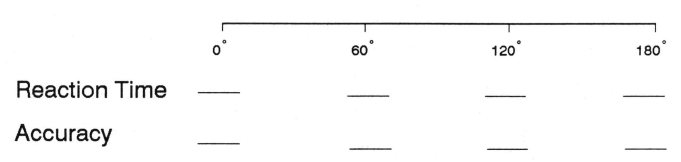

Absolute Angle of Rotation (in degrees)

	0°	60°	120°	180°
Reaction Time	___	___	___	___
Accuracy	___	___	___	___

Cell entries are MEAN CORRECT REACTION TIME (msec) and MEAN PERCENT CORRECT

Mental Rotation of Images

Individual Data

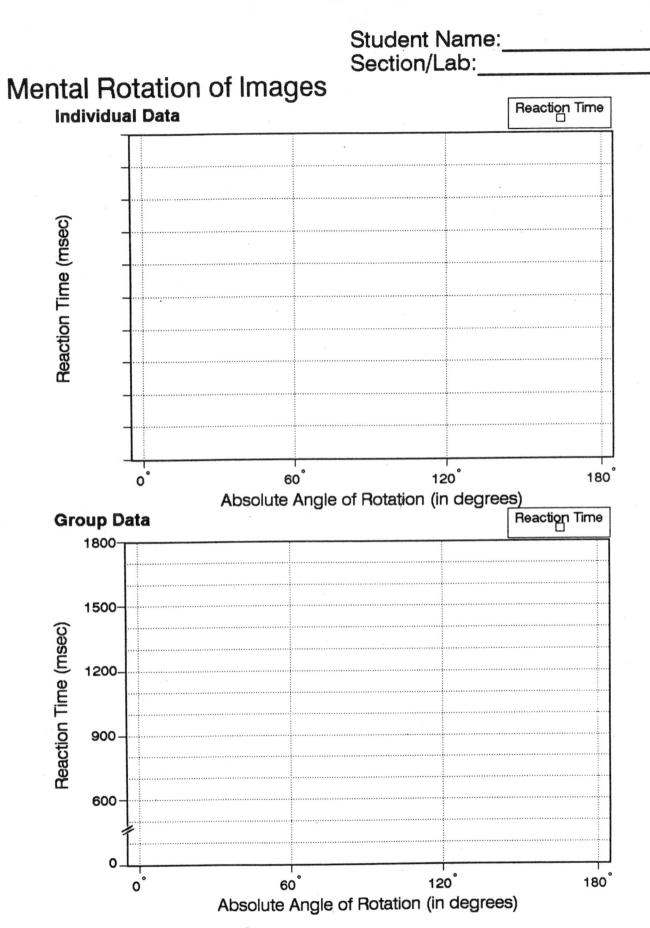

1.7 Attentional Interference and the Stroop Effect

Abstract

Selective attention is the ability to focus on one dimension of a stimulus while ignoring another. Sometimes, though, we fail to select, processing the information from both dimensions at once. The classic instance of this is the **Stroop effect**. Here, color words are presented in colored ink (e.g., the word RED in green ink). When subjects are told to ignore the word and name the ink color aloud (i.e., say "green"), they are slow and error-prone relative to a control condition (e.g., xxx in green ink). What is especially striking is that when the task is to read the word and ignore the ink color, subjects show virtually no interference: They read the word "green" out loud just as fast when it is printed in red ink as when it is printed in control black ink. Stroop interference during color naming is evidence of the unintended processing of the word, something that we apparently cannot avoid doing. It tells us that we process both dimensions -- color and word -- in parallel, and suggests that the more familiar processes involved in reading are harder to ignore than the less familiar processes involved in color naming.

First demonstrated by J. Ridley Stroop (1935) over half a century ago, the Stroop task has become one of the best known and most frequently employed measures in cognitive psychology (see MacLeod, 1991, for a review). The fascination with the task stems from at least two sources: (1) it is a very large and highly replicable effect, and (2) as yet, nobody has been able to adequately explain it.

Why should the to-be-ignored word interfere with naming the color? For many years, two possible answers were proposed. Both rely on the assumption of *parallel processing*, that we process both the color and the word at the same time. In the *relative speed of processing* account (e.g., Morton & Chambers, 1973), the bottleneck is seen as being at the response stage. Basically, only one response can be given at a time and if the wrong dimension reaches the response stage first, then interference results as you try to remove it and replace it with the right dimension. Not surprisingly, words are processed faster than colors can be named because of our extensive practice at reading (see Fraisse, 1969). Thus, the fundamental *asymmetry* -- that words interfere with color naming but colors do not interfere with word reading -- is readily explained by the fact that words are processed faster than colors, the essence of the relative speed of processing account.

The second account relies on the concept of *automaticity* (see Experiment 2.13). Through extensive practice, our everyday skills require less and less attention. Some may even reach a stage where they no longer require attention at all, becoming completely *automatic* processes. Examples would be typing or driving a car ... or *reading*. Other skills still require attention, and are called *controlled* processes. Examples could be programming your VCR or dancing, if you have not had a lot of experience with either. The basic idea is that once a particular skill has become automatic we cannot "turn it off". (A good illustration of this is to try *not* reading signs along a highway.) How does this relate to the Stroop effect? Naming the ink color is a controlled task; word reading is automatic. When you are told to name the ink color, the word is automatically processed and interferes. However, when you are told to read the word, there is little problem created by the ink color. Once again, the fundamental asymmetry of the Stroop effect is explained, but in a quite different way.

Which explanation is right? We still do not really know, but we are closer. There is increasing evidence that the relative speed of processing account is not an adequate explanation (e.g., Glaser & Glaser, 1982; Dunbar & MacLeod, 1984). There are also suggestions of problems with the automaticity explanation (e.g., Kahneman & Chajczyk, 1983). Whereas the criticisms of the relative speed of processing view have led to its rejection by many researchers, the automaticity view, in modified form, still seems to be a reasonable explanation. In the very recent past, these descriptive sorts of explanations have been augmented by new kinds of computer models that try to simulate the Stroop effect and to explain it in a very rigorous way (e.g., Cohen, Dunbar, & McClelland, 1990; Phaf, Van der Heijden, & Hudson, 1990). No doubt the Stroop effect will continue to fascinate psychologists for some time to come.

In this experiment, you will experience the Stroop effect first hand. For those of you with color monitors, your task will be to identify the color of ink in which words (or control Xs) are printed. We have also introduced a *congruent* condition (e.g., the word RED in red ink) to demonstrate the "flip side" of interference -- facilitation. People are faster to name the ink color when it agrees with the "irrelevant" word.

For those of you with monochrome monitors, we have included a variation on the Stroop effect that uses spatial location in place of color (Logan, 1980). (Note that those with color monitors can actually try both versions.) In the spatial analog, your task is to indicate where a word is located with respect to a central fixation point (i.e., indicate "above", "below", "left", or "right"). The trick is that the word itself can be ABOVE, BELOW, LEFT, or RIGHT (or a control row of Xs). Once again, mismatches between word and position (e.g., the word LEFT to the right of the fixation point) should produce interference whereas matches (e.g., the word LEFT to the left of fixation) should result in facilitation, corresponding to what we see in the more familiar color-word version of the Stroop effect.

Method

The Color-Word Version (Color Monitors Only)

In this experiment, you will do 108 trials of the Stroop task, divided into 3 blocks of 36 trials each. Within each block, randomly intermingled, there will be 12 control trials (xxxx in color), 12 congruent trials (the word and color matching), and 12 incongruent trials (the word and color mismatching). Each trial will consist of a fixation point (a '+') followed by the colored word which will stay on the screen until you respond.

Your task is **always** to ignore the word (or row of Xs) and to name the color in which it is printed. You should try to respond as quickly as you can while still avoiding errors. (If you find yourself making frequent errors, you are probably trying to go too fast.) You will respond using the numeric keypad on the right side of the keyboard. Before beginning, it will be helpful if you label the keys that you will use for responding, as shown in Figure 1.7.1. You will need either some transparent tape and four colored squares or four colored key caps -- red, blue, green, and yellow. Cut the colored squares out, and then tape them onto the keys as follows: 2=blue, 4=green, 6=red, 8=yellow. You will be responding to the ink color on the screen by pressing the key with the same ink color on the keypad.

Figure 1.7.1 Response keys to be used for the Stroop task

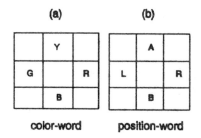

color-word   position-word

The Keypad. (a) For color-word, the letters indicate where to place color patches: 2=blue, 4=green, 6=red, 8=yellow. *Be sure to use color patches, not words.* (b) For position-word, the letters indicate the directions: 2 = below, 4 = left, 6 = right, 8 = above. The arrows on these keys should serve as adequate reminders, so no labels are required.

The Position-Word Version (Monochrome or Color Monitors)

In this experiment, you will do 108 trials of a Stroop-like task, divided into 3 blocks of 36 trials each. Within each block, randomly intermingled, there will be 12 control trials (xxxx in some position), 12 congruent trials (the word and position matching), and 12 incongruent trials (the word and position mismatching). Each trial will consist of a fixation point (a '+') followed by the word -- LEFT, RIGHT, ABOVE, or BELOW -- in one of the four positions (left, right, above, or below the central fixation point) which will stay on the screen until you respond.

Your task is **always** to ignore the word (or row of Xs) and to indicate the position in which it is printed. You should try to respond as quickly as you can while still avoiding errors. (If you find yourself making frequent errors, you are probably trying to go too fast.) You will respond using the numeric keypad on the right side of the keyboard. The keys you will use are the intuitive ones, so you should not have to label them. As Figure 1b shows, they are: 2=below, 4=left, 6=right, 8=above. You will be responding to the item's position on the screen by pressing the key of the same location on the keypad.

Multiple-Item Stroop Version (Color Monitors Only)

In this version, you will replicate closely the original task used by Stroop in his Experiment 2, in which the stimuli were printed on sheets of paper, and the subject named the colors out loud. You will see 36 stimuli displayed at once, and must name the colors in which each is displayed, pressing the spacebar to indicate when you have finished. There will be nine trials of that kind, which differ only in the nature of the 36 stimuli. Each list will be made up of either control trials (xxx in color), congruent trials (the word and color match), or incongruent trials (the word and color mismatch). You will press a key to display the 36 stimuli, then name the colors out loud as fast as you can, then press a key again to indicate when you have finished. Your task is **always** to ignore the word (or row of x's) and to name the color in which it is printed. You should try to respond as quickly as possible while still avoiding errors.

There will be three blocks of three trials each. Each block of three trials will have one control list, one congruent list, and one incongruent list, with the order of those trials randomized within each block. Within each block of three trials, the trials correspond in the following way. For each trial where there are incongruent color words as stimuli, there is a corresponding trial with x's, with the number of x's in each of the 36 positions matched to the number of letters in the incongruent trial. For example, if the first stimulus on an incongruent trial was the word yellow, the first stimulus on the corresponding neutral trial would be xxxxxx, thus matching the two trial types for length of the stimuli. For each incongruent trial, the congruent trial stimuli will be in the same colors, but each word displayed will match the color in which it is displayed.

This version can be completed either by yourself or with a partner. If you do not have a partner, you should not keep track of errors (but you should try to avoid making them). If you do have a partner, that person will serve as student experimenter. The experimenter will keep track of the number of errors you make on each trial and will enter them on the computer when prompted. To perform this experiment with a partner, you will need to obtain copies of the score sheets from your instructor. The student experimenter will be told at the beginning of each block of trials which score sheet to use.

Instructions for Running the Experiment

To run this experiment, insert Disk 1 into Drive A: of your computer and enter the MEL Lab as instructed in Section 0.2. Select **Perception** from the topic menu and **Attentional Interference and the Stroop Effect** from the specific experiment menu. Before the experiment begins you will be asked to pick a version of the experiment to run. Instructions on the computer screen will then explain the experiment and how to perform the task. Practice trials are presented for the Color-word and Position-word versions. Note that you must get 24 out of the 30 practice trials for the Color-word version and 8 out of the 10 practice trials for the Position-word version correct before you can begin the 108 trials of the actual experiment. The Multiple-item version presents no practice trials and 9 actual trials. *Reaction time* is important for this experiment, so please respond as quickly and accurately as you can to each stimulus. *Materials needed*: Pencil and paper (if no printer is available) to copy down the results reported in the table at the end of the experiment; tape and colored squares or colored key-caps if you are running the Color-word version; score sheets if you are running the Multiple-item version with a student experimenter. *Things to notice*: What effect does the relation between the word and the color have on your time to respond to the color? What effect does making an error on one trial have on your time to respond on the next trial?

Expected Running Time = 18 minutes (Color-word and Position-word versions); 15 minutes (Multiple-item Version)

Questions

1. What is the major dependent variable for this experiment? Are there any other (potential) dependent variables?

2. What is the independent variable? How many levels does it have?

3. What are some control variables used in this experiment?

4. How does the magnitude of interference compare to that of facilitation? If they are different, why might this be the case?

5. Normally, the Stroop task is done with oral responding into a microphone, instead of with key pressing. What difference(s) do you think this might produce, and why?

Advanced Questions

1. How might you go about designing experiments to test the relative speed of processing vs. the automaticity explanations of the Stroop effect?

2. What would be the effect of using words other than color words (e.g., HORSE or LEMON printed in red ink) in the color-word version of the Stroop effect? See Klein (1964).

Extension Experiments

1. Imagine examining the Stroop effect with children at ages 4, 5, 6, 7, and 8. What do you think would happen to the Stroop effect from prior to the ability to read until after the child is reading quite fluently? See Schiller (1966) and Comalli et al. (1962).

2. What do you think would happen if you showed subjects pictures of objects that had the wrong words printed on them (e.g., a picture of a dog with the word CAT printed on it)? Would you get interference? If so, would interference occur in reading the word or in naming the picture? See Lupker (1979).

3. What would you expect to happen to Stroop interference if you turned the words upside down or made them difficult to read in some other way? See Dunbar & MacLeod (1984). How would this be handled by the relative speed vs. automaticity explanations?

References

Cohen, J. D., Dunbar, K., & McClelland, J. L. (1990). On the control of automatic processes: A parallel distributed processing account of the Stroop effect. *Psychological Review, 97*, 332-361.

Comalli, P. E., Jr., Wapner, S., & Werner, H. (1962). Interference effects of Stroop color-word test in childhood, adulthood, and aging. *Journal of General Psychology, 100*, 47-53.

Dunbar, K., & MacLeod, C. M. (1984). A horse race of a different color: Stroop interference patterns with transformed words. *Journal of Experimental Psychology: Human Perception and Performance, 10*, 622-639.

Fraisse, P. (1969). Why is naming longer than reading? *Acta Psychologica, 30*, 96-103.

Glaser, M. O., & Glaser, W. R. (1982). Time course analysis of the Stroop phenomenon. *Journal of Experimental Psychology: Human Perception and Performance, 8*, 875-894.

Klein, G. S. (1964). Semantic power measured through the interference of words with color-naming. *American Journal of Psychology, 77*, 576-588.

Logan, G. D. (1980). Attention and automaticity in Stroop and priming tasks: Theory and data. *Cognitive Psychology, 12*, 523-553.

Lupker, S. J. (1979). The semantic nature of response competition in the picture-word interference task. *Memory and Cognition, 7*, 485-495.

MacLeod, C. M. (1991). Half a century of research on the Stroop effect: An integrative review. *Psychological Bulletin, 109*, 163-203.

Macleod, C. M., & Dunbar, K. (1988). Training and Stroop-like interference: Evidence for a continuum of automaticity. *Journal of Experimental Psychology: Learning, Memory, and Cognition, 14*, 126-135.

Morton, J., & Chambers, S. M. (1973). Selective attention to words and colours. *Quarterly Journal of Experimental Psychology, 25*, 387-397.

Phaf, R. H., Van der Heijden, A. H. C., & Hudson, P. T. W. (1990). SLAM: A connectionist model for attention in visual selection tasks. *Cognitive Psychology, 22*, 273-341.

Schiller, P. H. (1966). Developmental study of color-word interference. *Journal of Experimental Psychology, 72*, 105-108.

Stroop, J. R. (1935). Studies of interference in serial verbal reactions. *Journal of Experimental Psychology, 18*, 643-662.

Thought Questions

1. When you made a mistake, was it usually on the incongruent trials? Did you respond incorrectly with the word that you were not supposed to read?

2. Did you ever respond to a stimulus with the **completely** wrong response (e.g., say "yellow" to the word RED in green ink, or "above" to the word LEFT in the bottom position)?

3. How similar do you think the flanker effect (Experiment 1.5) and the Stroop effect are? How would you go about finding out precisely?

Stroop Effect

Individual Data

Please indicate which version of the experiment you performed:

Version 1: Color-Word   ___

Version 2: Position-Word   ___

Version 3: Multiple-item   ___

Condition

	Congruent	Control	Incongruent
Reaction Time	___	___	___
Percent Correct *	___	___	___

* recorded only if student experimenter is used in Version 3

Cell entries are MEAN CORRECT REACTION TIME** and

MEAN PERCENT CORRECT

** Reaction time is reported in milliseconds in Versions 1 & 2 and in seconds in Version 3.

MEL Lab: Student Workbook v.1.6; © PST - Do not reproduce

The Stroop Effect

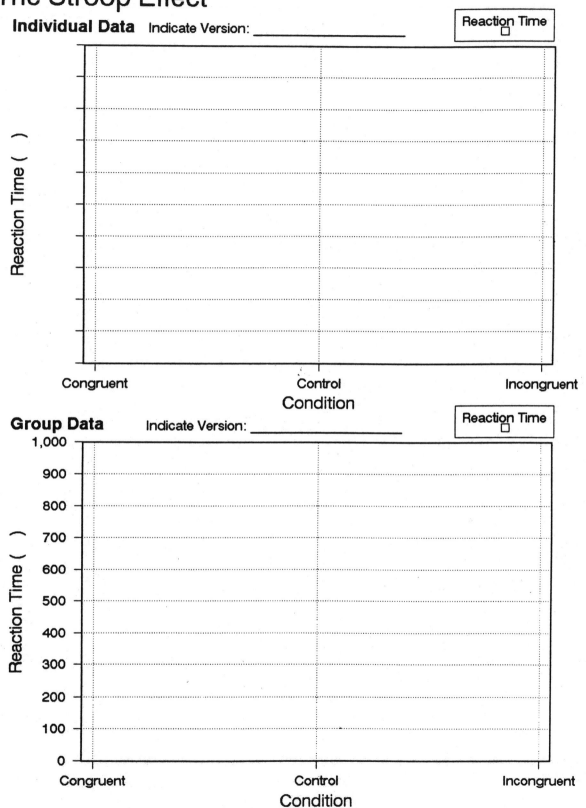

Individual Data   Indicate Version:_____

Reaction Time
☐

Reaction Time ( )

Condition

Congruent   Control   Incongruent

Group Data   Indicate Version:_____

Reaction Time
☐

1,000
900
800
700
600
500
400
300
200
100
0

Reaction Time ( )

Condition

Congruent   Control   Incongruent

2 Experiments in Cognition

Cognition is thinking, and thinking is central to psychology. Thinking is made up of many processes, and the study of cognition is the study of those many different processes that make up thinking, including memory, problem-solving, language, imagery, and reading. Many early studies of thinking asked subjects to report the contents of their consciousness as they performed various tasks. That method of "trained introspection" ultimately failed, because there was no way to verify the reports, and hence no way to solve disagreements. Because of that failure, many psychologists followed the lead of John Watson's Behaviorism in declaring that psychology simply could not study the mind.

However, by the 1960's it had become clear that Watson had thrown the baby of cognition out with the bath water of introspection. Modern cognitive psychology continues to reject introspection as a scientific method, but finds that there are good approaches to the study of mind. Researchers can use external measures to identify component cognitive processes. Two of the most important such measures have been the study of *errors* in memory or problem-solving, and the study of *reaction time*, or the time needed to perform a cognitive task. These methods have become standard for cognitive psychology, yielding many insights into how cognition works. By comparing the time needed to make decisions under varying conditions, for example, we can explore how people search through short-term memory, how they make inferences linking sentences as they read, or how memory is organized. The study of errors under varying conditions of an experiment can help us measure the duration of short-term memory, the role of imagery in problem-solving, or the best way to rehearse material that we need to remember for a long time.

In this section of the Manual, a number of experiments and exercises explore many of the approaches modern psychology uses to study the nature of cognition.

2.1 Lexical Decisions

Abstract

A number of models of the organization of knowledge in memory treat memory as a network of specific memories connected together by links. Most assume that when we remember something we "activate" that location in memory, and this activation spreads down the links between that location and others to which it is linked. In this exercise, the lexical decision task of Meyer and Schvaneveldt (1971) is replicated. Subjects must make judgments about whether a string of letters is or is not a common word. Generally, a word is more quickly identified as such if it follows a related word (BUTTER following BREAD) than if it follows an unrelated word (DOCTOR following BREAD). This result is interpreted as supporting "spreading activation" models of memory organization.

How can we study the organization of memory? Early psychological studies of memory were principally concerned with the recall or recognition of recently learned material. The material to be learned was often nonsense syllables, such as DAQ, which were assumed to have little previous meaning associated with them. But much of our memory involves things we have learned long ago and have recalled frequently. In fact, we don't usually think about reading or writing or talking as being memory tasks, but that is just what they are--at least in part. Using or recognizing a word requires the use of memory, albeit usually very familiar memory. One way to study the organization of this sort of memory is to use a reaction time task, instead of the traditional study-test task. One approach to studying memory organization using reaction times has been to determine how long it takes people to recognize a word in various contexts.

Meyer and Schvaneveldt (1971) performed such a reaction time experiment using a "lexical decision" task. A lexical decision involves deciding whether a string of letters is a word or not, and in the lexical decision task of Meyer and Schvaneveldt the subjects saw two letter strings at once and had to indicate as quickly as possible whether both were words. Their finding, which provides strong support for the notion of spreading activation, was that if both letter strings were words, subjects were much faster if the words were related. For example, if the top word were NURSE, you would be faster at deciding that the bottom string of letters is a word if it were DOCTOR than if it were BUTTER.

Meyer and Schvaneveldt interpreted these differences in reaction times (RT's) as indicating how "closely" two words are stored in memory. If you think of memory as a network of words linked to other associated words, then if two words are close together in the network, "activating" one by recognizing it may result in that activation spreading to other, nearby words. If seeing NURSE leads to partial activation of words close to it in the network, then DOCTOR should receive such activation. Now when DOCTOR is seen, it requires less time to recognize it, because it is already partially activated. Seeing NURSE would not activate a word farther away in the network, such as BUTTER, and so the time to recognize it would not be affected. Reaction time then becomes a sensitive measure of the degree of association of two words or concepts.

Method

In this experiment, subjects are presented with two letter strings, one appearing a few lines above the other. The task is to decide to press one key if *both* letter strings form words, and to press another key otherwise (that is, if either or both letter strings are nonwords). Trials on which both strings form words make up 50 of the 98 trials. Within those trials, half consist of two unrelated words, while half consist of two related words. Of the 48 trials where one or both letter strings are nonwords, 16 each (in random order) are word above nonword, nonword above word, or two nonwords. Nonwords were constructed by using common words, but replacing one or two letters to form a nonword letter string that is orthographically (i.e., visually similar letters) similar to a real word.

Instructions for Running the Experiment

To run this experiment, insert Disk 1 into your computer and enter the MEL Lab as instructed in Section 0.2. Select **Cognition** from the topic menu and **Lexical Decisions** from the specific experiment menu. Instructions on the computer screen will then explain the experiment and what keys to use for your responses. Note that you must get 8 of the 10 practice trials right before you can begin the 98 trials of the actual experiment. (If you miss more than 2 practice trials, you will have to repeat them.) *Reaction time is important* for this experiment, so please respond as quickly and accurately as you can to each stimulus. *Materials needed*: Pencil and paper, if no printer is available, to copy down the results reported in the table at the end of the experiment. *Things to notice*: You will see two sets of letters on each trial, and must decide if *both* are words. When both letter sets are words, do some pairs of words seem easier than others?

Expected Running Time = 12 minutes

Questions

1. What is the dependent variable(s) in this experiment?

2. What is the independent variable?

3. What are some important control variables?

4. What are the results of this experiment? Specifically, is there any difference in the speed of the lexical decision when the target is a word and the other letter string is a nonword, related word, or unrelated word?

5. What is the main difference between this experiment and Meyer and Schvaneveldt's (1971) Experiment 1? What about their Experiment 2? Do these differences seem to matter for the overall result?

6. Is there a speed-accuracy trade-off of RT and error rates? That is, are faster RT's associated with higher error rates? What sorts of problems could this cause for interpretation of the pattern of RT's if such a trade-off occurred?

Advanced Questions

1. Meyer, Schvaneveldt, and Ruddy (1975) reported a similar experiment, but one in which the visual quality of the words was degraded by partially masking them. Using the additive factors logic of Sternberg (1969, and see Section 2.3 of this manual), how might you interpret the interaction they found between stimulus quality and whether the words were related or not?

2. Tulving and Gold (1963) have also shown an effect of context on word recognition. What is their finding, and how might it relate to Meyer and Schvaneveldt's experiment?

3. Is Morton's (1969) logogen model of word recognition compatible with the results of this experiment? Does that model contradict Meyer and Schvaneveldt's "spreading activation" model?

4. Meyer and Schvaneveldt (1971) found faster RT's when a nonword appeared above a word than when a word appeared above a nonword, even though the same response was made to each. How might that difference be explained? (See their Discussion.)

5. Meyer and Schvaneveldt (1971) also reported far more errors when a nonword appeared above a word than when

a word appeared above a nonword. Relate this to the experiment on response competition (Eriksen & Eriksen, 1974).

Extension Experiments

1. See Advanced Question number 1. What is the effect of degrading the stimulus words?

2. Is priming secondary associations in a network a sequential process or a parallel process? A word like "river" would prime "boat" which would prime "deck." Is the priming sequential (i.e., at 100 msec "boat" is primed but not until 200 msec is "deck" primed) or parallel (i.e., both "boat" and "deck" are primed at the same time reaching a peak at 100 msec) but with the secondary association weaker?

3. Meyer and Schvaneveldt's (1971) Experiment 2 used a slightly different version of this task, which made it a *same-different* judgement of whether both strings were words or nonwords. Meyer, Schvaneveldt, and Ruddy (1975) used *successive* presentations of the two letter strings in each pair, with subjects responding to each one separately, indicating whether it was a word or nonword. Do these procedural changes matter for the general pattern of the results?

4. Meyer and his colleagues have used *pairs* of words/nonwords in various formats. Suppose that the experiment consisted of *single* trials, with each involving a word-nonword judgement. Would NURSE be responded to faster if preceded by DOCTOR in this case? Perhaps more interestingly, would the facilitation in responding drop off if there were another trial in between? Would this depend on the nature of that trial (whether word or nonword)? Does the facilitation drop with time, even if no other word intervenes?

5. Do opposite words (antonyms) prime each other (hot-cold)? How would you discriminate the positive and negative priming effects?

References

Eriksen, B. A., & Eriksen, C. W. (1974). Effects of noise letters upon the identification of a target letter in a nonsearch task. *Perception and Psychophysics, 16*, 143-149.

Meyer, D. E., & Schvaneveldt, R. W. (1971). Facilitation in recognizing pairs of words: Evidence of a dependence upon retrieval operations. *Journal of Experimental Psychology, 90*, 227-234.

Meyer, D. E., Schvaneveldt, R. W., & Ruddy, M. G. (1975). Loci of contextual effects on visual word recognition. In P. M. A. Rabbit & S. Dornic (Eds.) *Attention and Performance V*. London: Academic Press.

Morton, J. (1969). Interaction of information in word recognition. *Psychological Review, 76*, 165-178.

Sternberg, S. (1969). Memory scanning: Mental processes revealed by reaction-time experiments. *American Scientist, 57*, 421-457.

Tulving, E. & Gold, C. (1963). Stimulus information and contextual information as determinants of tachistoscopic recognition of words. *Journal of Experimental Psychology, 66*, 319-327.

1.   On trials when two words were presented, did it seem to be easier if the words were related?

2.   If the top letter string was a word, did you sometimes anticipate that the bottom one would also be a word? If so, did that seem to slow you down? Did it seem to cause you to make more errors?

Lexical Decision

Individual Data

Type of Strings

Word Related Word	Word Unrelated Word	Word Nonword	Nonword Word	Nonword Nonword

Reaction Time

——— ——— ——— ——— ———

Accuracy

——— ——— ——— ——— ———

Cell entries are MEAN CORRECT REACTION TIME (msec) and

MEAN PERCENT CORRECT

Lexical Decision

Individual Data

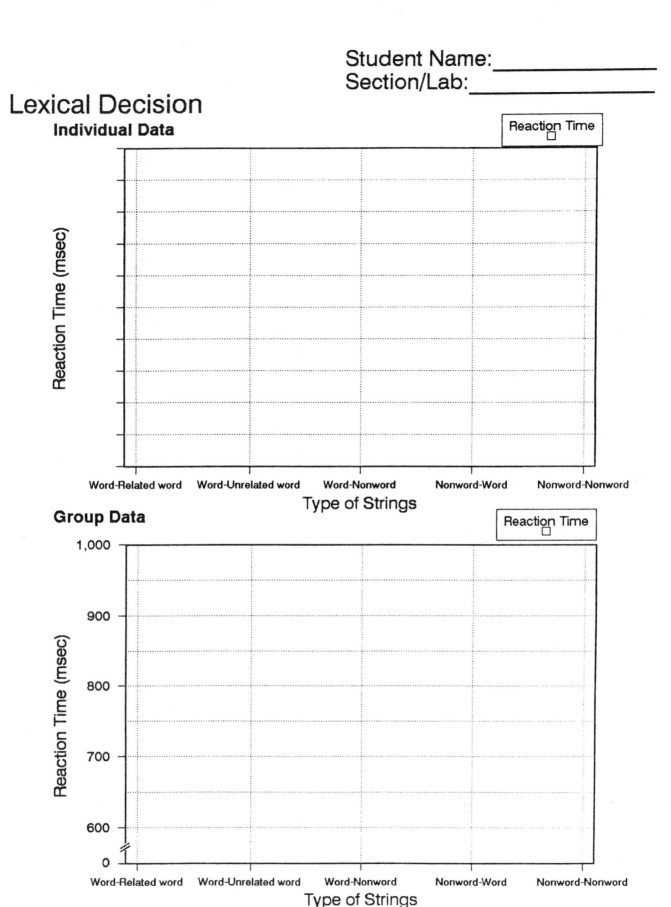

2.2 Scanning Short-Term Memory

Abstract

Sternberg (1966) proposed a method of studying how people search short-term memory to determine whether certain information is present. This experiment replicates his, to determine whether we search STM one item at a time (serially) or all at once (in parallel), and to determine whether the search stops when the item is located (self-terminating) or must continue through the entire contents of STM (exhaustive). This experiment illustrates reaction-time methodology, the study of internal cognitive processes, and the testing of alternative hypotheses. In addition, the typical finding of exhaustive search illustrates the limitations of generalizing from intuitions, as opposed to formal testing of hypotheses.

A question of considerable interest to cognitive psychologists is the nature of the process of searching short-term memory (STM). Suppose you are given a set of numbers to remember, and are permitted to rehearse them by saying them over and over to yourself. At various times you are given a number and must decide whether that number is one of the ones you were first given. In order to do this, you must somehow search the items you are rehearsing in STM in order to decide whether the test item is among them. The experiment described below uses this task to examine the nature of the search process in STM.

Sternberg (1966, 1969) developed a procedure that permits a test of two questions about the nature of the search of STM. The first question was whether the contents of STM are searched all at once (parallel search) or one item after another (serial search). The second question concerned whether the search stops when the item searched for is found (self-terminating search) or whether all items in STM must be compared to the item searched for (exhaustive search). After a description of the task Sternberg used to study search of STM, we will return to these two questions, and the sorts of predictions about experimental results that come from them.

Sternberg's task was a simple one. The subject is given a list of from one to six digits, called the *memory set*, which he or she is permitted to rehearse. A few seconds later, the subject sees a single digit (called the *probe* digit) and must indicate, by pressing one of two buttons, whether that probe digit is or is not a member of the memory set. The dependent variable is reaction time (RT), or how long it takes the subject to make a decision and press the appropriate button. As in most RT experiments, the subjects are instructed to press the button as quickly as possible without making many errors (typically 5% or less). The independent variable is the size of the memory set (1-6 digits), which varies from trial to trial. On half of the trials the probe is a member of the memory set (positive trials) and on half it is not (negative trials).

Serial vs. parallel search.

Sternberg's first question was whether subjects search the whole memory set at once, or whether they must search through the memory set one item at a time. An analogy might help to make this distinction clearer. Suppose you had to visually search a short shelf of books for a particular book. You might, for example, have your textbooks all together in one place. If you are looking for your calculus text, you might just glance at the whole set of books at once and be able to tell whether the calculus book was among them (e.g., the calculus book has a distinctive color). This would be a parallel search. But suppose the books were several volumes of an encyclopedia--all the same size and color and *not* in the correct order--and you had to decide whether the E-G volume was among them. Now you would likely have to look at each book in turn to make a decision. This would be a serial search.

Getting back to search of STM, how can we tell which sort of search people actually do? Sternberg reasoned as follows: If you search serially, then the more items there are to search, the longer it should take. That is, RT should increase as the memory set size increases. On the other hand, if you can search all the items at once, it should not matter how many there are--RT should be the same for any memory set size (up to the capacity of STM). The test is now a simple one--does RT increase with memory set size (indicating serial search) or not (indicating parallel search)?

Figure 2.2.1 Serial versus parallel search

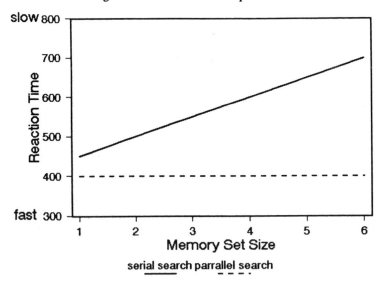

Exhaustive vs. self-terminating search.

The second question Sternberg's experiment was designed to answer was whether the search through STM (assuming it is a serial search) *stops* when a match is found between the probe and an item in the memory set, or whether it must continue through the whole memory set. Again, an analogy to a small shelf of books might be useful. Suppose you have several volumes of an encyclopedia on a shelf, and you must decide whether the E-G volume is among them. You have to search one volume at a time, looking at the letters on the cover. If the E-G volume is *not* on the shelf, you must search through all of the books before you can be sure it is not there. But if the E-G volume *is* on the shelf, you will probably quit looking when you have found it. An important point to note is that you *must* do an exhaustive search if the book you are looking for is not on the shelf--the only way you can know it is not there is to look at each book.

What, then, are the predictions for search of STM? We know that you *must* do an exhaustive search if the probe is negative. That is, the only way you can be sure the probe is *not* in the memory set is to compare it to *all* members of the set. For a positive probe, on the other hand, you might be able to do a self-terminating search, and stop searching when you find a match between the probe and an item in the memory set. What happens, then, as we increase memory set size? Since we are assuming that the search is serial, the RT will increase as memory set size increases. We know that the search must be exhaustive for negative probes. So if you do an exhaustive search on all trials, then the increase in RT as memory set size increases should be the same for positive and negative probes.

What would happen if you use a self-terminating search? Suppose the memory set size was 3 digits. On a third of the trials the probe would match the first digit you compared it to, and the search would end. On a third of the trials the probe would match the second digit it was compared to and the search would end, while on a third of the trials a match would not be found until the third comparison. Thus, on average you would have to make only two comparisons, instead of the three required for an exhaustive search. The average number of comparisons required for exhaustive and self-terminating searches is shown in Figure 2.2.2.

Figure 2.2.2 Self-terminating versus exhaustive search

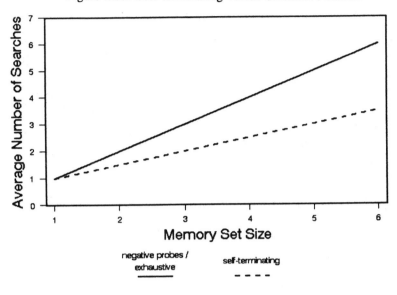

If we assume that each comparison takes the same amount of time, then RT for positive probes will increase with memory set size only half as fast as RT for negative probes if the search is self-terminating. If the search is exhaustive, on the other hand, RT will increase the same for both negative and positive probes, as memory set size increases.

At this point, you should think about the questions raised and the predictions made about RT and memory set size. Think about the task as described above, and try to decide for yourself what you think the result will be. Will RT increase as memory set size increases, suggesting a serial search? If it does, will RT increase more for negative probes than for positive ones, indicating a self-terminating search? Or will it increase the same amount for positive probes as for negative probes, indicating an exhaustive search? Why would you continue searching when you have found what you are looking for?

Method

The general procedure is that you will be given a set of numbers to remember (the memory set), varying from a single digit to five digits. You should remember these by rehearsing them (saying them to yourself). When you have seen the memory set, you will press the indicated key to start a trial. You will see a single digit displayed (the probe), and you must indicate whether it is a member of the memory set or not, by pressing the appropriate keys. There are 10 practice trials and 180 experimental trials. Memory sets of size 1, 3, or 5 digits occur equally often in random order. Probes are divided randomly and equally between members of the memory set (positive probes) and nonmembers (negative probes).

Each memory set will be displayed until you press the space bar to begin the trials, so that you have plenty of time to begin rehearsing the correct set of letters. Probe digits will appear just above a fixation mark, so that you will not have to guess at their location, and they will be displayed for 200 msec, which should be long enough to permit easy identification of the probe. After responding, you will receive feedback about RT and accuracy.

Discussion

What conclusion do you reach with regard to whether the search of STM is serial or parallel? Sternberg found that RT did increase with memory set size. For his subjects, each additional item in STM added about 38 msec to the RT, and he concluded that the search of STM is serial--one item at a time, rather than all at once.

Assuming that you also found an increase in RT with increases in memory set size, you should now address the second question--is the search self-terminating or exhaustive? Sternberg argued that exhaustive search is indicated if the slopes of the lines for positive and negative probes are the same. He found that the slopes (increases in RT as memory set size is increased) were nearly identical for positive and negative probes, indicating an exhaustive search.

The Sternberg task has been used by many investigators, and his basic findings have been replicated many times. For this task, search of STM seems to be a serial, exhaustive search. (In other tasks where search times exceed about one second, however, self-terminating search becomes more common.)

Instructions for Running the Experiment

To run this experiment, insert Disk 1 into your computer and enter the MEL Lab as instructed in Section 0.2. Select **Cognition** from the topic menu and **Scanning Short-Term Memory** from the specific experiment menu. Instructions on the computer screen will then explain the experiment and what keys to use for your responses. Note that you must get 8 of the 10 practice trials right before you can begin the 180 trials of the actual experiment. (If you miss more than 2 practice trials, you will have to repeat them.) *Reaction time is important* for this experiment, so please respond as quickly and accurately as you can to each stimulus. *Materials needed*: Pencil and paper, if no printer is available, to copy down the results reported in the table at the end of the experiment. *Things to notice*: What does the search of STM seem to involve? That is, what does it feel like you are doing as you search STM for the target letters?

Expected Running Time = 24 minutes

Questions

1. What is the dependent variable in this experiment?

2. What are the independent variables? Is this a within- or between-subjects design?

3. What are the major control variables?

4. Does the evidence from this experiment suggest a serial search or a parallel search? Why?

5. Does the evidence from this experiment suggest a self-terminating search, or an exhaustive search? Why?

6. Compare your group data to the data reported in Sternberg (1969, Figure 1). Graph the points from Sternberg's figure onto the plot of your group data. Are the overall RT's about the same? If not, what factors could affect the difference?

Advanced Questions

1. Does it make sense to use an exhaustive search? At first glance it probably doesn't seem to. After all, if you are looking for your calculus textbook among the half-dozen books on your desk, you probably stop looking when you find it! The evidence suggests rather strongly, though, that when searching STM you compare the probe to *all*

members of the memory set, even if you have already found a match. Is there a possibility that an exhaustive search might actually be faster than a self-terminating one? Here's a hint: Assume that making a comparison and making a decision about that comparison (deciding if there was a match) are two different stages in information processing that might take different amounts of time.

2. Sternberg argued that a serial search would be indicated if there is an increase in RT as memory set size increased--that is, if the slope is not zero. If the slope is zero, a parallel search would be indicated. Is this argument correct? Suppose that you have only a certain quantity of attention available in STM, and that it is divided equally among the items to be searched, and that the search is actually parallel. If you make these assumptions, what would you predict about changes in RT as memory set size increases? See Baddeley (1976, pp. 146-147) for a discussion of this type of model.

3. Another experiment in this series examines automatic processing. If you have already done that experiment, you might consider what would happen to search of STM as you do the same memory set over and over ("consistent mapping"). Would the search still be serial and exhaustive? Experiments reported by Schneider and Shiffrin (1977) or Simpson (1972) might help you answer this question.

4. The points representing mean RT for the memory set sizes usually fall in a straight line--each added item in the memory set adds a constant amount of time to overall RT. You can write the equation for a straight line in the general form

$$Y = a + bX.$$

For our data, this becomes

$$RT = a + bS, \text{ where S is the memory set size.}$$

That is, reaction time is some value "a" plus some value "b" multiplied by the memory set size. "A" is called the *intercept* of the line and "b" is called the *slope*.

What is the formula for your group data? How do you interpret the intercept and slope? That is, what do these numbers *mean*? If your slope and intercept are markedly different from Sternberg's reported data (Sternberg, 1969, Figure 1), what do you think might cause that difference?

5. Using Sternberg's procedure Corballis, Kirby, and Miller (1972) found a strong serial position effect for memory set sizes of 4 and 6. That is, RT was fastest for the first and last items of the list and slowest for the middle items. Is this consistent with a serial, exhaustive search of STM? Why or why not?

Extension Experiments

1. How does the comparison process change as a function of the complexity of the material to be searched (e.g., letters, numbers, words, and pictures, as well as single colors or shapes and conjunctions of colors and shapes)? See Teichner and Krebs (1974), Briggs and Johnson (1973), and Fisk and Schneider (1983).

2. How does the comparison process change as a function of degree of practice, whether the memory set changes often or not? See Schneider and Shiffrin (1977) and Kristofferson (1972a,b).

3. As you increase the number of items in the memory set (and hence the number of comparisons that must be made), do you expect a shift from exhaustive to self-terminating search? Can subjects be *trained* to make a self-terminating or exhaustive search? See Schneider and Shiffrin (1977, p. 27, 32).

4. In the present experiment you compared one to six items in memory to a single display item (probe). What would happen if you compared one memory item to four display items? See Atkinson, Holmgren, and Juola (1969), Teichner and Krebs (1972), and Schneider and Shiffrin (1977). How might processing vary with changes in the number of memory elements and the number of display elements? Might either memory or display comparison processes be slower (Schneider & Shiffrin, 1977, p. 28)? Could you process the *display* exhaustively while self-terminating in memory?

References

Atkinson, R. C., Holmgren, J. E. & Juola, J. F. (1969). Processing time as influenced by the number of items in the visual display. *Perception and Psychophysics, 6,* 321-326.

Briggs, G. E. and Johnsen, A. M. (1973). On the nature of central processes in choice reactions. *Memory and Cognition, 1,* 91-100.

Baddeley, A. D. (1976). *The psychology of memory.* New York: Basic Books.

Corballis, M. C., Kirby, J., & Miller, A. (1972). Access to elements of a memorized list. *Journal of Experimental Psychology, 94,* 185-190.

Fisk, A. D. & Schneider, W. (1983). Category and word search: Generalizing search principles to complex processing. *Journal of Experimental Psychology: Learning, Memory, and Cognition, 9,* 177-195.

Kristofferson, M. (1972a). Effects of practice on character classification performance. *Canadian Journal of Psychology, 26,* 54-60.

Kristofferson, M. (1972b). When item recognition and visual search functions are similar. *Perception and Psychophysics, 12,* 379-384

Miller, G. A. (1956). The magical number seven, plus or minus two: Some limits on our capacity for processing information. *Psychological Review, 63,* 81-97.

Murdoch, B. B., Jr. (1961). The retention of individual items. *Journal of Experimental Psychology, 62,* 618-625.

Peterson, L. R. & Peterson, M. J. (1959). Short-term retention of individual verbal items. *Journal of Experimental Psychology, 58,* 193-198.

Schneider, W. & Shiffrin, R. M. (1977). Controlled and automatic human information processing: I. Detection, search, and attention. *Psychological Review, 84,* 1-66.

Shiffrin, R. M. & Schneider, W. (1977). Controlled and automatic human information processing: II. Perceptual learning, automatic attending, and a general theory. *Psychological Review, 84,* 127-189.

Shiffrin, R. M. (1988). Attention. In R. C. Atkinson, R. J. Herrnstein, G. Lindzey & R. D. Luce (Eds.), *Steven's handbook of experimental psychology, Volume 2: Learning and cognition.* New York: John Wiley & Sons.

Simpson, P. J. (1972). High-speed memory scanning: Stability and generality. *Journal of Experimental Psychology, 96,* 239-246.

Sternberg, S. (1966). High-speed scanning in human memory. *Science, 153,* 652-654.

Sternberg, S. (1969). Memory scanning: Mental processes revealed by reaction-time experiments. *American Scientist, 57,* 421-457.

Teichner, W. H. & Krebs, M. J. (1974). Visual search for simple targets. *Psychological Bulletin, 81,* 15-28.

Thought Questions

1. Did the task seem harder to do when there were more letters in the memory set?

2. Did you sometimes realize that you were about to press the wrong key, but too late to be able to stop the movement?

3. Did you feel that you were comparing the probe letter to the letters in memory one at a time or all at once?

Scanning Short-Term Memory

Individual Data

Memory Set Size

	1	3	5
Positive Probes ("yes")	——	——	——
Negative Probes ("no")	——	——	——

Cell entries are MEAN CORRECT REACTION TIME (msec)

Memory Set Size

	1	3	5
Positive Probes ("yes")	——	——	——
Negative Probes ("no")	——	——	——

Cell entries are MEAN PERCENT CORRECT

Correlations between mean correct reaction time and memory set size:

Positive probes ("yes") = _____   Negative probes ("no") = _____

Slopes of the functions relating

mean correct reaction time and memory set size (msec):

Positive probes ("yes") = _____   Negative probes ("no") = _____

Y-intercepts of the functions relating

mean correct reaction time and memory set size (msec):

Positive probes ("yes") = _____   Negative probes ("no") = _____

Slope ratio (msec) (Negative probe/Positive Probe) = _____

Scanning Short-Term Memory

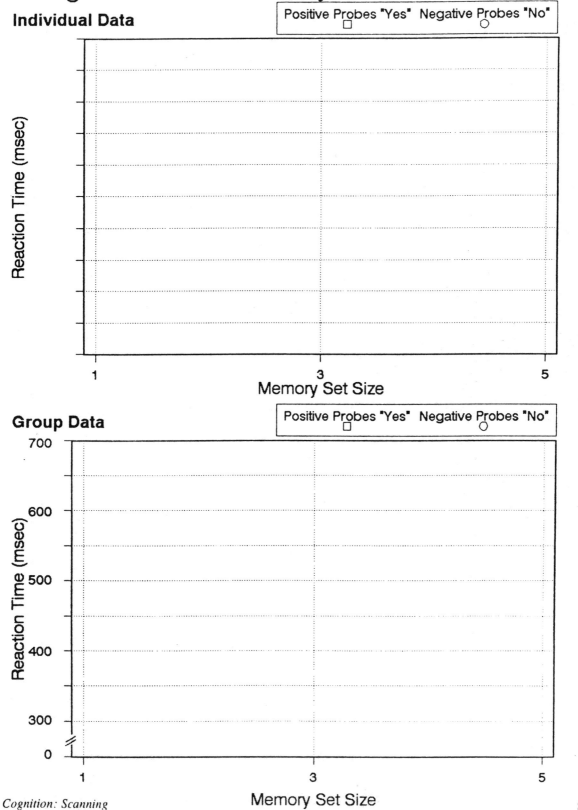

Individual Data

Positive Probes "Yes" □   Negative Probes "No" ○

Reaction Time (msec)

1   3   5

Memory Set Size

Group Data

Positive Probes "Yes" □   Negative Probes "No" ○

Reaction Time (msec)

700

600

500

400

300

0

1   3   5

Memory Set Size

2.3 Additive Factors Methodology

Abstract

Additive factors methodology allows testing of internal stages of cognitive processes. This permits separating the component stages of encoding, comparing and responding even though the dependent measure--the time it takes the subject to respond--is always the sum of the times for the three stages. Additive factors methodology assumes the processing occurs in a series of processing stages carried out in sequence, with each stage being completed before the next begins. This technique relies on an examination of the interaction of the effects of two different experimental manipulations. If those manipulations affect different stages of processing, they should have additive effects on the time needed to complete the task. If, on the other hand, two manipulations affect the same stage, their effects should interact. Examination of the joint manipulation of two variables can thus be used to determine the validity of the stages proposed by information-processing models of cognition. This methodology is illustrated in relation to the search of short-term memory to determine whether a target letter is part of the memory set the subject has just seen.

How can we measure cognitive processes going on inside your head? One possibility would be to measure brain activity, but there are severe practical, as well as theoretical, problems associated with such measures. Cognitive psychologists are often interested in describing the stages of processing involved in mental activities. For example, when you search for a book on a shelf you must encode the visual patterns of what you see into some sort of internal representation, then compare those patterns to the mental image of the book you are seeking. Finally, you must actually reach for and retrieve the book when you find it. These activities comprise a series of stages, each of which must be completed before the next is begun. Sternberg (1969) was concerned with how we can determine the nature of the stages of a mental process, such as a simple comparison. This laboratory exercise is a demonstration of the method Sternberg devised to study stages of mental processing, which he called *additive factors methodology*.

Additive factors logic is concerned with showing that certain mental processes take place in a series of stages. Sternberg's immediate interest was his model of search of STM, but the same logic applies to any model of a process that involves a series of discrete stages. To show that there really are a series of discrete stages, Sternberg manipulated two variables, each of which was assumed to influence a different stage of processing. He argued that if there really were two separate stages that he could manipulate with these variables, then the total time of all the stages (reaction time) might change as either of the variables was changed, but there would be no *interaction*. That is, the effects of the two variables will be independent of each other. If you change one condition of the experiment response time will increase (or decrease) independently of the other condition. If, on the other hand, the two variables really affected the same stage, then they would not be independent of one another, and there would be an interaction. For example, changing one condition would have an effect by itself, but an even bigger effect if another condition were also changed.

Before turning to a more formal treatment of additive factors, an analogy might be helpful to show why no interaction would occur if different stages were being independently manipulated, and why an interaction would occur if they were not independent. Suppose you were measuring the total time you spent getting gasoline each time you went to the gas station. That total time would be the sum of three stages: *waiting time* before you get to a pump, *pumping time*, and *paying time*. How long it takes you to complete getting gasoline will depend on how long each of these stages takes. Different factors would affect each stage. Waiting time would depend on how many cars were ahead of you and how many pumps there were. Pumping time would depend on the rate of flow of the gasoline and how much you were buying. Paying time would depend on the number of people ahead of you and how many cashiers were on hand.

We can first examine the effect of manipulating variables that affect two *different* stages. The first variable is the waiting time--we compare the total wait on three different occasions. Assume that the only thing different about these three stops at the gas station was the number of cars ahead of you. On one occasion there were none, while on other occasions there were 5 or 10 cars ahead of you. Clearly, the more cars there were ahead of you, the longer the total time, as represented in Figure 2.3.1.

Figure 2.3.1 Stages of processing in the gas station example

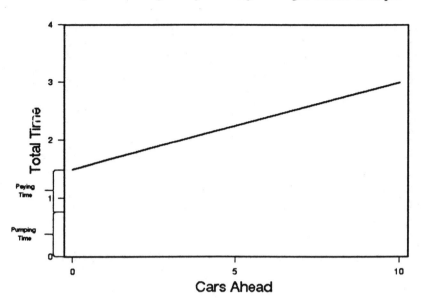

The second variable is pumping time, again measured on three occasions. Assume that the waiting time and paying time were constant, but that on one occasion you only needed two gallons of gas, while on others you needed ten or twenty. The more gas you needed, the longer it would take, as shown in the Figure 2.3.2. Notice that we have also shown how long it would take if you bought zero gallons. That is the sum of how long you waited for the cars ahead of you in line and how long you waited to pay, if you only bought a penny's worth of gasoline (that is, essentially none).

Now we can combine these two effects and see what happens as we vary *both* the number of cars ahead of you and the amount of gasoline you are buying. Paying time is still constant. This situation is illustrated in Figure 2.3.3. On the left is a graph of total time (Y axis), with number of cars ahead of you on the X axis. Each line then represents a different amount of gasoline needed. On the right are the same data values, but with the amount of gasoline needed on the X axis and different lines representing different numbers of cars ahead of you. Notice that in both cases the lines are parallel. That shows that there is no interaction. The number of cars ahead of you and the amount of gasoline you need each have an effect on total time, but their effects are independent. The two factors or variables affect different stages, and so their separate effects are *additive*--each one adds a separate amount to total time.

Let us turn now to another situation, in which we manipulate two variables that affect the *same* stage--in this case, the pumping stage. The first variable is the speed of the pump--how much gasoline is pumped per minute. On one occasion, you get a very fast pump, on another a medium pump, and on another a slow pump. The slower the pump, the more time it takes. Pumping time is a function of pump speed. This is illustrated in Figure 2.3.4.

The second variable is the amount of gasoline needed. Again, we compare two, five, and ten gallons, the same

Figure 2.3.2 Times for three stages as function of gallons pumped

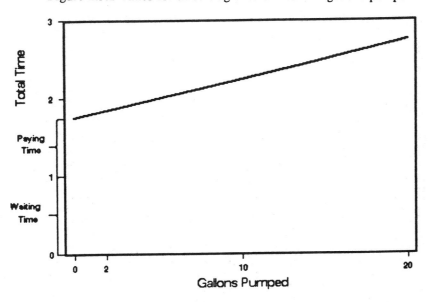

Figure 2.3.3 Additive factors of pumping time and number of cars

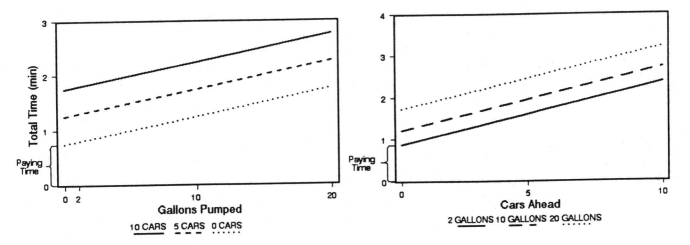

comparison as in Figure 2.3.2.

Having looked at the separate effects of these two variables--pump speed and gallons needed--we can now look at what happens when they both vary. Figure 2.3.5 presents the result. On the left, total time is graphed as a function of gallons needed (X axis), with each line representing a different pump speed. On the right, total time is shown with pump speed on the X axis, and each line representing a different number of gallons needed. These two figures have the same information, but both are included so that you can see that either is appropriate.

The main point to notice is that the lines are not parallel--there is an interaction. On a good day, when you only need a little gasoline and get a good pump, everything is fine, and either a slow pump or the need for a lot of gasoline will increase total time slightly. But notice what the *combination* of a slow pump and the need for a lot of gasoline does. You could be there a long time! Why the interaction? Because both variables affect the same

Figure 2.3.4 Total time as a function of pump speed

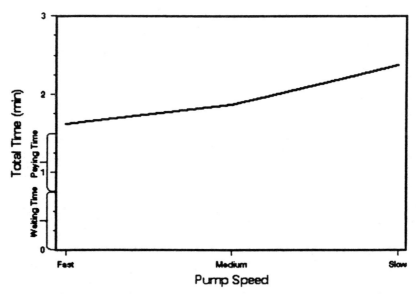

Figure 2.3.5 Interaction of pump speed by gallons pumped

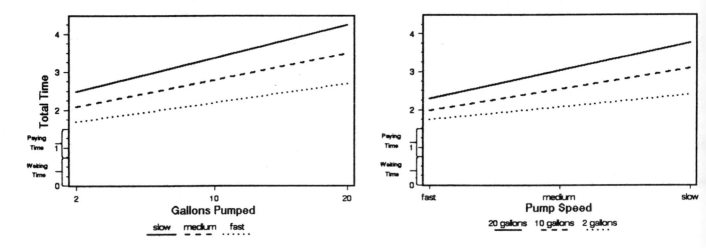

stage. These factors, or variables, are said to be *multiplicative* because the effect each has depends upon the other--a slow pump takes longer, but the more gasoline you have to pump, the more time it adds.

The gasoline-buying example was intended to show you the basics of additive factors logic. If two variables affect the different stages, their effects should be additive, but if they affect the same stage, their effects should interact. We will return to this analogy when we see how Sternberg applied this additive factors logic to confirm his stage model of search of STM.

Recall from the laboratory exercise on Scanning Short-Term Memory (Section 2.2) that the Sternberg (1966) memory search experiment was concerned with two issues. One was whether the search through items in short-term memory (STM) is serial (one at a time) or parallel (all at once). The other issue was whether the serial search is self-terminating (stopping when a match was found) or exhaustive (continuing to the end, even if a match was found). On the basis of experiments like this, Sternberg (1969) proposed a model of the search of short-term memory that treated the process as a series of discrete stages of processing, with each stage being completed before the next begins. The first stage is *stimulus encoding*, or putting a representation of the stimulus into memory for purposes of comparison to the members of the memory set. The next stage is that of the *comparisons* themselves (actually a series of substages--one for each comparison required). Next comes a *binary decision* stage, where a binary ("yes"/"no") decision is made. This is followed by a *response organization* stage, where the appropriate button-press is organized. The actual mechanical *response* is then carried out. Total reaction time (RT) is the sum of the processing time for each stage, plus the time to carry out the response.

Figure 2.3.6 Stages of processing. Adapted from Sternberg (1969, Figure 8).

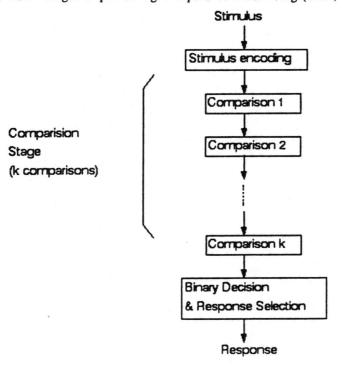

How do you verify the existence of these separate stages? The attempt to decompose RT into the durations of a series of stages has a long history in psychology. Donders (1868/1969), a Dutch physiologist, proposed the *subtractive method*. The basic idea of this approach is to measure RT on two tasks that differ only in the presence or absence of a single stage. The difference between the RT's for these two tasks would then be a measure of the duration of that stage. For example, Donders compared the mean RT's for a simple RT task (a single response is made when the stimulus is detected) and a choice RT task (one of several stimuli occurs and the appropriate response is chosen and executed). The difference between these two tasks is that the first requires only a stimulus detection stage and a response execution stage, while the second adds a stimulus identification stage and a response selection stage. This difference in RT was taken as measuring the duration of these two "extra" stages. (It lumps them together, of course, and doesn't measure how long each of them takes alone.) This approach to measuring the duration of stages of processing remained popular for some time (e.g. Jastrow, 1892). A problem arose for this method, however. Suppose that inserting a new stage also affected how long the other stages took? If this were the case, you would not have a pure measure of the time of the inserted stage. For example, in our gas station analogy, if you don't pump any gas, you also don't have to pay. Paying time is not totally independent of pumping time. The validity of "pure insertion" was difficult to demonstrate (Kulpe, 1895), and eventually led Woodworth (1938, cited in Sternberg, 1969), in his *Experimental Psychology* to advocate discarding the method altogether. In the second edition of this book Woodworth and Schlosberg (1954) relegate mention of this method to an "historical sketch." Reaction time remained important, but not as a measure of the duration of stages of mental processing.

Sternberg proposed the *additive factors* methodology as a way to overcome this difficulty, and verify his stage model of search of STM. This method discards what Sternberg calls the *assumption of pure insertion* for a "weaker and more plausible *assumption of selective influence*." Rather than trying to insert or remove a processing stage without affecting other stages, Sternberg sought to find ways to influence the duration of one stage without influencing other stages. This new method is not concerned with measuring the duration of each stage, but rather with verifying a particular stage model by providing evidence that the stages exist and are independent of one another.

Here's the logic: Recall the memory search task. The subject is given a small set of letters to remembered, then probed by being shown a letter. The subject must respond differently (press a different button) depending on whether the letter is or is not a member of the memory set. Total RT, according to Sternberg's model, is the sum of encoding, comparison, decision, and response organization stages, plus the time to make the overt response. Suppose we identify factors that influence the various stages. If the stages are truly independent, then manipulating the factors in an experiment should result *only* in a "main effect" of one or the other factor (or both), but there should be no interaction. Let's take a simple example. We know already that memory set size affects RT. It is reasonable to assume that this is because the comparison stage must make more comparisons. A factor that would influence the overt response would be how far you had to move to reach the response keys. If you have your finger on the button you should be faster than if you start each trial with your hand beside the keyboard. If we did an experiment in which we manipulated memory set size and response distance, we would expect to get a result like the idealized one in Figure 2.3.7. There is a clear effect of memory set size--RT increases as you must make more comparisons. There is an equally clear effect of response distance--the further you have to move, the longer it takes. But there is no interaction--the lines are parallel. These factors are *additive*. They each add their own constant amount to RT, but the *combination* has no effect. We have strong evidence, therefore, that the comparison stage and the overt response are independent, separate stages, each of which adds some amount to overall RT. (In terms of our earlier analogy to time in line at a gas station, this would be like increasing the number of cars and slowing the pump speed. Each would have an effect, but the combination would have no effect beyond that of the individual variables.)

Figure 2.3.7 Additive factors: memory set size and response type

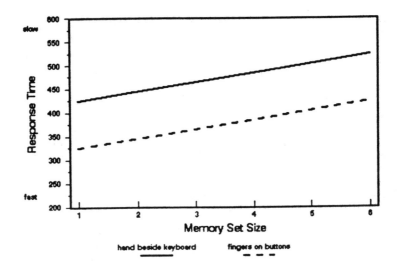

Here is another example illustrating an interaction. Suppose I manipulate stimulus discriminability in two ways. One is by using small versus large letters and the other is by the presence or absence of a "mask" that partly obscures the stimulus. It seems reasonable that both of these factors would influence the encoding stage, and so should interact. Idealized results of such an experiment are presented in Figure 2.3.8. Note that small letters, being harder

MEL Lab: Student Workbook v.1.6; © PST - Do not reproduce

to see, result in slower RT's, and that the mask also increases RT because it, too, makes it harder to see. But what happens when we combine a small letter and a mask? That ought to result in even worse performance, as indeed the graph indicates. The interaction occurs because both factors affect the same stage. (Again, recall the analogy of pump speed and amount of gasoline needed showing a stronger effect when combined than either showed alone.)

Figure 2.3.8 Interaction of letter size and masking

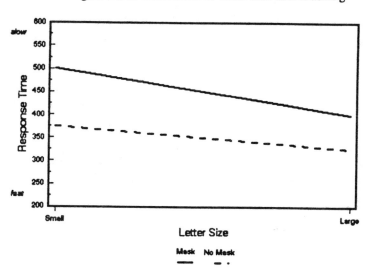

To summarize, two experimental manipulations that affect the same stage will interact, while two manipulations that affect different stages will be additive. With this logic in mind, Sternberg sought to find factors that would affect various stages in an additive fashion. If successful, he would have strong evidence for his model of a series of discrete stages of processing in the search of STM. The experiment described below replicates one of Sternberg's experiments, testing for additivity in factors affecting encoding ("quality" of the stimulus--degraded or not) and comparison (memory set size).

McClelland (1979) has provided an elaborate analysis of additive and interactive effects. Sternberg's additive factors method assumes processing is done in discrete stages (e.g., the perceptual stage outputs nothing to the comparison stage until perceptual processing is complete). McClelland examined cascaded processes where input is cascaded through several stages quickly before one stage is complete (e.g., the perceptual stage outputs partial information to the comparison stage while the perceptual stage is still clarifying the stimulus). To use the fueling example, a cascaded process would be paying for the fuel as it is pumped (.e.g, pay a dollar as each gallon is pumped). The pumping and paying stages are no longer discrete. For cascaded processes interactions can occur even for variables that affect different stages. This complicates interpretation and is the subject of current research. For this exercise, we will limit analysis to additive factors methodology, assuming discrete stages of processing.

Method

The general method used is the same as in the first memory search experiment, but with the addition of a second factor of stimulus discriminability. This is manipulated by adding a pattern mask to the stimulus letter that makes it harder to recognize. Half of the 144 trials have the mask and half do not. Masked and non-masked trials are selected at random. The pattern mask will be turned on and off each 20 msec while the probe letter is displayed. Memory set sizes of 1, 2 and 4 will occur equally often, in random order.

Instructions for Running the Experiment

To run this experiment, insert Disk 1 into your computer and enter the MEL Lab as instructed in Section 0.2. Select **Cognition** from the topic menu and **Additive Factors Methodology** from the specific experiment menu. Instructions on the computer screen will then explain the experiment and indicate which keys to use for your responses. Note that you must get 8 of the 10 practice trials right before you can begin the 144 trials of the actual experiment. (If you miss more than 2 practice trials, you will have to repeat them.) *Reaction time is important* for this experiment, so please respond as quickly and accurately as you can to each stimulus. *Materials needed*: Pencil and paper, if no printer is available, to copy down the results reported in the table at the end of the experiment. *Things to notice*: What effect does the mask have on how easily the letters are recognized?

Expected Running Time = 20 minutes

Questions

1. What is the dependent variable in this experiment?

2. What are the independent variables?

3. What are important control variables?

4. What are your findings? Are the lines parallel, or is there an interaction? What specific stages are affected by each independent variable?

5. Sternberg (1969) actually found an interaction between stimulus clarity and memory set size for the *first* session of testing of his subjects. This interaction disappeared in the second session. What did he suggest accounted for this finding?

6. Sternberg (1969, p. 438) suggested that a factor affecting the binary decision stage is response type--whether the response indicated a positive probe or a negative probe. You have already examined the combined effects of probe type and memory set size, when you did the experiment on *Search of Short-Term Memory*. What do those data say about the separability of the serial comparison and binary decision stages?

7. Design an experiment to test the "gas station" analogy. Specifically, how would you determine whether pumping time and paying time were really separate stages? (the alternative might be if you had to pay continuously as you pumped--say, a dime at a time. In that case pumping time and paying time would be the same stage.) Keep in mind that you can only measure the total amount of time the car was in the station. Graph the results you would expect from various manipulations.

Advanced Questions

1. In this experiment it is expected that you will have demonstrated separability of the stimulus encoding and serial comparison stages. In the previous experiment on *Search of Short-Term Memory* you likely demonstrated separability of the serial comparison and binary decision stages. If stimulus encoding and serial comparison are separate stages, and serial comparison and binary decision are also, it should be the case that stimulus encoding and binary decision stages are also separable. Since this experiment employed positive and negative probes, it should be possible to directly test the separability of stimulus encoding and binary decision. Perform that test. What is the result?

2. Some doubts have been raised about the validity of stage models of information processing. These alternative models assume that a stage might begin to send its output to the next stage before it is complete. McClelland (1979)

proposed a "cascade" model and Eriksen and Schultz (1979) argued for a "continuous flow" model. How might these models interpret the findings of additive factors studies?

Extension Experiments

1. What other factors could you manipulate to try to determine whether other pairs of stages could be shown to be independent? Sternberg (1969, p. 438) mentioned several. For a more recent discussion of a number of studies using additive factors methodology, see Wickens (1984).

References

Donders, F. C. (1869/1969). On the speed of mental processes. In W. G. Koster (Ed. & Trans.) *Attention and Human Performance II. Acta Psychologica, 30*, 412-431.

Eriksen, C. W. & Schultz, D. W. (1979). Information processing in visual search: A continuous-flow conception and experimental results. *Perception and Psychophysics, 25*, 249-263.

Fisher, D. L. (1982). Limited channels models of automatic detection: Capacity and scanning in visual search. *Psychological Review, 89*, 662-692.

Jastrow, J. (1892). Classification time. *American Journal of Psychology, 4*, 411-415.

Kulpe, O. (1895). *Outlines of Psychology.* New York: MacMillan.

McClelland, J. L. (1979). On the time relations of mental processes: An examination of systems of processes in cascade. *Psychological Review, 86*, 287-330.

Sternberg, S. (1966). High-speed scanning in human memory. *Science, 153*, 652-654.

Sternberg, S. (1969). Memory scanning: Mental processes revealed   by reaction-time experiments. *American Scientist, 57*, 421-457.

Wickens, C. D. (1984). *Engineering Psychology and Human Performance.* Columbus, OH: Merrill.

Woodworth, R. S. (1938). *Experimental Psychology.* New York: Holt.

Woodworth, R. S. & Schlosberg, H. (1954). *Experimental Psychology.* New York: Holt, Rinehart, & Winston.

Thought Questions

1. When the probe letter was "fuzzy," did it take you longer before you could tell what the letter was?

2. Once you had figured out what a "fuzzy" letter was, was it any harder to compare it to the letters in memory than if it had been seen clearly?

Additive Factors Methodology

Individual Data

Memory Set Size

	1	2	4
Not Masked			
Positive Probes ("yes")	——	——	——
Negative Probes ("no")	——	——	——
Masked			
Positive Probes ("yes")	——	——	——
Negative Probes ("no")	——	——	——

Cell entries are MEAN CORRECT REACTION TIME (msec)

Memory Set Size

	1	2	4
Not Masked			
Positive Probes ("yes")	——	——	——
Negative Probes ("no")	——	——	——
Masked			
Positive Probes ("yes")	——	——	——
Negative Probes ("no")	——	——	——

Cell entries are MEAN PERCENT CORRECT

Additive Factors Methodology
Individual Data

Data for NOT MASKED DISPLAYS

Correlations between mean correct reaction time and memory set size:
Positive probes ("yes") =_____ Negative probes ("no") =_____

Slopes of the functions relating
mean correct reaction time and memory set size (msec):
Positive probes ("yes") =_____ Negative probes ("no") =_____

Y-intercepts of the functions relating
mean correct reaction time and memory set size (msec):
Positive probes ("yes") =_____ Negative probes ("no") =_____

Slope ratio (msec) (Negative/Positive) =_____

Data for MASKED DISPLAYS

Correlations between mean correct reaction time and memory set size:
Positive probes ("yes") =_____ Negative probes ("no") =_____

Slopes of the functions relating
mean correct reaction time and memory set size (msec):
Positive probes ("yes") =_____ Negative probes ("no") =_____

Y-intercepts of the functions relating
mean correct reaction time and memory set size (msec):
Positive probes ("yes") =_____ Negative probes ("no") =_____

Slope ratio (msec) (Negative/Positive) =_____

Additive Factors Methodology

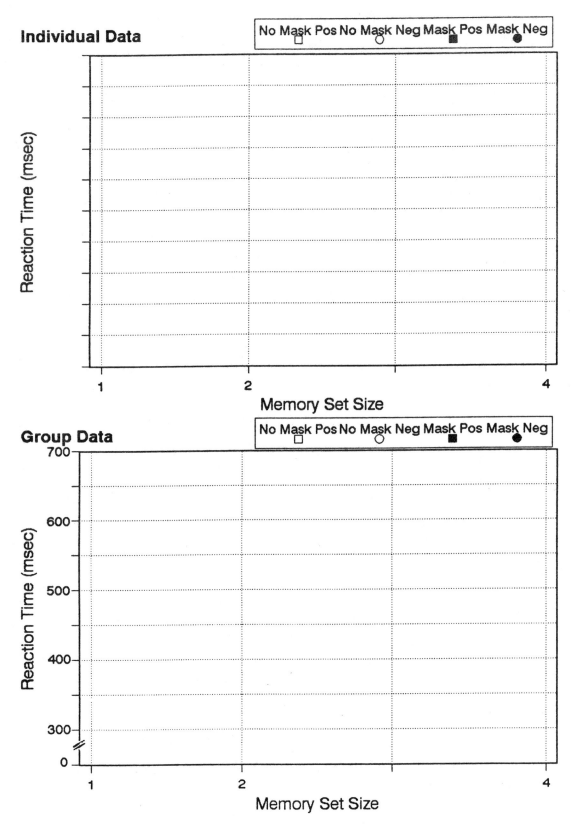

Individual Data

| No Mask Pos □ | No Mask Neg ○ | Mask Pos ■ | Mask Neg ● |

Reaction Time (msec)

Memory Set Size

Group Data

| No Mask Pos □ | No Mask Neg ○ | Mask Pos ■ | Mask Neg ● |

Reaction Time (msec)

Memory Set Size

2.4 Sentence-Picture Comparison

Abstract

Clark and Chase (1972) proposed a model of how we compare sentences and pictures to determine whether the sentence is true of the picture or not. In this exercise, one of their experiments is replicated in which a sentence appears, followed by a picture. Chase and Clark argued that the sentence and picture must be encoded into mental representations of the same type for comparison. According to their model, the sentence and the picture are each converted into propositions and then compared. By varying the sentences in several ways, it is possible to show that their theory provides a good fit to the data. Sentences were either positive or negative ("is" or "isn't"), true or false in relation to the picture, and used either a marked or an unmarked adjective. Their theory makes some specific predictions about the patterns of reaction times obtained, which are used to test the theory. The additive factors logic can be applied to testing the assumption of a series of stages of processing leading to the decision about whether the sentence is true of the picture.

In this experiment, you will replicate a study by Clark and Chase (1972), which examined the process by which one compares a sentence and a picture to determine whether the sentence accurately describes the picture. The sentences are simple ones, like:

The star is above the plus.

The pictures are of the form:

```
*   or   +
+        *
```

For this sentence, of course, the answer would be "true" for the picture on the left and "false" for the other.

The sentences and pictures vary in a number of ways. The pictures can be either of those shown above, while the sentences can be true or false, positive or negative (is or isn't), and contain the word "above" or "below." You will be examining the pattern of reaction time latencies (RT's) for these various conditions to test Clark and Chase's theory of how we do this task.

In the experiment by Clark and Chase that you are replicating, they were concerned with the process of sentence-picture comparison when the sentence is presented first. Their model of this process requires some modification when the picture is presented first, but we won't be concerned with that situation. Clark and Chase postulated four stages in the process of comparing the sentence and picture, which are outlined below. They are: forming a mental representation of the sentence, forming a mental representation of the picture, comparing those representations, and making a response.

When a mental representation of the sentence is formed, it is assumed that the representation is stored as a set of propositions (a proposition may be thought of a simple statement). The sentence, "Star is above Plus" (or Plus is above Star) requires a single proposition; Star isn't above Plus requires two--"Star is above Plus": and "It is false." For this reason, a negative sentence will take longer to encode or form a representation than a positive sentence.

In the process of forming the mental representation, above and below will be treated somewhat differently, according to this model. *Above* is assumed to be the normal ("unmarked") statement, while *below* is the less direct statement, called a semantically marked form. The linguistic analysis that leads to this assumption is beyond the scope of this presentation (see Clark, 1971, for a detailed discussion of marking), but the prediction it makes is that the time to encode *below* will be longer than the time to encode *above*. To perhaps make this distinction more meaningful, think about how you describe such relationships. Which would you find the more natural way to describe a ceiling and floor: *The floor is below the ceiling*, or *The ceiling is above the floor*? Try this with other objects that could be above or below one another, and you will likely find that you are generally more comfortable saying *A is above B* than saying *B is below A*, even though the two sentences mean the same thing.

In the next stage of the process, a mental representation of the picture is formed. Clark and Chase assumed that the picture is encoded as a proposition (statement) in such a way that a picture with the star on top will be encoded *star above plus* if the sentence had *above* as the relationship, and as *plus below star* if the sentence had *below* as the relationship.

In the third stage, the two representations (of the sentence and picture) are compared, but they cannot simply be compared for surface identity. The propositions for *Star is not above Plus* are *Star above Plus* and *False*. But these propositions are true of the picture encoded as *Plus above star*. So, this third stage must involve a series of steps in making the comparisons, not just a check for identity of the encoded propositions. These comparisons involved first checking to see whether the subjects of the propositions match, and then checking to see whether there is a *False* proposition for the sentence.

Figure 2.4.1 is taken from Clark and Chase (1972), and illustrates the steps in the process in flow-chart form.

Figure 2.4.1 Stages of processing in sentence-picture comparison.
(Redrawn from Clark & Chase 1972, Table 1).

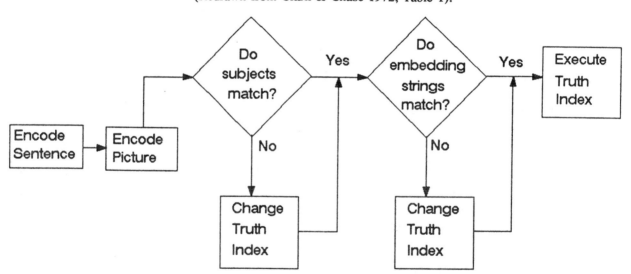

In the final stage, a response is made, based on whether the outcome of the previous stages was *True* or *False*. This stage is assumed to add a constant amount of time to RT, since a True or False response would require the same time to execute.

The exact predictions from this model are quite involved, but for our purposes they can be summarized as follows:

1. A sentence with *Below* will require longer to process than one with *Above*, resulting in longer RT.

MEL Lab: Student Workbook v.1.6; © *PST - Do not reproduce*

2. Negative sentences will take longer than positive ones (*Isn't* takes longer to process than *Is*).

3. False sentences will take longer to process than true ones (a mismatch requires extra processing time).

Method

The experiment for this exercise replicates Clark and Chase's (1972) Experiment 1. In this experiment, subjects see a sentence, followed by a picture. The task is simply to indicate, by pressing the appropriate keys, whether the sentence is a true statement about the picture or a false one. The pictures are of a star (*) and a plus (+), one above the other. On half of the trials, the star is above the plus, with the other half reversed. The sentences describe the relationship between the star and the plus, varying in whether they are true or false in relation to the actual picture, in whether they are positive or negative statements, and in whether the relation is stated as "above" or "below." The resulting 16 sentences (two each for the eight trial types) are presented 10 times each, after an initial practice block of 10 trials. The order of the conditions within the 160 trials is random.

Responses are to be made quickly but accurately.

Instructions for Running the Experiment

To run this experiment, insert Disk 1 into your computer and enter the MEL Lab as instructed in Section 0.2. Select **Cognition** from the topic menu and **Sentence-Picture Comparison** from the specific experiment menu. Instructions on the computer screen will then explain the experiment and what keys to use for your responses. Note that you must get 8 of the 10 practice trials right before you can begin the 160 trials of the actual experiment. (If you miss more than 2 practice trials, you will have to repeat them.) *Reaction time is important* for this experiment, so please respond as quickly and accurately as you can to each stimulus. *Materials needed*: Pencil and paper, if no printer is available, to copy down the results reported in the table at the end of the experiment. *Things to notice*: How do you seem to be doing this task? That is, what mental acts do you perform in making your decisions?

Expected Running Time = 20 minutes

Questions

1. What is the dependent variable in this experiment?

2. What are the independent variables?

3. What are some important control variables? Describe the use of randomization in this experiment.

4. Describe your results. For each independent variable, state whether there was a main effect. State what interactions occurred and describe them.

5. Are your data consistent with those of Clark and Chase?

Advanced Questions

1. Discuss the results of this experiment in terms of *additive factors logic*. (See the laboratory exercise "Additive Factors Methodology.") Do your data (and those of Clark and Chase, 1972) permit the drawing of conclusions about the reality of the proposed stages?

Extension Experiments

1. What is the effect of presenting the picture first, and then the sentence? See Clark and Chase's (1972) Experiment 2.

2. Clark and Chase (1972) presented their sentences and pictures simultaneously, with the sentence on the left, and instructed their subjects to read the sentence first (Experiment 1). In another experiment they varied the instructions and the left-to-right order of the sentence and picture. Gough (1966, and see Clark and Chase, p. 502) has reported a similar experiment, but with the sentence appearing three seconds before the picture (presumably enough time to complete encoding it). Does the timing matter? Could the effects of reading time on the verification task be measured by placing it under the subject's control?

References

Gough, P. R. (1966). The verification of sentences: The effects of delay of evidence and sentence length. *Journal of Verbal Learning and Verbal Behavior, 5,* 492-496.

Clark, H. H., & Chase, W. G. (1972). On the process of comparing sentences against pictures. *Cognitive Psychology, 3,* 472-517.

Clark, H. H. (1971). More about "Adjectives, Comparatives, and Syllogisms": A Reply to Huttenlocher and Higgins. *Psychological Review, 78,* 505-514.

1. Which seemed harder, sentences with "is" or those with "isn't?"

2. Which seemed harder, true sentences or false ones?

3. Which seemed harder, sentences with "above" or those with "below?"

Sentence-Picture Comparison

Individual Data

Congruency

	True		False
Sentence Type:			
Positive (is)	___		___
Negative (isn't)	___		___

Cell entries are MEAN CORRECT REACTION TIME (msec)

Sentence-Picture Comparison

Individual Data

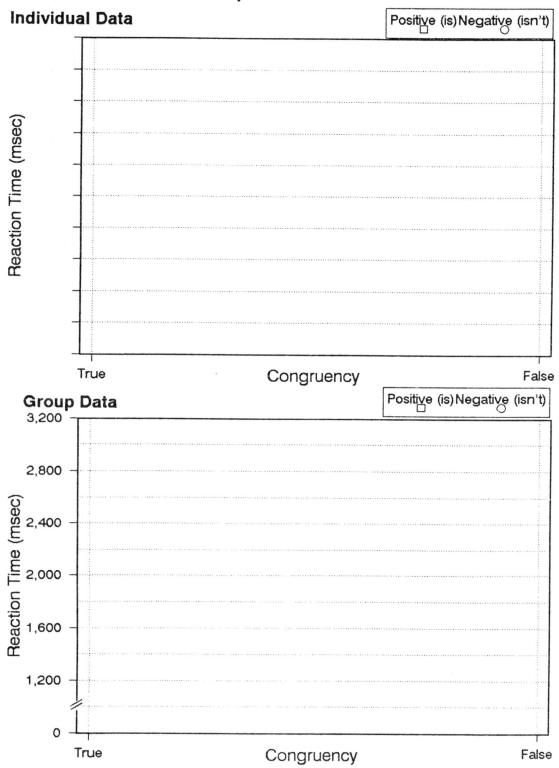

Reaction Time (msec)

Positive (is) □ Negative (isn't) ○

True   Congruency   False

Group Data

Positive (is) □ Negative (isn't) ○

Reaction Time (msec)

3,200

2,800

2,400

2,000

1,600

1,200

0

True   Congruency   False

MEL Lab: Student Workbook v.1.6; © PST - Do not reproduce

2.5 The Symbolic Distance Effect

Abstract

This exercise concerns the process of comparing two objects (here, animals) for size, when the objects themselves are not present, but rather must be remembered, and is designed to illustrate the symbolic distance and congruity effects. The symbolic distance effect is reflected in faster RT's for two animals that are very different in size than for two that are similar. The congruity effect occurs when judgments of "Which is smaller?" are made faster for two small animals than for two large ones, while judgments of "Which is larger?" show the opposite pattern. Discussion of the issue of whether the comparisons are based on imagery or propositional coding makes it clear that this issue cannot (yet) be resolved.

Relational judgments are a common form of cognitive process in everyday life. These are judgments of largest, heaviest, greenest, or greatest in whatever dimension is of interest. Whenever you say that one person is taller than another, or that one object is above another, you are making a relational judgement. The study of these types of judgments has been of interest to psychologists for some time. In a typical experiment, subjects are asked to compare two animals in size, judging either which is larger or which is smaller of two animals. Of course, the subjects are seeing either the animal names or pictures of them. Thus the relational judgement is based on *memory*, rather being a direct perceptual judgement. In addition to studying relational judgments *per se*, experiments like this can also help us learn something about how concepts (such as *animal* or *dog*) are stored in memory. A standard finding in experiments of this type is that the greater the difference in size of the two animals, the faster a subject can answer the question (Moyer, 1973). This has been termed the *symbolic distance effect* (Moyer & Bayer, 1976). An interesting finding in regard to this effect is that it takes less time to answer "Which is smaller?" than "Which is larger?" if the objects to be compared are both small. If both objects are large, it takes longer to answer "Which is smaller?" This finding is known as the *congruity effect*.

Two general classes of explanations have been offered for the symbolic distance effect. One is based on imagery (Paivio, 1975). This explanation assumes that we have an analog representation of the objects stored in memory. When the subject sees SQUIRREL and ELEPHANT, he or she calls up an image of each, and compares them for size. According to this explanation, the image is analogous to the actual object in important ways, such as relative size.

A second class of explanation assumes that we store in memory a set of propositions about the objects. In this context, you can think of a proposition as a basic statement, like "Elephants are large," or "Squirrels are small." One type of information we have stored about elephants is that they are large, and similarly, we have stored the information that squirrels are small. We can compare these stored facts in order to answer the question, and thus don't need images. (Clearly there would be many other propositions stored with each animal beyond just size, but that doesn't change the basic point.)

This argument over the basic explanation of the symbolic distance effect is ongoing, and no final answer seems likely for some time. In regard to this issue, Adams (1980) has commented, "Some may find theoretical indecisiveness like this uncomfortable, but it does not bother scientists very much because the world is clouded with uncertainty in their eyes and they are tolerant of it. At any moment, given the facts available, a scientist will pass tentative judgments on the mechanisms that are required to explain the facts, and then will get on with the job of research to refine the judgments and reduce the uncertainty" (p. 283).

Method

Each subject completes the entire experiment, which consists of 264 trials, half of which are *larger* judgments, and half of which are *smaller*. The animals to be rated are taken from Čech and Shoben (1985). Six small animals (flea, snail, mouse, chipmunk, rabbit, and beaver, in ascending order) and six large animals (sheep, crocodile, lion, horse, rhino, elephant) are used as stimulus words. On each trial, two animal names are presented, above and below a fixation mark. Each animal is paired with each other animal twice. On one pairing, the larger animal is listed above the fixation, while on the other pairing, the larger one is below the fixation.

In half of the experiment, subjects are instructed to answer "Which is larger?" by indicating either the top (above fixation) or bottom name. In the other half of the experiment, they are asked to indicate which is smaller. Order of the judgments is counterbalanced.

Instructions for Running the Experiment

To run this experiment, insert Disk 1 into your computer and enter the MEL Lab as instructed in Section 0.2. Select **Cognition** from the topic menu and **The Symbolic Distance Effect** from the specific experiment menu. Instructions on the computer screen will then explain the experiment and what keys to use for your responses. Note that you must get 8 of the 10 practice trials right before you can begin the 264 trials of the actual experiment. (If you miss more than two practice trials, you will have to repeat them.) *Reaction time is important* for this experiment, so please respond as quickly and accurately as you can to each stimulus. *Materials needed*: Pencil and paper, if no printer is available, to copy down the results reported in the table at the end of the experiment. *Things to notice*: How do you do this task? Be prepared to explain what you were doing mentally to decide which animal was larger or smaller. *Remember*: a lion is bigger than a crocodile. (You will know the rest of them.)

Expected Running Time = 30 minutes

Questions

1. What is the dependent variable for this experiment?

2. What are the independent variables?

3. What are some important control variables?

4. Is there a symbolic distance effect? What pattern in the data indicates this?

5. Is there a congruity effect? What pattern in the data indicates this?

6. Do you feel that you are using imagery to make the judgment, or are you using propositional information about the animals?

7. Čech and Shoben (1985) report two experiments on symbolic magnitude comparisons that had subjects make relational judgments about the same animals as in the experiment for this exercise, but instead of using *all* the animals, they used only the small animals (Experiment 1) or only the large ones (Experiment 2). What did they find?

Advanced Questions

1. Parkman (1971) did an experiment similar to this one, but instead of animal names, he presented pairs of digits (0 to 9), and asked subjects to indicate which was larger. He found the usual symbolic distance effect. It can be argued on this basis that imagery is a poor explanation. Why should your image of a "9" be bigger than your image of a "4?" Something else must be going on. Can you think of a reply to this finding that argues that this finding does not rule out an analog representation?

2. In the experiment on "Sentence-Picture Comparison" (Section 2.4), subjects must decide whether a relational statement is true or false in regard to a picture. Note that this is not *a memory experiment*, but rather requires judgments or verifications of currently visible information. What is the role of imagery in this experiment?

Extension Experiments

1. Suppose that the animals to be compared were only the small animals used in this experiment. In this case "rabbit" and "beaver" are the largest animals. Would a congruity effect occur, such that "larger" judgments about this pair were made faster than "smaller" judgments? See Čech and Shoben (1985).

2. In the experiment for this exercise only a limited number of animal names were used. Would the results change if members of different categories were compared for size (e.g. SNAIL-LAMP)? See Paivio (1975) for this and several other interesting manipulations of this basic experiment.

References

Adams, J. A. (1980). *Learning and memory: An introduction.* Homewood, IL: Dorsey Press.

Čech, C., & Shoben, E. J. (1985). Context effects in symbolic magnitude comparisons. *Journal of Experimental Psychology: Learning, Memory, and Cognition, 11,* 299-315.

Moyer, R. S. (1973). Comparing objects in memory: Evidence suggesting an internal psychophysics. *Perception and Psychophysics, 13,* 180-184.

Moyer, R. S. & Bayer, R. H. (1976). Mental comparison and the symbolic distance effect. *Cognitive Psychology, 8,* 228-246.

Paivio, A. (1975). Perceptual comparisons through the mind's eye. *Memory and Cognition, 3,* 635-647.

Parkman, J. M. (1971). Temporal aspects of digit and letter inequality judgments. *Journal of Experimental Psychology, 91,* 191-205.

Thought Questions

1. Did you feel that you compared the animals visually?

2. Were animals that are nearly the same size (FLEA-SNAIL) harder to judge than animals that are very different (FLEA-ELEPHANT)?

The Symbolic Distance Effect

Individual Data

Question:	Animal Pair Type		
	Both Large	Both Small	Mixed
Which is Larger?	——	——	——
Which is Smaller?	——	——	——

Cell entries are MEAN CORRECT REACTION TIME (msec)

The Symbolic Distance Effect

Individual Data

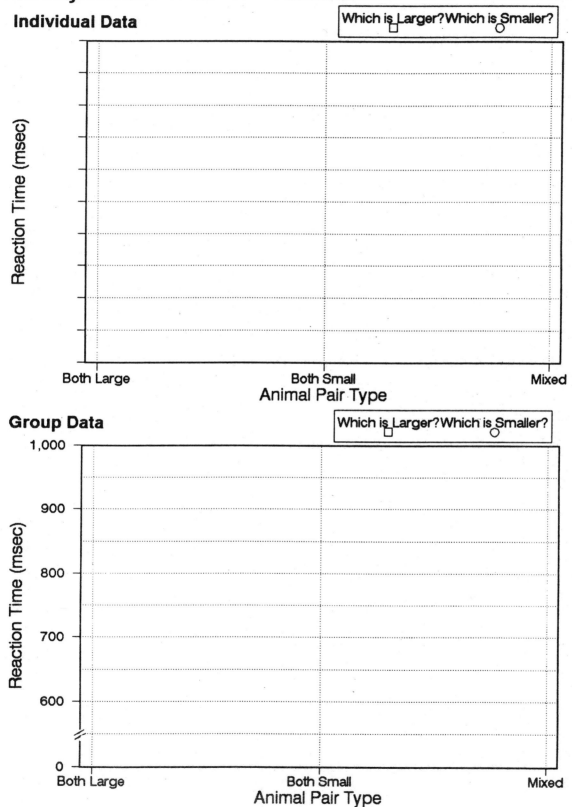

The Symbolic Distance Effect

Ordinal Distance refers to the number of positions apart two animals in the list are in size. It is calculated by numbering the animals from smallest to largest, and then taking the difference between any pair of animals as the ordinal distance for that pair. For example, FLEA (#1) and SNAIL (#2) differ by one position (ordinal distance = 1), as do SHEEP (#7) and CROCODILE (#8). The ordinal distance between FLEA (#1) and ELEPHANT (#12) is 11.

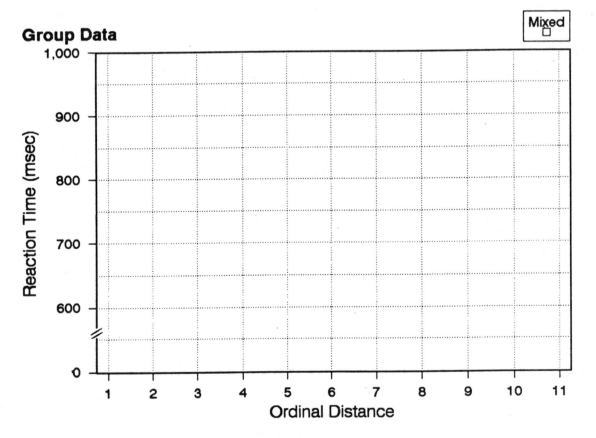

Group Data

Mixed ☐

2.6 Short-term Memory

Abstract

Short-term memory (STM) refers to the memory associated with very brief delays before recall. The typical finding is a rapid drop in recall of brief lists with delays out to about 20 seconds, if rehearsal is prevented. In this exercise, students replicate the classic experiment of Peterson and Peterson (1959), which first brought prominent attention to a class of memory phenomena that have been of central interest to cognitive psychology ever since.

Early studies of human memory involved examining how well people could learn and remember lists of words or nonsense syllables over relatively long periods--hours or days. Then, in 1958, Brown reported an interesting finding. In one condition of a larger experiment, he found that there was a decrement in recall of single pairs of consonants when there was only a five-second delay. This suggests that there may be another mechanism operating other than the traditional conception of memory. Peterson and Peterson (1959) extended Brown's finding, and systematically tested for recall of simple materials after brief delays. A major innovation of this type of study was that of preventing rehearsal. Subjects allowed to rehearse the list of letters or words to be remembered in an experiment on memory show no decline in recall with increased delay before testing. But when the delay before recall is filled with some mental activity that prevents rehearsal, recall drops dramatically, even over a very brief interval. This finding of Peterson and Peterson's is what you will be attempting to replicate in this experiment.

Figure 2.6.1 Recall as a function of delay before recall. Graphed from data tabled in Peterson & Peterson (1959)

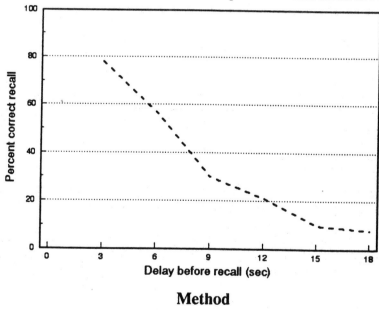

Method

There are two versions of this experiment, and your instructor will tell you which to perform. One version replicates Peterson and Peterson's procedure almost exactly. On each trial a set of three consonants (called a CCC trigram) is read out loud to the subject by a human experimenter, who then also reads out loud a three-digit number. The subject must then count backwards by threes (out loud) from that number. A tone sounds every second, and subjects are to try to count backwards in time to the tone (that is, one subtraction every second). They continue to count backwards for either 3, 9, or 18 seconds, until told to stop. They then must try to recall the CCC trigram. There are 45 trials - 15 at each delay.

The other version of this experiment has the computer act as experimenter throughout. The subject sees the trigram presented on the screen, and then the number from which to count backwards. In this version, the subject must type in the answers to their subtractions. The delays before recall and the number of trials are identical to the other version.

Instructions for Running the Experiment

To run this experiment, insert Disk 1 into your computer and enter the MEL Lab as instructed in Section 0.2. Select **Cognition** from the topic menu and **Short-Term Memory** from the specific experiment menu. Your instructor will assign you to complete one of the two versions of this experiment, and you will choose which version to do at the beginning of the experiment. Instructions on the computer screen will then explain the experiment and what keys to use for your responses. There are no practice trials for this experiment. On each trial, you will be given three letters to remember, perform the subtraction task for 3 to 18 seconds, and then try to remember the letters. Speed of responding is *not* important. *Materials needed*: Pencil and paper, if no printer is available, to copy down the results reported in the table at the end of the experiment. *Things to notice*: What effect did the subtraction task have on your memory for the letters? Did the time you spent on the subtraction task play a role?

Expected Running Time = 24 minutes

Questions

1. What is the dependent variable?

2. What is the independent variable?

3. What are some important control variables?

4. Does recall drop off as delay is increased? Peterson and Peterson found a dramatic decline in recall, with only about a 15% recall rate for an 18-second delay. They reported recall of about 70% for a 3-second delay.

5. If your class performed both versions of this experiment, were they both successful at replicating Peterson and Peterson's results? If not, how do the two versions of the counting-backwards-by-threes differ? (If you only completed one version of the task, you might want to perform the other version in demonstration mode, just to see how it was done).

6. What would be the effect of having the subject recall three letters that formed a word (CAT), instead of three consonants? What about three, three-letter words? Murdoch (1961) performed such an experiment, and you should examine his results.

Advanced Questions

1. One early claim about the nature of encoding of information in STM was that it is *acoustic* in nature. That is, even though you *see* the stimulus visually, you represent the letters by their *sound*. What evidence supports this claim? See Conrad (1964) and the experiment on perceptual matching (Section 1.4 of this workbook).

MEL Lab: Student Workbook v.1.6; © PST - Do not reproduce

2. Is STM restricted to auditory codes? See Posner and Keele (1967), or the experiment titled "Perceptual Matching" (Section 1.4).

Extension Experiments

1. In addition to the *duration* of STM measured in this exercise, you might also want to measure the *capacity*, using a technique like the digit-span test. See Miller (1956).

2. Are three three-letter words treated the same in STM as nine letters or as three words? See Murdoch (1961).

3. What would happen if you only did three or four trials per subject, with no practice trials, and had a different group of subjects for each delay? This procedure produces some interesting results, and illustrates proactive interference in STM. See Keppel and Underwood (1962). For an additional interesting wrinkle on this experiment that illustrates release from proactive interference, see Wickens (1970).

4. How does familiarity with the stimuli affect processing? If you did the three-word version of the task, how would decay vary for frequent words (e.g., cat, tree) and infrequent words (e.g., kiwi, mango)?

References

Brown J. (1958). Some tests of the decay theory of immediate memory. *Quarterly Journal of Experimental Psychology, 10*, 12-21.

Conrad, R. (1964). Acoustic confusions in immediate memory. *British Journal of Psychology, 55*, 75-84.

Keppel, G. & Underwood, B. J. (1962). Proactive inhibition in short-term retention of single items. *Journal of Verbal Learning and Verbal Behavior, 1*, 153-161.

Miller, G. A. (1956). The magical number seven, plus or minus two: Some limits on our capacity for processing information. *Psychological Review, 63*, 81-97.

Murdoch, B. B., Jr. (1961). The retention of individual items. *Journal of Experimental Psychology, 62*, 618-625.

Peterson, L. R., & Peterson, M. J. (1959). Short-term retention of individual verbal items. *Journal of Experimental Psychology, 58*, 193-198.

Wickens, D. D. (1970). Encoding categories of words: An empirical approach to meaning. *Psychological Review, 77*, 1-15.

1.   Did you try to rehearse the letters by repeating them to yourself?

2.   Were you able to rehearse successfully even while counting backwards by threes?

Short-Term Memory

Individual Data

Please indicate which version of the experiment you performed:
Version 1: Experimenter = Computer _____
Version 2: Experimenter = Partner _____

	Delay (sec)		
	3	**9**	**18**
Recall	____	____	____
Subtraction Task *	____	____	____

not recorded in Version 2

Cell entries are MEAN PERCENT CORRECT

Short Term Memory

Individual Data

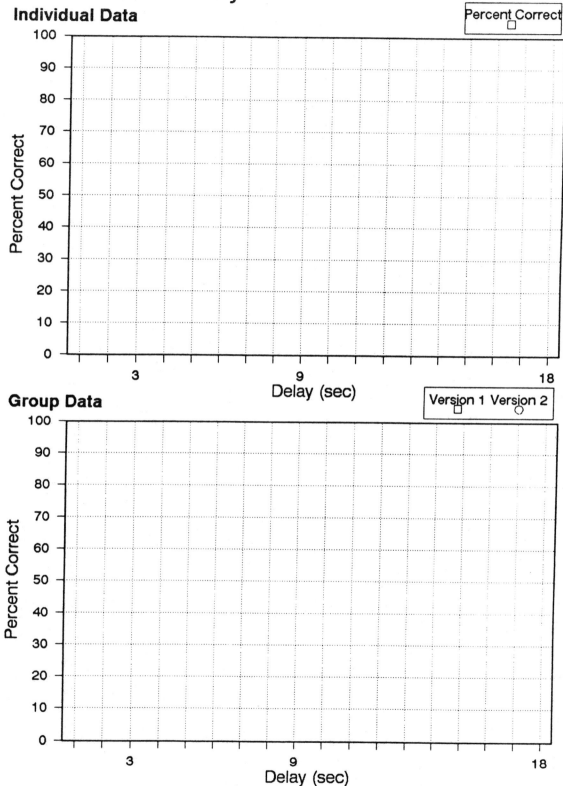

Percent Correct □

Group Data — Version 1 □   Version 2 ○

2.7 Free Recall and the Serial Position Effect

Abstract

The serial position effect refers to the good recall for the first few and last few words in a list presented once, and the relatively poor recall of words in the middle. One possible explanation for this effect is that the first few words have enough rehearsal to store them in Long-Term Memory (LTM) and the last few words are still available in Short-term Memory (STM). Words in the middle are no longer in STM, but are not rehearsed well enough to transfer them to LTM. In this exercise two tests are made of this explanation. One is to determine whether a delay without rehearsal will reduce the recency effect (the good recall of the last few words). The second test determines whether preventing adequate rehearsal of the first few words will reduce the primacy effect (good recall of the first few words). An important implication of this experiment is that it provides evidence that STM and LTM are separate storage mechanisms.

It has been known for some time that free recall of a list of unrelated words shows a *serial position effect*. Free recall refers to instructions to recall the words in any order. Good recall of the first few words in the list is called *primacy*, while good recall of the last few words is called *recency*. These are illustrated in Figure 2.7.1.

Figure 2.7.1 Idealized form of the serial position curve

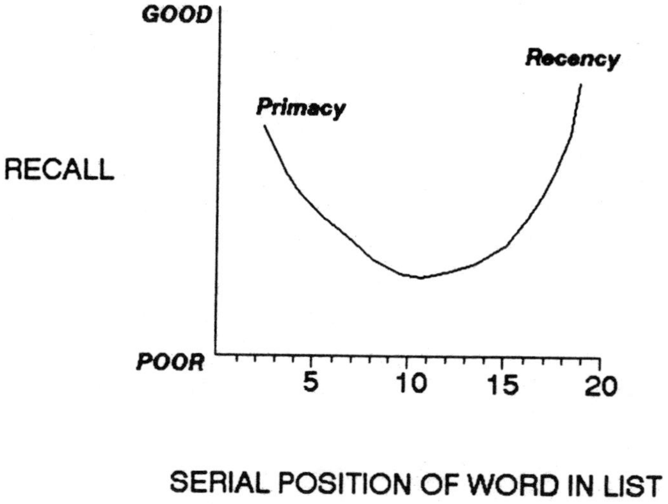

SERIAL POSITION OF WORD IN LIST

This exercise is concerned primarily with testing a theory proposed to explain the serial position effect. Recall from the exercise on measuring the duration of short-term memory (STM) that such a memory system had begun to be seriously studied in the late 1950's (Brown, 1958; Peterson & Peterson, 1959). Studies of the serial position effect began in earnest at about the same time. One theory that was developed to explain it was that the first few words on a list receive sufficient rehearsal to be transferred to long-term memory (LTM). At recall, those words are retrieved from LTM. The last few words on the list, however, would still be in STM. When the list ends and the subjects are told to recall the list, those words are still in STM and can be recalled from there. Words in the middle of the list exhibit poor recall because they could not be adequately rehearsed for storage in LTM (due to interference from the previous words), but they were no longer available in STM.

Glanzer and Cunitz (1966) offered a test of that theory. They reasoned that we already knew from studies of LTM what some of the variables are that affect it, such as meaningfulness of the material, number of presentations, and presentation rate. If one of these was manipulated in an experiment, and it produced a change in primacy, without affecting recency, then this would support the notion that primacy is due to LTM storage of the first few words. Similarly, they reasoned that we already knew how to manipulate STM. A delay imposed between presentation of the items and their recall will effectively "wipe out" STM if rehearsal is prevented, as Peterson and Peterson (1959) had shown. The experiment for this exercise replicates some of the conditions of Glanzer and Cunitz' Experiments 1 and 2. The variable they chose to affect LTM was presentation rate, while that chosen to affect STM was length of delay before recall.

Method

In this experiment, subjects are presented with lists of 20 words. After each list is presented, subjects will have two minutes in which to try to recall as many words as possible in any order. Recall will be done by having the subject enter the first and last letter of each word recalled. All word lists consist of common nouns.

Lists are presented under each of three conditions. The first is a control condition. Words are presented at a rate of one word every two seconds, and recall occurs immediately after presentation of the last word. In a second condition (speeded-presentation) the rate of presentation is increased, in order to try to minimize transfer to LTM. Words are presented at the rate of two per second, again with immediate recall. In the third condition (delayed-recall) there is a delay before recall, in order to manipulate STM. Words are presented at the rate of one every two seconds, as in the control condition, but a 30-second delay is imposed before recall. In order to prevent rehearsal, the delay period is filled with a distractor task (speeded judgement of whether 3-digit numbers are greater or less than 500). Four lists of each type are presented, in random order.

Instructions for Running the Experiment

To run this experiment, insert Disk 1 into your computer and enter the MEL Lab as instructed in Section 0.2. Select **Cognition** from the topic menu and **Free Recall and the Serial Position Effect** from the specific experiment menu. Instructions on the computer screen will then explain the experiment and what keys to use for your responses. In this experiment, you will see a list of 20 words, and then be asked to recall as many as possible *in any order* shortly after seeing the list. There are twelve lists. *Materials needed*: Pencil and paper, if no printer is available, to copy down the results reported in the table at the end of the experiment. *Things to notice*: What effect does speed of presentation have on recall? What effect does a delay before recall have?

Expected Running Time = 35 minutes

Questions

1. What is the dependent variable for this experiment?

2. What is the independent variable?

3. What are some important control variables?

4. What are the results? Is primacy affected by rate of presentation? Is recency affected by delay?

5. Murdock (1962) compared different lengths of lists presented at either one word per second or one word every two seconds. Is there an effect of speed of presentation on the 20-word lists? What is that effect?

6. Postman and Phillips (1965) independently performed an experiment that manipulated the length of the delay before recall. Were their results congruent with those of Glanzer and Cunitz?

MEL Lab: Student Workbook v.1.6; © *PST - Do not reproduce*

Advanced Questions

1. The results of this experiment have been used to argue that STM and LTM are two independent memory systems. What other arguments have been advanced to support this position? Note that there are both behavioral and neurological findings that suggest such a distinction.

2. While results of this experiment have been taken as support for a dual-memory system, there are some contradictory findings. What are some of these? See Bjork and Whitten (1974).

3. What is the effect on serial positions curves of requiring ordered recall? That is, what is the result if subjects must recall the words in order? See Raffel (1936) or Deese (1957).

Extension Experiments

1. One explanation for the levels-of-processing effect (Craik & Lockhart, 1972) is that greater elaboration makes items in memory more distinct, and thus less likely to be confused with others (Eysenck, M. W. & Eysenck, M. C., 1980). What would be the effect on the serial position curve of making a single item in the middle of the list very distinct?

2. What is the effect of having subjects make a final recall of as many words as they can from *all* of the lists studied in a single session? Craik (1970) reported finding what has been called negative recency.

3. How does learning vary as a function of the presentation duration (e.g., present items for 1, 2, 4 or 8 seconds) or list length (e.g., 12, 24, or 48 word lists).

References

Bjork, R. A. & Whitten, W. B. (1974). Recency-sensitive retrieval processes in long-term free recall. *Cognitive Psychology, 6*, 173-189.

Brown J. (1958). Some tests of the decay theory of immediate memory. *Quarterly Journal of Experimental Psychology, 10*, 12-21.

Craik, F. I. M. (1970). The fate of primary memory items in free recall. *Journal of Verbal Learning and Verbal Behavior, 9*, 143-148.

Deese, J. (1957). Serial organization in the recall of disconnected items. *Psychological Reports, 3*, 577-582.

Eysenck, M. W. & Eysenck, M. C. (1980). Effects of processing depth, distinctiveness, and word frequency on retention. *British Journal of Psychology, 71*, 263-274.

Glanzer, M. & Cunitz, A. R. (1966). Two storage mechanisms in free recall. *Journal of Verbal Learning and Verbal Behavior, 5*, 351-360.

Murdock, B. B., Jr. (1962). The serial position effect of free recall. *Journal of Experimental Psychology, 64*, 482-488.

Peterson, L. R., & Peterson, M. J. (1959). Short-term retention of individual verbal items. *Journal of Experimental Psychology, 58*, 193-198.

Postman, L. & Phillips, L. W. (1965). Short-term temporal changes in free recall. *Quarterly Journal of Experimental Psychology, 17*, 132-138.

Raffel, G. (1936). Two determinants of the effects of primacy. *American Journal of Psychology, 48*, 654-657.

Thought Questions

1. Were the first few words on each list usually easy to remember or hard to remember?

2. Were the last few words on each list usually easy to remember or hard to remember?

3. Were the words in the middle of the lists usually easy to remember or hard to remember?

Free Recall and Serial Position Effect

Individual Data

Serial Position	Presentation Type		
	Control	Speeded	Delayed
1	____	____	____
2	____	____	____
3	____	____	____
4	____	____	____
5	____	____	____
6	____	____	____
7	____	____	____
8	____	____	____
9	____	____	____
10	____	____	____
11	____	____	____
12	____	____	____
13	____	____	____
14	____	____	____
15	____	____	____
16	____	____	____
17	____	____	____
18	____	____	____
19	____	____	____
20	____	____	____

Math Accuracy = ____

(Note: the SERIAL POSITION is the horizontal axis on the plot)
Cell entries are MEAN PERCENT CORRECT

Free Recall and Serial Position Effect

Individual Data

Control Speeded Delayed

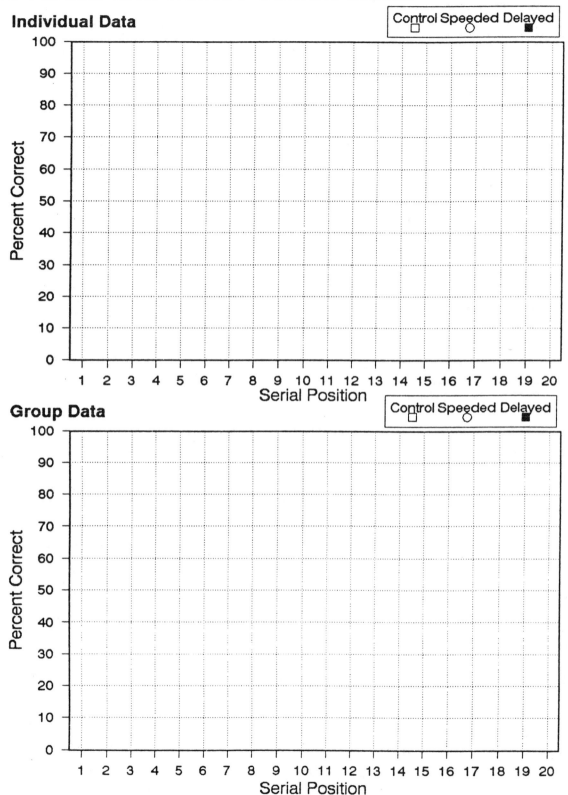

Group Data

Control Speeded Delayed

2.8 Organization in Memory as an Aid to Recall

Abstract

This exercise concerns the effects of organization on learning and recall, and replicates a study by Bower, Clark, Lesgold, and Winzenz (1969). Subjects study four lists of words for one minute each, then have five minutes for free recall. The study and recall are then repeated. The lists (totalling 104 words) are either hierarchically organized by categories or are randomly ordered. The typical result is a striking difference in recall between the organized and random conditions. Recall is better for the second presentation for both groups. This experiment is intended to provide a starting point for discussions of memory, to demonstrate the importance of organization, and to illustrate a simple **factorial** design.

The effect of organization on memory has long been studied. Materials that are arranged in a meaningful manner are thought by most of us to be easier to remember. However, Bower, Clark, Lesgold, and Winzenz (1969) noted that many previous experiments had shown only a fairly weak effect when comparing memory for organized and random word lists. They felt that a well-designed experiment should show organization to be a powerful variable for recall. In this exercise, you will replicate that experiment.

Why should organization matter? If you have completed the exercise on Recognition, Recall, and Encoding Specificity (Section 2.10), you will recall the importance given there to *retrieval cues*. One effect of organization on memory is that it provides better retrieval cues. Recalling one word can sometimes provide a retrieval cue for another, but only if they are related in memory. But there is more than just a *retrieval* effect involved. *Storage* or encoding is also affected by organization, because organized material suggests strongly how and where the material should be stored. One limitation to learning isolated facts is that we don't know "where" in memory to store them (and then, on retrieval, might have a hard time figuring out where to look for them). When materials are organized, on the other hand, we can more easily and quickly decide where it fits best in memory. Thus encoding is improved, as well as retrieval.

Method

This experiment replicates Bower et al.'s (1969) Experiment 1 with some modification. Subjects study four lists of 26 words each for one minute per list. At the end of the four minutes of study time, subjects are given five minutes for free recall (i.e., recall in any order) to write down as many of the words as they can remember. As soon as the recall period is completed, the whole procedure is repeated a second time: the same four lists to study for one minute each, with five minutes for free recall. After the second recall period, an alphabetized list of all 104 words is presented so that the subjects can verify which words were correct. They enter both the number recalled correctly and the number of intrusions, or false recalls, for each recall period.

Conditions are counterbalanced by subject number. Subjects in one condition (organized lists) see four lists of words arranged in a hierarchical fashion, with a heading at the top, subheadings below that, and three or four words in each subcategory below that. Subjects in the other condition (unorganized lists) see the same 104 words in the same physical arrangement, but with the words rearranged randomly. Subjects are instructed to recall all words, including the headings.

Instructions for Running the Experiment

To run this experiment, insert Disk 1 into your computer and enter the MEL Lab as instructed in Section 0.2. Select **Cognition** from the topic menu and **Organization in Memory as an Aid to Recall** from the specific experiment menu. Instructions on the computer screen will then explain the experiment and what keys to use for your responses. This experiment involves studying lists of words and then trying to recall them in any order you can. This experiment is concerned with the accuracy of memory, so please stress accuracy and *not* speed of responding. *Materials needed:* You will need two sheets of paper and a pen or pencil to record your responses in the recall part of the experiment. Your instructor may ask you to turn in the recall sheets. You will compare your recall sheets to the list of words presented on the computer screen, and enter both the number of words you recalled and the number of intrusions (false recalls). *Things to notice*: Are you able to use the hierarchical organization to aid you in encoding and retrieval?

Expected Running Time = 25 minutes

Questions

1. What is the dependent variable for this experiment?

2. What are the independent variables? Are these between- or within-subjects variables?

3. What are some important control variables?

4. What are the results of the experiment? If there was an interaction, describe why it occurred.

5. Examine the recall sheets for the disorganized group. Did subjects sometimes recall a word and then recall other, related words? If this happened, how does this fit with the notion of spreading activation in memory? (See the exercise on Lexical Decision (Section 2.1)).

6. One of the organized lists was taken from Bower, et al's (1969) article. Which one was it?

7. Bower et al. (1969) also report a similar experiment that employed a recognition test instead of a recall test. What was the result?

Extension Experiments

1. The experiment you performed used conceptual (categorical) hierarchies. Would organization affect the learning of associative hierarchies in the same way? See Bower et al. (1969).

2. Would the same effect be seen if a recognition test were employed? See Bower et al. (1969).

References

Bower, G. H., Clark, M., Lesgold, A., & Winzenz, D. (1969). Hierarchical retrieval schemes in recall of categorized word lists. *Journal of Verbal Learning and Verbal Behavior, 8,* 323-343.
Tulving, E. & Pearlstone, Z. (1966). Availability versus accessibility of information in memory for words. *Journal of Verbal Learning and Verbal Behavior, 5,* 381-391.

Thought Questions

1. Did the way the words were organized seem to matter?

2. Did recall improve the second time through the lists?

Organization in Memory as an Aid to Recall

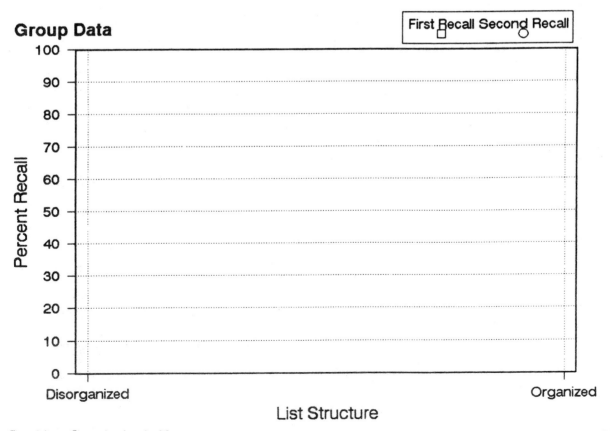

Group Data

First Recall □ Second Recall ○

Percent Recall

100
90
80
70
60
50
40
30
20
10
0

Disorganized   Organized

List Structure

2.9 Mnemonics: Aids to Memory

Abstract

Mnemonic techniques have been known for centuries, and psychologists have added to our knowledge of their use by careful experiments, verifying that they do aid memory. In this exercise, three methods of memorizing are compared--rote learning, the method of loci, and the pegword method. The role of mental imagery in memorization is also stressed.

Mnemonics are memory devices--tricks, if you will. There are a number of different mnemonics that can aid memory for lists of words. In the experiment detailed below, you will be taught to use two of them, called the pegword method and the method of loci (pronounced LOW-sigh, plural of locus, which means location). Both methods make use of imagery. In the method of loci, you memorize a list of words by imagining yourself placing the objects named in various locations. To recall the words, you imagine yourself walking around to the locations and retrieving the objects. The pegword method makes use of a little rhyme that you must first learn. To memorize a list of words, you form an image of the object named interacting with the word in the rhyme.

The method of loci has an ancient tradition. In his treatise on rhetoric, *De Oratore* (trans. 1959, cited in Adams, 1980), the Roman Cicero, who lived in the first century B.C., wrote an account of the discovery of the method of loci. The poet Simonides attended a banquet where he read a lyric poem in honor of the host. Later, he was called out of the hall for a brief time.

But in the interval of his absence the roof of the hall where Scopas was giving the banquet fell in, crushing Scopas himself and his relations underneath the ruins and killing them; and when their friends wanted to bury them but were altogether unable to know them apart as they had been completely crushed, the story goes that Simonides was enabled by his recollection of the place in which each of them had been reclining at table to identify them for separate internment; and that this circumstance suggested to him the discovery of the truth that the best aid to clearness of memory consists in orderly arrangement. He inferred that persons desiring to train this faculty must select localities and form mental images of the facts they wish to remember and store those images in the localities (Cicero, trans. 1959, cited in Adams, 1980).

The pegword method is a variant of the method of loci, in which an image of each word to be remembered is "stored" with an image of another word used in a rhyme: e.g., "One is a gun, Two is a shoe," etc. (Bower & Reitman, 1972).

Method

In this experiment, you will learn nine lists of ten words each. Three lists each will be learned using the method of loci, the pegword method, and rote learning. The latter is a control condition for comparison to the other methods. All three methods are described in detail below. When you call up this experiment on the computer, you will be shown a list of words, all displayed at once, and told which method to use. You will have one minute to study the list. At the end of that time, the computer will prompt you to begin another task (indicating whether numbers displayed on the screen are greater than or less than 500), which will continue for 30 seconds. You will have two minutes (timed by the computer) to recall as many words as you can (in any order). All three lists for a given mnemonic will occur together, with the order of the three mnemonics counterbalanced.

In order to prepare for this experiment, you must first learn the mnemonics to be used.

Rote learning. In rote learning, you simply try to memorize the list of words by saying them over and over to yourself. You may already know better ways to memorize than this, but please *do not* use them. Just try to learn by repetition.

The method of loci. Before trying to use this method, you should prepare a list of 10 locations you are familiar with. Ten locations in your family home would work, or you can choose some other area you know well. The locations should be in the order you would encounter them when taking a walk through the area you have chosen. Write down the locations you choose: the couch in the living room; the oven and refrigerator, the bathtub, etc. Spend a few minutes practicing a mental walk through the house (or wherever), visiting each location in turn, until you can do this correctly without looking at your list. When you are instructed to learn a list of words by the method of loci, you should imagine that you are walking through the area, placing the objects on or in the locations you've memorized. For the example just given, if the first word was horse, your might imagine a horse climbing up on the couch in the living room, if the next word is bicycle, you might imagine taking your bicycle apart and putting it in the oven, and so on. At the time of recall, you should imagine yourself visiting each location in turn, and write down the item found there. (Since you will be learning three lists by this method, it is possible that you will get confused. Some people report that they can avoid this confusion by "removing" the objects at the time of recall. Take the horse off the couch, the bicycle out of the oven, etc.)

The pegword method. Before using this method, you must first memorize a little rhyme, which follows. This set of pegwords is taken from Bower and Reitmen (1972). You can substitute other rhyming words, if you prefer, such as "Seven is heaven."

> One is a gun.
> Two is a shoe.
> Three is a tree.
> Four is a door.
> Five is knives.
> Six is sticks.
> Seven is oven.
> Eight is plate.
> Nine is wine.
> Ten is hen.

When you are given a list of words to learn by this method, you should form an image of each word in turn interacting with the pegword from the rhyme. If the first word is horse, you might imagine someone shooting a horse with a gun. If the next word is bicycle, you might imagine a bicycle with shoes instead of tires, or imagine yourself riding a bicycle with your shoes in the basket, instead of on your feet. Any image will do, so long as there is some sort of interaction between the pegword and the word to be remembered. At the time of recall, recall the rhyme first. That way you will easily recall the pegword, and that should serve as a cue to recalling the word from the list.

Instructions for Running the Experiment

To run this experiment, insert Disk 1 into your computer and enter the MEL Lab as instructed in Section 0.2. Select **Cognition** from the topic menu and **Mnemonics: Aids to Memory** from the specific experiment menu. Instructions on the computer screen will then explain the experiment and what keys to use for your responses. *Before beginning*: be sure that you have read the descriptions of the mnemonic techniques, and have spent some time practicing the rhyme for the peg-word method and the locations you will use for the method of loci. *Materials needed*: Pencil and paper, if no printer is available, to copy down the results reported in the table at the end of the experiment. *Things to notice*: Does one method seem to work better than the others?

Expected Running Time = 45 minutes

Questions

1. What is the dependent variable in this experiment?

2. What is the independent variable?

3. What are some important control variables? Why were you required to judge numbers as greater than or less than 500 for 30 seconds after each list was studied?

4. Which method(s) lead to the best recall? The worst?

5. What is it about an image that makes it effective as a cue for recall? It has been suggested that bizarre images are easier to recall. Would you regard the images you formed as bizarre? You were instructed to form *interacting* images. Would non-interacting images work as well? For a test of the roles of interaction and bizarreness, see Wollen, Weber, and Lowry (1972).

Advanced Questions

1. Why do these methods work? Bower (1970) presents a detailed analysis of these mnemonics. You might want to consider how you could test some of his claims.

2. What problems would you encounter with longer lists? Try to extend the pegword rhyme to more than 10 items. Bower and Reitmen (1972) present one possible extension. You might want to compare your extended rhyme to theirs for effectiveness.

3. What happens if you forget the location where you placed an object, or make a mistake on the pegword rhyme?

4. Are there limitations to these methods? That is, would they work as well for all types of materials?

5. You might want to consider the use of these methods for the learning of multiple lists. Bower and Reitman provide some experimental evidence concerning this issue.

6. What other mnemonic techniques can you think of? One that works rather well is external storage--write it down so you can look it up later. (Note that this is a dangerous strategy for taking most exams!) A method that seems to work well for learning words in a foreign language is the keyword method (Atkinson & Raugh, 1975).

7. You were instructed to use visual imagery in these experiments. Are other modalities possible? For a fascinating account of imagery in many modalities, you should read A. R. Luria's (1976) "little book about a vast memory", which describes the mnemonics used by S., a professional mnemonist who seemed unable to forget.

Extension Experiments

1. One way to extend this study is by including other methods, such as the keyword method (Atkinson & Raugh, 1975). Can you show that certain methods are best for certain types of materials?

2. What happens when a location or pegword must be re-used? Bower and Reitman (1972) report studies where the same set of locations or pegwords were used in the learning of multiple lists. They called their technique "progressive elaboration."

3. How might the serial position curve differ if the subject uses mnemonics to remember the word?

References

Adams, J. A. (1980). *Learning and memory.* Homewood (IL): Dorsey Press.

Atkinson, R. C. & Raugh, M. R. (1975). An application of the mnemonic keyword method to the acquisition of Russian vocabulary. *Journal of Experimental Psychology: Human Learning and Memory, 104,* 126-133.

Baddeley, A. (1982). *Your memory: A user's guide.* New York: Macmillan Publishing Co.

Bellezza, F. S. (1982). *Improve your memory skills.* Englewood Cliffs, NJ: Prentice-Hall.

Bower, G. H. (1970). Analysis of a mnemonic device. *American Scientist, 58,* 496-510.

Bower, G. H. & Reitman, J. S. (1972). Mnemonic elaboration in multilist learning. *Journal of Verbal Learning and Verbal Behavior, 11,* 478-485.

Cicero (1959). *De Oratore* (Books I and II). (Rev. ed.) (E. W. Sutton & H. Rackman, trans.). Cambridge: Harvard University Press.

Glanzer, M. & Cunitz, A. R. (1966). Two storage mechanisms in free recall. *Journal of Verbal Learning and Verbal Behavior, 5,* 351-360.

Luria, A. R. (1976). *The mind of a mnemonist.* (L. Solotaroff, trans.). Chicago: Henry Regnery.

Wollen, K. A., Weber, A., & Lowry, D. H. (1972). Bizarreness versus interaction of mental images as determinants of learning. *Cognitive Psychology, 3,* 518-523.

Yates, F. A. (1966). *The art of memory.* Chicago: The University of Chicago Press.

1. Which mnemonic technique seemed to lead to the best memory?

2. Which seemed to lead to the worst memory?

Mnemonics: Aids to Memory

Individual Data

Please note: the order in which the three mnemonic techniques are presented is varied between subjects. Therefore, the order in which the techniques are listed in the table and plot may not match the order in which you used the techinques.

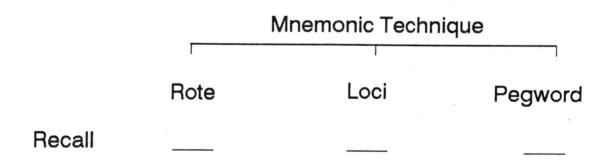

	Mnemonic Technique		
	Rote	Loci	Pegword
Recall	____	____	____

Cell entries are MEAN PERCENTAGE RECALLED

Student Name:______________
Section/Lab:______________

Mnemonics

Individual Data

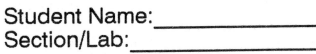

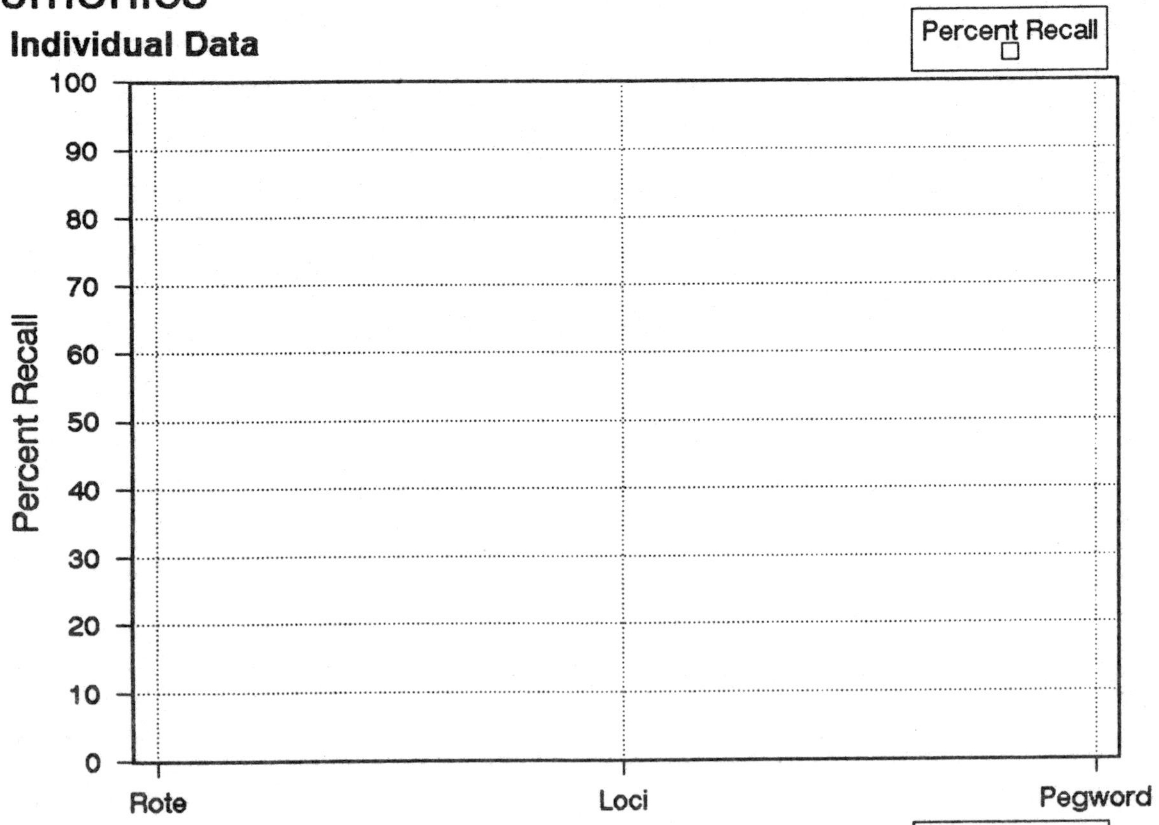
Percent Recall
Percent Recall
100
90
80
70
60
50
40
30
20
10
0
Rote
Loci
Pegword

Group Data

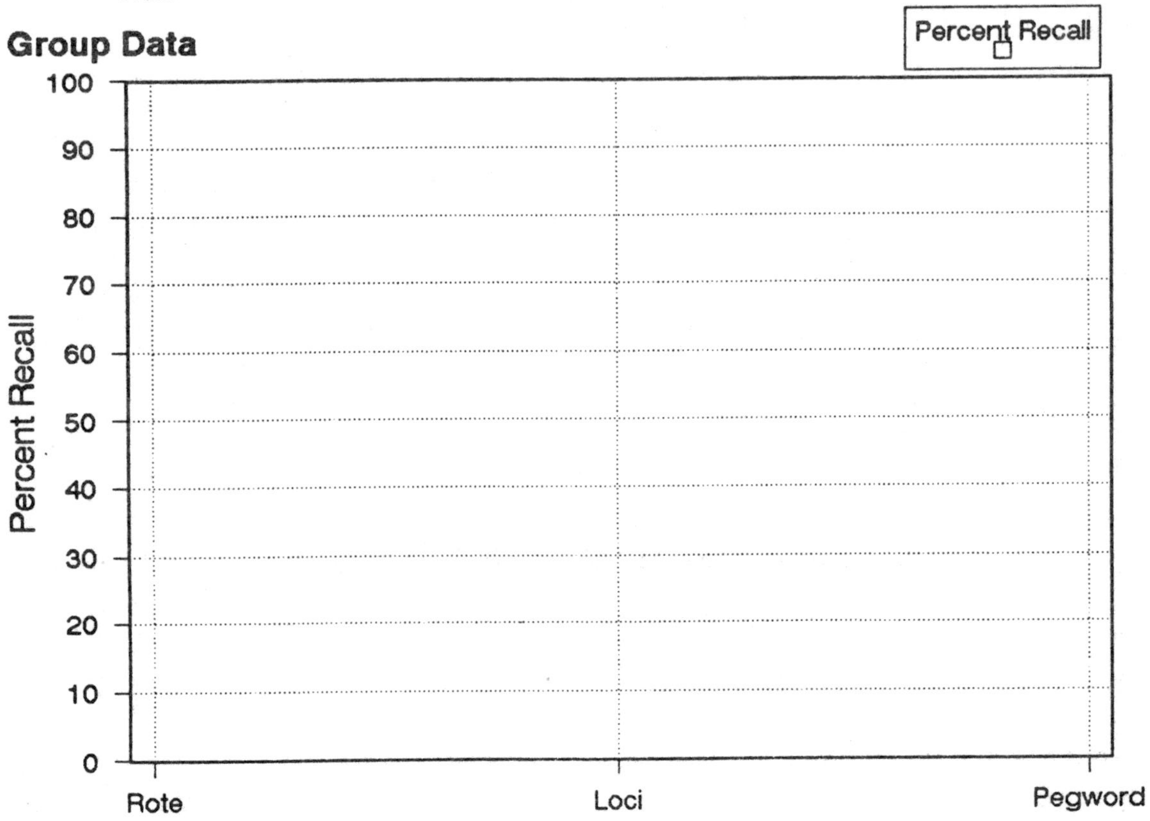
Percent Recall
Percent Recall
100
90
80
70
60
50
40
30
20
10
0
Rote
Loci
Pegword

2.10 Recall, Recognition, and Encoding Specificity

Abstract

Recall and recognition tests of memory for learned word lists are demonstrated. While recognition is better than recall in most situations, the experiment in this exercise demonstrates that under certain circumstances we can recall words that we cannot recognize. This replicates the Tulving and Thomson's (1972) experiment designed to test "episodic" and "tagging" theories of memory for word lists. The roles of context and retrieval cues in memory are illustrated.

Which is easier, recall or recognition? Most people's intuitive belief is that recognition is easier, and psychologists long ago confirmed that belief with laboratory studies of recall and recognition. Anyone who has studied a foreign language knows that you can learn to understand the language much earlier than you can speak it. Most of us have had the experience of not being able to recall someone's name, but recognizing it instantly when we see or hear it. And most students prefer multiple choice exams to essay exams because they feel more confident that they will recognize the right answer among several choices than they will recall the information. All three of these examples illustrate that recognition is usually easier than recall. But why is recognition easier? One theory is that recall requires that you *generate* a possible item, then recognize it as correct or not. Thus recall adds a step to the process, and if you fail to generate the right answer, you cannot recognize it (Kintsch, 1971).

That theory is an appealing one, but there are some experimental results that question it. This experiment is a replication of Tulving and Thompson's (1973) demonstration that there are circumstances under which you can recall items from memory that you cannot recognize. (For the sake of time, this version uses some of the simplifications suggested by Watkins and Tulving, 1975). The rather unexpected result suggests that the generate/recognize theory of recall is wrong, because that theory seems to always imply that recognition performance will be superior to recall. Tulving has proposed a different theory of why recognition is usually easier than recall that can account for recognition failure as well. His theory is based on the principle of *encoding specificity*. This principle states that memory works best when the context of remembering is the same as the context of encoding. The context of encoding is everything you are experiencing at the time you encode something into memory. If the context at the time of remembering is the same, that provides retrieval cues that help you remember. The reason recognition is usually easier than recall is because having the to-be-remembered item present provides a retrieval cue. Recognition is thus cued recall. This theory suggests that you might recall an item you cannot recognize if there are more retrieval cues present in the recall task than in the recognition task.

Method

Subjects will be given a list of 24 pairs of words. The left-hand member of each pair will be called a cue, and will be displayed in upper-case letters. The right-hand member will be called the target, and will be displayed in lower-case letters. Subjects will be given one minute to study the word lists, and will be instructed that when they are tested for recall the cue words will be present, though it is not required that the target words be matched to the cues. After the study time, subjects will actually be tested first for recognition. The recognition test will consist of the target words and three words strongly associated with each. Subjects are to indicate any words that they recognize from the previously studied list. Subjects will then be given the recall test they were previously told about.

The word lists used for this experiment employ the target words and weak cues from Tulving and Thompson's (1973, p. 361) List A. The recognition test distractors were generated by having students in Introductory Psychology classes write down three associates for each target word. The three most frequently occurring associates, along with the target words, make up the recognition test.

Discussion

The main point of interest is whether recognition or recall was best. Tulving and Thompson, as well as later investigators, found that recall was best for this task. Their interpretation was that seeing the word in a different context in the recognition task provided few retrieval cues, whereas the cue words that were paired with the target words on original learning act as retrieval cues (albeit fairly weak ones) for the recall task.

Instructions for Running the Experiment

To run this experiment, insert Disk 1 into your computer and enter the MEL Lab as instructed in Section 0.2. Select **Cognition** from the topic menu and **Recall, Recognition, and Encoding Specificity** from the specific experiment menu. Instructions on the computer screen will then explain the experiment and what keys to use for your responses. This experiment involves reviewing a list of words and then trying to recall them in any order you can. Speed of responses does not matter, only accuracy. *Materials needed*: Pencil and paper, if no printer is available, to copy down the results reported in the table at the end of the experiment. *Things to notice*: Which seems easier in this task, recall or recognition of the list of words?

Expected Running Time = 15 minutes

Questions

1. What is the dependent variable?

2. What is the independent variable?

3. What are the control variables?

4. What are the results? Is recall consistently better than recognition under these conditions?

5. Watkins and Tulving (1975) reported that, in experiments like this one, subjects often fail to recognize words that they can remember. They claimed that this evidence rules out a "tagging theory" of recognition and recall, and is in favor of an "episodic theory." What are those theories, and why do their data support episodic over tagging theory? (Note: see the first two paragraphs of Watkins and Tulving's Summary on page 5 of Watkins and Tulving, 1975.)

Advanced Questions

1. Watkins and Tulving make the strong claim that tagging theory always predicts better recognition than recall. Is that claim justifiable?

2. Would this experiment work the same way with memory for non-verbal items? Or does it rely on some peculiarity of the verbal materials used? (See Winograd & Rivers-Bulkeley, 1977.)

3. What aspects of context act as retrieval cues? In this experiment, the cue words were part of the context of encoding, and were useful as retrieval cues because they helped reinstate the same context during retrieval. A number of studies suggest that many aspects of the context, including physiological states and the physical surroundings, can be useful in aiding recall if they are the same at the time of recall as at the time of encoding. You might want to examine studies of *state-dependent learning* by Bower, Eich, and others to help answer this question.

4. Watkins and Tulving (1975, Experiment 5) used the sign test to analyze their data in terms of whether recall or recognition was best. Another approach is to compare the mean scores for recall and recognition using the dependent-samples *t*-test (or repeated-measures ANOVA). Is there any advantage to one over the other?

Extension Experiments

1. The distractor words used in the recognition test of this experiment were all semantically related to the test items. Would you obtain different results if you used distractors that were not related in meaning to the test items? See Watkins and Tulving (1975, Experiment 5).

2. Does the order of the tests (recognition and then recall) matter for the outcome of this experiment?

3. Can subjects sometimes recognize words that they previously could not? Wallace (1978) argued that failure to recognize words you can recall is actually a special case of a more general class of context effects, which includes recognition failure of words that can later be recognized.

References

Kintsch, W. (1971). Models for free recall and recognition. In D. A. Norman (Ed.), *Models of human memory*. New York: Academic Press.

Tulving, E. & Thompson, D. M. (1973). Encoding specificity and retrieval processes in episodic memory. *Psychological Review, 80*, 352-373.

Wallace, W. P. (1978). Recognition failure of recallable words and recognizable words. *Journal of Experimental Psychology: Human Learning and Memory, 4*, 441-452.

Watkins, M. J. & Tulving, E. (1975). Episodic memory: When recognition fails. *Journal of Experimental Psychology: General, 104*, 5-29.

Winograd, E. & Rivers-Bulkely, N. T. (1977). Effects of changing context on remembering faces. *Journal of Experimental Psychology: Human Learning and Memory, 3*, 397-405.

1.   Which seemed easier, recall or recognition?

2.   Did you remember some words on the recall test that you did not remember during the recognition test?

Recall, Recognition, and Encoding Specificity

Individual Data

Test Type

	Recognition	Recall
Correct	____	____
Intrusions	____	____

Cell entries are MEAN PERCENTAGE RECALLED

Recall, Recognition, and Encoding Specificity

Individual Data

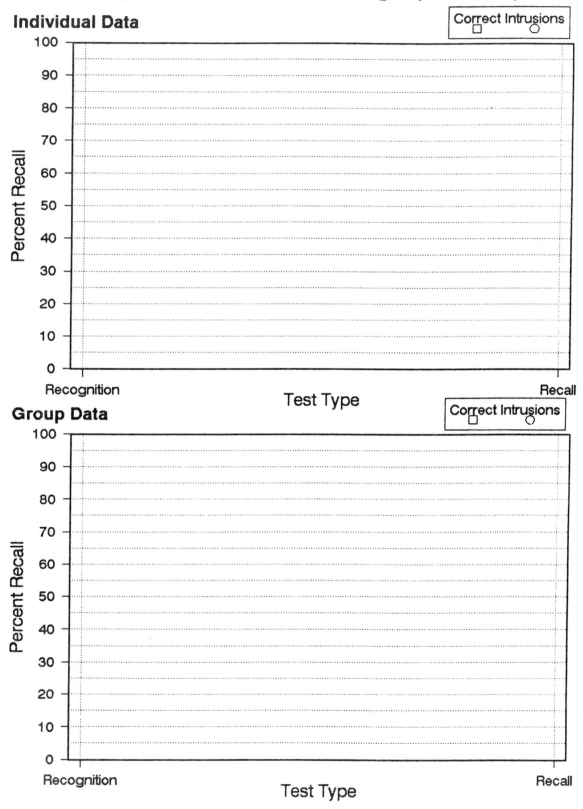

Correct Intrusions
□ ○

Percent Recall

100
90
80
70
60
50
40
30
20
10
0

Recognition   Test Type   Recall

Group Data

Correct Intrusions
□ ○

Percent Recall

100
90
80
70
60
50
40
30
20
10
0

Recognition   Test Type   Recall

2.11 Spacing and Rehearsal Patterns in Learning

Abstract

A simple sort of learning that we all engage in is the paired-associates learning of a person's name and face. But what is the best pattern of rehearsing, so that we can recall the person's name some time later? Landauer and Bjork (1978) performed an experiment to test their suggestion that the best rehearsal strategy for this task is to rehearse (think of the person's face and name) very quickly after first meeting them, and then wait progressively longer and longer before subsequent rehearsals. Their argument is that each recall thus strengthens the memory trace so that it will still be intact after a longer and longer period of time. In this exercise, Landauer and Bjork's experiment is replicated.

A social situation we all encounter is that of meeting new people whose names we want or need to remember later. How can you effectively learn the person's name? You could rely on external memory aids, such as writing down the name and a description of the face for later study. Or you might follow the learning theorist Edwin Guthrie's advice and shout the name loudly while looking right in the person's face. (While this might or might not help you learn the person's name, it would absolutely guarantee that person would never forget you!) One thing you probably try to do in this situation is to say the person's name over to yourself, mentally associating it with the person's appearance, repeating this process several times. As Landauer and Bjork (1978) note, this sort of rehearsal amounts to a series of self-administered tests. When you rehearse the name a few seconds after hearing it, you are elaborating it in an effort to be able to recall it later. When you repeat this process a few minutes later you are testing yourself on your ability to recall the name. The longer you wait before this first self-test, the less likely you are to be able to recall the name. But if you do recall the name, this test-trial will itself strengthen your memory, making later recall more likely. The issue for this experiment is to determine the best spacing of these self-tests. Should you test your memory several times very quickly after meeting someone? Should you space the tests over time? If so, what would be the best pattern of tests? The same issues are relevant to memorizing material for an exam. How should you space looking at the facts while cramming?

An experiment by Landauer and Bjork addressed these questions in an effort to find the optimal rehearsal strategy. They suggested that the optimal strategy would be to test at expanding intervals. They reasoned that an early first test would be more likely to succeed than a later one. This act of recall would provide a repetition of the information, thus strengthening the memory for the next recall test. The next test would be successful after a longer interval, leading to still stronger memory, and so on. Their Experiment I was concerned with recall of last names, when first names were given as cues. This is very similar to the real-world situation of being given a person's first and last names when you are introduced, but then hearing only their first name in later conversation. Their Experiment II studied pairing of names and faces, which is like the real-world situation of meeting a number of people at once--a situation where most of us perform rather badly. The present experiment replicates Landauer and Bjork's Experiment I, but suggestions are made in the Extension Experiments section for how you might do the other experiment.

Method

In this experiment, you will be shown a series of names. The first time each name appears, it will include both the first and last name. The other times it appears, you will only be shown the first name, and you are to fill in the last name. Each name will be shown for 9 seconds, which is the time you have for studying that name or for recalling it. There will be a series of 50 such trials (study and recall combined). In all, you will "meet" 16 people. There will then be a 30 minute wait, followed by a final test of each of the names.

During the acquisition phase two names will be presented in each condition. Three of these conditions are Uniform, with approximately equal spacing between the recall trials. Uniform Short has spacings of 1,2,3 and 2,4,6 (where the numbers represent the number of trials after the initial presentation: 2,4,6 thus indicates that the tests occurred on the second, fourth, and sixth trials following first presentation). Uniform Medium has spacings of 5,10,15 and 6,12,18, while Uniform Long has spacings of 10,20,30 and 12,22,36. Another condition is Expanding, in which the spacing between recall attempts is longer each time (1,5,15 and 2,7,17). Another is Contracting, where the spacing between recall attempts shortens each time (11,16,18 and 11,15,16). As Landauer and Bjork note, Uniform Short is what people most often do: simply repeating the name several times to themselves in short succession. A control condition presents two names once only, testing for recall either 1 or 2 trials later. Two other conditions serve mainly as fillers, to permit accurate spacing of the other recall attempts. Two names are presented once each but never tested, while two other names are presented twice each but never tested.

The final phase of the experiment follows a thirty-minute break and consists of a single presentation of each first name and tests for recall of the corresponding last name.

(The list of names in this experiment is one of those used in the original experiment by Landauer and Bjork, and we thank Prof. Thomas Landauer for supplying it.)

Figure 2.11.1 Proportion of names recalled for various types of spacing. Data are from Landauer & Bjork, 1978.

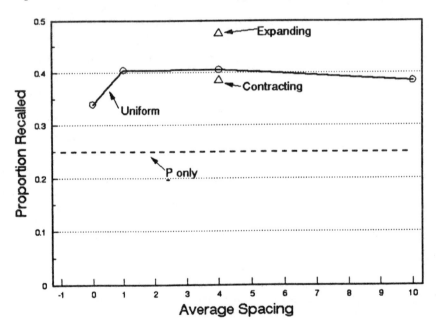

Instructions for Running the Experiment

To run this experiment, insert Disk 1 into your computer and enter the MEL Lab as instructed in Section 0.2. Select **Cognition** from the topic menu and **Spacing and Rehearsal Patterns in Learning** from the specific experiment menu. Instructions on the computer screen will then explain the experiment and what keys to use for your responses. This experiment has 10 practice trials and 50 test trials. Each "trial" involves presenting a name. On some trials there will be a first and last name, and you should use the few seconds they are on the screen to try to remember the last name. On most trials you will see only a first name, and must type in the last name that you previously saw with it. After you finish that part of the experiment, there will be a 30-minute break (timed by the computer), after which you will be shown each first name and asked to enter the corresponding last name. Accuracy

MEL Lab: Student Workbook v.1.6; © *PST - Do not reproduce*

of recall should be stressed, and speed of responding does *not* matter. *Materials needed*: Pencil and paper, if no printer is available, to copy down the results reported in the table at the end of the experiment. *Things to notice*: Does the spacing of the recall trials for each name matter? *Please note*: The computer will tell you when you have come to the 30-minute break before the final recall. Feel free to get up and move around during that time, but be careful of two things: (1) Make sure no one else uses the computer during that time. If you are leaving the room, it would be wise to put a sign on the computer telling others that it is in use. (2) Make sure you are back in 30 minutes to begin the final recall portion of the experiment.

Expected Running Time = 20 minutes (plus 30 minute break)

Questions

1. What is the dependent variable for this experiment?

2. What is the independent variable?

3. What are some important control variables?

4. What is the pattern of results? Are the expanding series learned better than the others? How does each group do relative to the presentation-only control?

5. Refer to Landauer and Bjork's article. Did they get the same result when subjects learned names to go along with faces? See their Experiment 2.

Advanced Questions

1. Landauer and Bjork also compared repeated testing (recall) with repeated presentation of the whole name (repetition). For Expanding rehearsal, testing was better than repetition. Why might this be so? What does this suggest about study methods for classes you are taking? Note that repeated testing requires you to practice *retrieval*, while repetition may involve only the practice of *encoding*.

2. Would these results on spacing effects generalize to situations other than paired-associate learning? Can you devise a test of spacing effects for learning materials from a lecture course? Since the time between a lecture and the test over the material presented may be several weeks, rather than the 30 minute delay in this experiment, would expanding patterns of studying over days or weeks be as effective as they are over the few minutes tested in this experiment?

Extension Experiments

1. This experiment uses paired-associate learning, where the first name is the stimulus term, and the last name is the response term on test trials. Would this same method work with stimuli other than names? You might want to try doing the same experiment, but using other stimuli. One type of paired-associate learning that you probably do (or will do) is learning the foreign equivalent of an English word, in a foreign language class. Such stimulus pairs could be used for this experiment--just substitute an English word for the first name and a word in a foreign language you are learning for the last name. If you get the same results, can you devise a good timing method to use in studying vocabulary items?

2. Does this method (spaced practice) work with materials such as phone numbers? What effect does rehearsal strategy have on people's *confidence* about their recall? See Landauer and Ross (1977).

3. How might spacing procedures work to learn technical terms such as the names of chemical compounds?

4. How would you compare the benefits of spacing to recall an item versus repeatedly reading it from your notes or being given the correct answer?

References

Dempster, F. N. (1988). The spacing effect: A case study in the failure to apply the results of psychological research. *American Psychologist, 43,* 627-634.

Greene, R. L. (1989). Spacing effects in memory: Evidence for a two-process account. *Journal of Experimental Psychology: Learning, Memory, and Cognition, 15,* 371-377.

Landauer, T. K. (1967). Interval between item repetitions and free recall memory. *Psychon. Sci. 8,* 439-440.

Landauer, T. K., & Ainslie, K. I. (1975). Exams and use as preservatives of course-acquired knowledge. *Journal of Educational Research, 69,* 99-104.

Landauer, T. K. & Bjork, R. A. (1978). Optimum rehearsal patterns and name learning. In M. M. Gruneberg, P. E. Morris & R. N. Sykes (Eds.), *Practical aspects of memory* (pp. 625-632).

Landauer, T. K., & Eldridge, L. (1967). Effect of tests without feedback and presentation-test interval in paired-associate learning. *Journal of Experimental Psychology, 75,* 290-298.

Landauer, T. K. & Ross, B. H. (1977). Can simple instructions to use spaced practice improve ability to remember a fact?: An experimental test using telephone numbers. *Bulletin of the Psychonomic Society, 10,* 215-218.

Landauer, T. K., & Rubin, N. (1966). Spacing of item repetitions in paired-associated learning. *Proceedings of the American Psychological Association,* pp. 91-92.

1. Did the spacing between presentations of a name seem to make any difference in ease of recall?

Spacing and Rehearsal Patterns in Learning

Individual Data

	Condition					
	Short	Medium	Long	Expanding	Contracting	Control
Acquisition	___	___	___	___	___	___
Final	___	___	___	___	___	___

Cell entries are MEAN PERCENT CORRECT

Spacing and Rehearsal Patterns in Learning

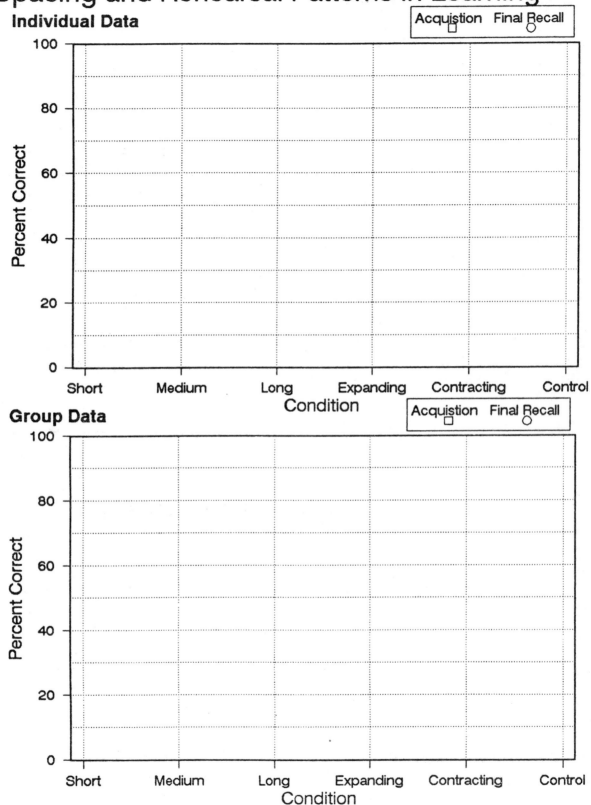

Individual Data

Acquistion ☐   Final Recall ○

Percent Correct

100 — 80 — 60 — 40 — 20 — 0

Condition: Short   Medium   Long   Expanding   Contracting   Control

Group Data

Acquistion ☐   Final Recall ○

Percent Correct

100 — 80 — 60 — 40 — 20 — 0

Condition: Short   Medium   Long   Expanding   Contracting   Control

2.12 The Generation Effect

Abstract

The "generation effect" refers to a common finding that words generated by a subject's own efforts are remembered better than those that are presented by the experimenter. Slamecka and Graf (1978) described the general phenomenon, and the experiment in this exercise replicates one of theirs. Some subjects see pairs of words related by some rule (e.g., rhymes or words in the same category). Other subjects see one word and a letter, and must generate the second word according to the rule. Both groups are then tested for recognition.

When cramming for an exam, what is the effectiveness of generating your own study notes versus using someone else's? When generating your own notes you have to think more carefully about the material. You must organize what you say and then write down the answer. In contrast, when reading someone else's notes, you may try just to memorize the answers to be able to repeat them in an exam.

The "generation effect" is a term given to a very robust finding in memory research: subjects remember words that they have generated themselves far better than words that were merely presented for study. Slamecka and Graf (1978) provided some basic tests of the phenomenon. Here is their basic experiment: Subjects were given lists of pairs of related words (e.g., long-short) and required to read each pair out loud. They were then tested for how well they remembered the right-hand member of each pair. That procedure is called the "read" condition. But some pairs of words had only the left-hand word and the first letter of the right-hand word (e.g., long-s). The subject had to think of a word that would fit and say that out loud. This is the "generate" condition. Again, there was a memory test. In many experiments under variations of this procedure, subjects' memory for words they have generated is better than for the same words when supplied by the experimenter in the read condition.

Other experimenters have extended the range of materials for which a generation effect is found. Jacoby (1978) found the effect with a problem-solving task like a crossword puzzle. Subjects were given a crossword-puzzle clue and a partial word. Again, subjects who had to solve the puzzle themselves performed better on a subsequent memory task than subjects who were given the solutions. The effect is not limited to memory for words, however, as shown by Gardiner and Rowley (1984). Their subjects were given multiplication problems that either required that they work out the solution themselves (generate) or had the correct solutions supplied (read). Again, the generation effect was clear: memory was better for problems the subjects solved themselves than for problems where the answer was supplied. However, the generation effect does not always occur. Interestingly, the effect does not seem to occur when the response terms (right-hand terms) are nonwords. McElroy and Slamecka (1982) had subjects read or generate pronounceable non-words by either a rhyming rule (*prab-f* is a cue to generate "frab") or a letter-transposition rule (take the first three letters of the stimulus term and add them to the first letter in backward order: *preet-t* is a cue to generate "terp"). In neither case did they find any advantage of generate over read conditions.

This sort of regularity in data compels attention. What is the basis for the effect? If you are already familiar with the "levels-of-processing" approach in memory, that might occur to you as a candidate. This approach says that how long you remember something is a function of how you processed it, with materials receiving deeper processing for meaning being remembered better. The generation effect could thus be interpreted as due to the deeper processing required of words that are generated as opposed to words that are merely read. This approach, and several variants of it (see McElroy & Slamecka, 1982), assume that semantic memory is the locus of the effect. (Semantic memory refers to memory for word meanings, as well as knowledge of the world.) Another class of explanations assumes that the difference is due to inherent differences in the two tasks--generating and reading. For example, Jacoby (1978) suggested that arousal might be heightened during generation as compared to during reading.

The generation effect remains a topic of considerable research, largely because it is clear that we do not yet have an accepted explanation. When one is found it is likely to considerably advance our understanding of the nature of memory.

Method

In this experiment, subjects either read or generate word pairs, and then are later asked to recognize those words. Word pairs are made up of common words, with the response term being related to the left-hand ("stimulus") word by one of five rules: rhyme, opposite, synonym, related, or in the same category. For the *read* conditions, both words of a pair are shown at once. For the *generate* condition, the left-hand word is presented along with the first letter of the response word. The subject must then type in the appropriate word. For the generate conditions, the rule to be applied in generating the response word is stated before that block of trials. After subjects read or generate words, a recognition test is presented for the right-hand words in each pair (the "response word"). Each subject receives 5 lists of 20 items each. Subjects in the generate condition may sometimes generate some word other than the one used for the read condition. When that occurs, they are tested using the word they generated. Subjects are assigned to either the read or generate condition by counterbalancing.

Instructions for Running the Experiment

To run this experiment, insert Disk 1 into your computer and enter the MEL Lab as instructed in Section 0.2. Select **Cognition** from the topic menu and **The Generation Effect** from the specific experiment menu. Instructions on the computer screen will then explain the experiment and what keys to use for your responses. This experiment involves either reading a list of words or generating a word-list, and then performing a recognition test. Speed of responses does not matter, only accuracy. *Materials needed*: Pencil and paper, if no printer is available, to copy down the results reported in the table at the end of the experiment.

Expected Running Time = 20 minutes

Questions

1. What is the dependent variable in this experiment?

2. What are the independent variables? Specify whether these are within- or between-subjects variables.

3. What are some important control variables?

4. Does a generation effect occur? If so, does it occur in all conditions? Specifically, are there any differences depending on the rule used?

5. Compare your results to those of Slamecka and Graf's (1978) Experiment 1. Is the mean percent recall about the same?

Advanced Questions

1. Slamecka and Katsaiti (1987) noted that there had not yet been a successful theoretical account of the phenomenon. While each suggested explanation can account for some of the facts, each has "fallen short of success in compelling a clearcut consensus about the matter" (p. 589). That is, of course, just the situation with any developing area of any science. But with time, some explanation should emerge that can encompass the results of many studies. Slamecka and Katsaiti offer such an explanation, though it is not exactly the sort they had hoped for. Discuss the importance of pure versus mixed lists. See Slamecka and Katsaiti (1987, p. 599) for a discussion. They cite Underwood's (1983) discussion as helpful. Does the generation effect ever occur with pure lists (that is, with

generate and read pairs in separate lists)? See Slamecka and Graf's (1978) Experiment 1, and the discussion of the issue on p. 605 of Slamecka and Katsaiti. Why should a recognition test show a generation effect with pure lists?

2. Slamecka and Katsaiti claim that various alternative explanations are ruled out by their results, since they fail to predict that pure lists and mixed lists would yield different results. What are those explanations, and how are they ruled out? See their discussion, beginning on p. 605.

3. What did Slamecka and Katsaiti find when they studied bilingual subjects? Why did those results lead to their experiments on selective displaced rehearsal?

Extension Experiments

1. An interesting extension experiment would be to perform Slamecka and Katsaiti's Experiment 3, which compared pure and mixed lists.

2. A comparison that Slamecka and Katsaiti discuss is that of recognition versus recall tests (see Advanced Question 1). Do these two types of tests lead to different results? If so, why?

3. Jacoby (1978) found a generation effect with a "problem-solving" task similar to a crossword puzzle, and Gardiner and Rowley (1984) found it with simple multiplication problems. What other sorts of situations might yield a generation effect?

References

Gardiner, J. M. & Rowley, J. M. C. (1984). A generation effect with numbers rather than words. *Memory and Cognition, 12,* 443-445.

Jacoby, L. L. (1978). On interpreting the effects of repetition: Solving a problem versus remembering a solution. *Journal of Verbal Learning and Verbal Behavior, 17,* 649-667.

McElroy, L. A. & Slamecka, N. J. (1982). Memorial consequences of generating nonwords: Implications for semantic-memory interpretations of the generation effect. *Journal of Verbal Learning and Verbal Behavior, 21,* 249-259.

Slamecka, N. J. & Graf, P. (1978). The generation effect: Delineation of a phenomenon. *Journal of Experimental Psychology: Human Learning and Memory, 6,* 592-604.

Slamecka, N. J. & Katsaiti, L. (1987). The generation effect as an artifact of selective displaced rehearsal. *Journal of Memory and Language, 26,* 589-607.

Underwood, B. J. (1983). *Attributes of memory.* Glenview (IL): Scott, Foresman.

The Generation Effect

Individual Data

Please note: The order in which the different list types are presented is varied between subjects. Therefore, the order in which the list types are listed in the table and on the plot may not match the order in which you encountered the list types.

Please indicate which version of the experiment you performed:

Version 1: Read-only _____

Version 2: Generate _✓_

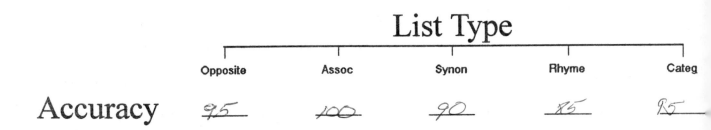

List Type

	Opposite	Assoc	Synon	Rhyme	Categ
Accuracy	95	100	90	85	85

Cell entries are MEAN PERCENTAGE RECALLED

The Generation Effect

Individual Data

Indicate Condition:_____
(Read-only or Generate)

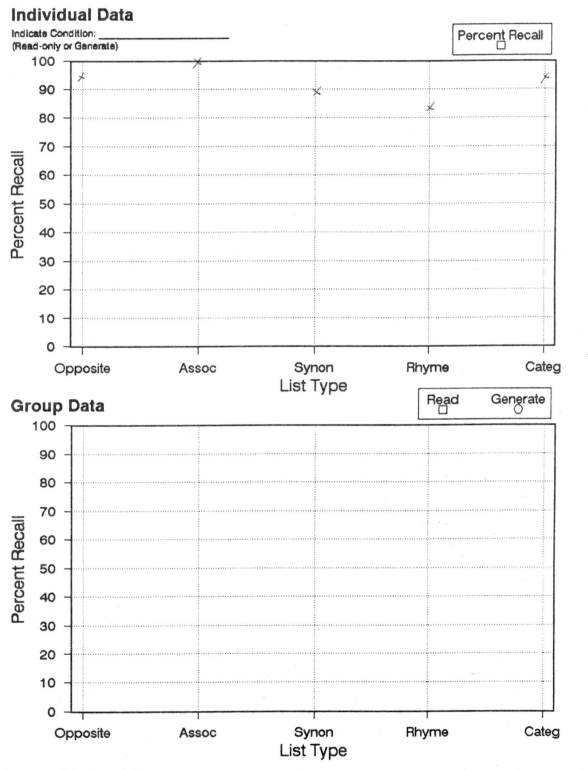

Percent Recall
□

Read Generate
□   ○

Group Data

2.13 Automatic versus Controlled Processing

Abstract

Many tasks of everyday life are so well-practiced that they become *automatic* and require virtually no attentional resources. An example would be putting your foot on the brake when you are approaching a stop sign. Other tasks, however, require a lot of attention. For example, the first time you ever drove a car, you probably had to think quite deliberately about what to do when you approached a stop sign. These types of tasks are called *controlled*. In addition to differing in the amount of attention they require, automatic processes are highly inflexible, while controlled processes are relatively easy to change. In this exercise, the acquisition of automatic processing is illustrated through the use of a category search task with either consistent or varied mapping (either the same or different categories). Consistent mapping promotes automatic processing through extended practice.

This exercise is concerned with *automatic* and *controlled* cognitive processing. Controlled processing occurs when we do cognitive acts that are not well practiced. This type of processing requires a lot of attention, but can be changed fairly easily. An example from everyday life would be following a recipe. You have to read each ingredient carefully, and pay attention to what you are doing. But you can also easily switch to another recipe and follow it, instead. Automatic processing, on the other hand, occurs only with large amounts of practice, and it is difficult to change. An example is writing the old year in dates during the month of January. This type of action is automatic, and difficult to change. In fact, the altering of writing the date requires controlled processing. In this exercise, the development of an automatic process from one that is initially controlled is illustrated.

A task that has been widely studied by experimental psychologists is the search of short-term memory. In this type of experiment, a subject is shown a set of letters (the *memory set*) and then shown a single letter (the *probe*). The subject's task is to decide whether that probe is a member of the memory set, and indicate the decision by pressing an appropriate key. In the usual version of this experiment (Sternberg, 1966, and see the experiment on Scanning STM, Section 2.2), the letters in the memory set are changed after every probe, or after every few probes. Subjects take longer to respond as the memory set size increases--that is, reaction time (RT) is an increasing function of the number of items to which the probe must be compared. This kind of search has all the hallmarks of controlled processing. It requires effort, the probe seems to be compared to the members of the memory set one at a time and it is easy to switch from one memory set to another.

Now suppose that you were given a great many trials with the same memory set on each trial. This is the basic experimental paradigm used by Schneider and Shiffrin, whose subjects had as many as 24 *hours* of practice. With this degree of practice, subjects become very good at doing the memory search--so good, in fact, that RT's are no longer for large memory sets than for small ones, suggesting that the subjects now are able to search the entire memory set at once (in parallel). This well-practiced search is now automatic. It requires little effort or attentional capacity. Also, this search is difficult to change--if a new memory set is given, it must be searched in a controlled manner. Similarly, the automatic search is hard to suppress--if a member of that memory set is now used as a distractor or negative probe with a new memory set, it will often be responded to incorrectly.

A similar task is used in the experiment detailed below. Here, the task is *category search*, where you are given a category (such as vehicles, or geographical features), and must decide whether probe words are or are not members of that category. One category will be *consistently mapped* (CM condition). You will get a lot of practice in searching for members of this category, and members of this category will never appear as negative probes when you are searching other categories. Other categories you will be given will have *varied mapping* (VM condition). That means that each one of these categories will receive relatively little practice, and a word might be a positive probe with one category, and be used as a negative probe with another. (A real-world example of consistent mapping is a stop sign. Note that the only response you make is to stop: a stop sign never means anything else.

A yield sign, on the other hand, illustrates varied mapping. If traffic is coming you respond by stopping, but if the intersection is clear you don't stop.)

How can we tell that a task is becoming automatic? One hallmark of automatic processes is that they require few attentional resources. One approach to the study of attention that has been fruitful is to treat attention as a resource--something that you have in a limited quantity (Kahneman, 1973). How well you can do two things at once is partly determined by the amount of attention it requires. Most adults can drive well enough to easily hold a conversation with a passenger in the car. In terms of this model of attention, driving is easy enough (after lots of practice) that it requires little attentional capacity. The spare capacity can be used to attend to the conversation. Note what happens, though, when you are driving on icy roads, or on a crowded, unfamiliar highway. In this situation, driving is not so easy, and requires more attentional resources, leaving little or no spare capacity for conversation. You might not reply or reply after some delay. This sort of model of attention as a limited resource suggests that we can use this same basic approach to studying attentional capacity. If a task is a difficult, controlled task it should require a lot of attentional capacity, and thus it should not be possible to do a second task at the same time (or at least not very well). On the other hand, if the task is automatic, requiring little capacity, you should be able to do a second task at the same time. Of course, the two tasks contain incompatible stimuli or responses--you can't look at two different places at once, or press two different keys at the same time with the same finger. This *dual-task methodology* has often been used in experiments of the kind illustrated in this exercise. In the version of the experiment that you will complete, automaticity is tested by giving you a more difficult version of the task in the last block. For the last block of trials the number of categories for which you are searching is increased to two, which should have the effect of exaggerating the differences between the CM and VM conditions.

Method

In this experiment, subjects will complete 10 practice trials, then 4 blocks of 72 trials each of a category search task. On each trial, a category is named, and then two words are presented above and below a central fixation. Subjects respond by indicating whether either of the words named a member of the category. There are eight categories, with six exemplars of each. Each category is searched for equally often, in random order. The categories are presented in one of two ways. Two of the categories are presented in the consistent mapping (CM) condition. The exemplars of these two categories *never* appear as distractor items when other categories are tested. Thus, when one of those exemplars appears, the correct response is always to indicate that they were in the category being searched for. The remaining categories are presented in the varied mapping (VM) condition. Exemplars of these categories may appear as positive probes for their own category or as negative probes (distractors) for the other VM categories. In the fourth block only, the memory set size will increase from one to two, i.e. two categories will be named on each trial.

Instructions for Running the Experiment

To run this experiment, insert Disk 1 into your computer and enter the MEL Lab as instructed in Section 0.2. Select **Cognition** from the topic menu and **Automatic versus Controlled Processing** from the specific experiment menu. Instructions on the computer screen will then explain the experiment and what keys to use for your responses. Because this experiment measures reaction time, please be sure to respond as quickly as you can while still maintaining a high level of accuracy. *Materials needed*: Pencil and paper, if no printer is available, to copy down the results reported in the table at the end of the experiment. *Things to notice*: For the consistently mapped (CM) condition, how does your performance change with extended practice?

Expected Running Time = 55 minutes

Questions

1. What is the dependent variable for this experiment?

2. What are the independent variables?

3. What are some important control variables?

4. Does the consistently mapped category search become automatic? What aspects of the data indicate this? Note that a great many trials are needed for fully-developed automaticity, and time may not have permitted enough in this experiment. There should still be some clear differences between your ability to search the CM category and the VM categories, though.

5. Automatic skills often seem impossible to acquire initially. For example, novice drivers may feel they will never learn to drive safely and carry on a conversation at the same time. Similarly, to a child, reading is so hard initially it seems impossible that one could read effortlessly for pleasure. Have you ever tried to play a musical instrument and felt this was too frustrating and that you would never learn the skill? This happens with many skills (e.g., typing, learning new computer programs, playing video games, mathematical operations). It is often surprising how good one can get in only 300 trials. However, several hundred trials of each component of a skill may take hundreds of hours of practice and the learning improvement may seem surprisingly slow. Given the need for extensive practice, how might human self-image and perseverance factors influence success of intellectually equivalent individuals? For example let us assume person X comes from a family that tells the student you are smart and have to work hard, and person Y from a family that feels no one succeeds in school and just getting by is all right. How will the performance of these two people vary initially in a college course, and in the next course that uses that course as a prerequisite? Although the initial abilities are equal, will differential development of automatic component skills produce different final abilities and self perceptions? How might you make students more appreciative of how much they can improve their performance with appropriate practice?

6. Certain skills require highly automatic component skills (e.g., reading, mathematics, programming, military piloting, air traffic control). How might the development of automatic processing be important in these skills (e.g., see Schneider, 1985; Laberge & Samuels, 1974)? Educational practice in the United States uses relatively little drill and practice compared with Oriental (e.g. Japan) or European (e.g., Germany) school systems. What risks are there of having too little consistent practice (see Laberge & Samuels, 1974; Schneider 1985)? How do we determine how much practice is enough?

Advanced Questions

1. What implications does this experiment have for long-term training of skills? You might want to consider motor skills, as well as more cognitive skills such as category search or recognition.

2. Schneider and Shiffrin (1977) argued that automatic and controlled processes represent two different modes of information processing. Where might each of these modes prove useful? That is, are there tasks for which one is clearly better than the other? Do most of the tasks studied by cognitive psychologists involve automatic processing? What everyday tasks require each of these modes of processing? Are there costs, as well as benefits, to automatic processing?

Extension Experiments

1. Run subjects for extended periods of practice (e.g., 2 hours of category search) and see if performance changes with really extended practice in the consistent and varied conditions. Examine what happens when you reverse the previously learned set (words which were originally trained as targets become distractors). See Schneider & Shiffrin, 1977 Experiment 2.

2. How might consistency be important in more complex real world tasks (e.g., processing order forms, see Myers & Fisk, 1987) or games (e.g., chess moves, see Fisk & Lloyd, 1988)? Design an experiment to examine learning of consistent and inconsistent rule sets.

3. Some designers fail to make computer interfaces consistent (e.g., to leave a program you might type the <Esc>, "EXIT", "QUIT" or "LOGOUT"). The need for consistency is an important reason for developing standards for computer systems. Develop an experiment with several related tasks with similar goals (see the experiment on telephone systems as an example, Section 4.1) with either consistent or inconsistent response mappings to map out the learning time as a function of the degree of consistency.

References

Fisk, A. D., & Lloyd, S. J. (1988). The role of stimulus-to-rule consistency in learning rapid application of spatial rules. *Human Factors, 30,* 35-49.

Fisk, A. D., & Schneider, W. (1983). Category and word search: Generalizing search principles to complex processing. *Journal of Experimental Psychology: Learning, Memory, and Cognition, 9,* 177-195.

Kahneman, D. (1973). *Attention and effort.* Englewood Cliff (NJ): Prentice-Hall.

LaBerge, D., & Samuels, S. J. (1974). Toward a theory of automatic information processing in reading. *Cognitive Psychology, 6,* 293-323.

Myers, G. L., & Fisk, A. D. (1987). Application of automatic and controlled processing theory to industrial training: The value of consistent competent training. *Human Factors, 29,* 255-268.

Schneider, W. (1985). Training high-performance skills: Fallacies and guidelines. *Human Factors, 27,* 285-300.

Schneider, W., Dumais, S. T., & Shiffrin, R. M. (1984). Automatic processing and attention. In R. Parasuraman, R. Davies, & R. J. Beatty (Eds.), *Varieties of attention* (pp. 1-27). New York Academic Press.

Schneider, W., & Fisk, A. D. (1984). Automatic category search and its transfer. *Journal of Experimental Psychology: Learning, Memory, and Cognition, 10,* 1-15.

Schneider, W. & Shiffrin, R. M. (1977). Controlled and automatic human information processing: I. Detection, search, and attention. *Psychological Review, 84,* 1-66.

Shiffrin, R. M. & Schneider, W. (1977). Controlled and automatic human information processing: II. Perceptual learning, automatic attending, and a general theory. *Psychological Review, 84,* 127-189.

Sternberg, S. (1966). High-speed scanning in human memory. *Science, 153,* 652-654.

Automatic versus Controlled Processing

Individual Data

	Block Number			
	1	2	3	4
Consistent Yes	___	___	___	___
Consistent No	___	___	___	___
Varied Yes	___	___	___	___
Varied No	___	___	___	___

Cell entries are MEAN CORRECT REACTION TIME (msec)

Automatic versus Controlled Processing

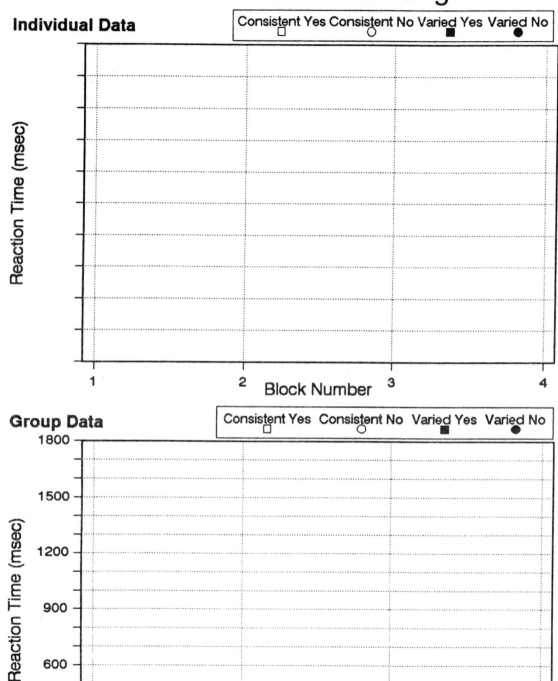

Individual Data

| Consistent Yes □ | Consistent No ○ | Varied Yes ■ | Varied No ● |

Reaction Time (msec)

Block Number

Group Data

| Consistent Yes □ | Consistent No ○ | Varied Yes ■ | Varied No ● |

Reaction Time (msec)

Block Number

2.14 Reading Comprehension: Linking Inferences

Abstract

Carpenter and Just (1977) have used reading time, in addition to eye-movement measures, to make inferences about the process of making inferences. When reading, we must often integrate information from successive sentences. Depending on how the sentences are phrased, these integrations or inferences may be more or less difficult, and those differences in difficulty should be reflected in reading time for the second sentence. In the experiment for this exercise subjects read series of sentences, checking each for any contradiction to previous sentences as the putative task. The real interest in the experiment is the reading time for a sentence that requires a bridging inference back to a previous sentence. Will it be a function of the number of intervening sentences? Will it be a function of the type of verb (direct or indirect) of the first sentence? Nouns referred to by indirect verbs should be harder to interpret, and lead to longer reading times, if the inference process affects reading time. In addition, the more recently the first sentence has been read, the more easily the inference should be made. These differences in reading time indicate the usefulness of reading time as a way to study lexical (i.e., specific word meaning) relationships.

In most reading, we must link the various sentences we read into a coherent, meaningful whole. In many cases, we must go beyond the direct information presented and make *inferences* in order to integrate or link two or more sentences. Carpenter and Just (1977) argue that "inferences based on lexical relations must take a certain amount of time to compute, and this time may well depend on the lexical relation involved." If the relationship is a simple one, it is presumed to require less time than if it were relatively complex.

In the experiment detailed below, the *reading time* for sentences is measured using serial presentation of sentences, with the subject controlling the onset of each sentence. It is assumed that the time a subject takes for each sentence reflects the time required to read and make sense of that sentence. (This assumption will not be correct for every sentence, but should be reasonable when the reading times for a number of sentences are averaged together.)

This experiment is based on Carpenter and Just's second experiment, which tested for differences in the time it takes to read sentences which differ in their lexical relationships to previous sentences in a series. Compare the following examples.

A. It was dark and stormy the night the millionaire died.
    The killer left no clues for the police to trace.

B. It was dark and stormy the night the millionaire was murdered.
    The killer left no clues for the police to trace.

Notice the difference. In A, the existence of a killer is not implied by the opening sentence. "Died" does not imply an agent or an object. In B, however, "the killer" has been *set up* by the verb "murdered," which does imply an agent (killer) or an object (murder weapon). Does this difference affect reading time? Carpenter and Just argued that it should, because more time must be spent integrating "the killer" into the context provided by the opening sentence in A than in B, where you presumably have a greater expectation of encountering information about the killer.

Carpenter and Just (1977) reported two main results of their experiments. They found an increase in reading time with increased lag between the opening and target sentences, as expected. Of most interest, however, was their finding of a greater reading time for the target sentence when the verb of the opening sentence was indirect. They concluded that this reflects the greater time required to integrate the target sentence with the previous information when the agent or object was not directly implied by the opening sentence.

Method

This experiment follows the method described by Carpenter and Just (1977), Experiment 2. On each trial, the subject sees a series of five sentences, presented one at a time, with each sentence remaining on the screen as the succeeding sentences are added. The subject has control over presentation of the sentences, pressing a key to see the next sentence. The ostensible task is to decide whether a sentence contradicts a previous sentence. If it does, the subject is to press the appropriate button. For half of the trials, either the third, fourth, or fifth sentence contradicts an earlier sentence.

The opening sentence of each series contains the verb of interest, which is either direct or indirect. An *indirect* verb is one that does not directly imply either an agent or an object, while a *direct* verb does make that implication. In the example above, "murdered" is directly related to "killer," while "died" is only indirectly related--it does not necessarily imply either an agent or an object. The actual target sentence is the one containing the agent or object, and this sentence follows the opening sentence with a lag of either zero or two sentences. Each lag occurs equally often, in random order. Direct and indirect opening sentences also occur equally often, in random order. The 32 opening sentences can each occur with either a direct or an indirect verb. Which verb is used for each specific sentence is counterbalanced so that if an opening sentence appears with a direct verb for odd-numbered subjects, that same sentence will appear with an indirect verb for the even-numbered subjects.

(The opening sentences and test sentences are taken from the original experiment of Carpenter and Just, and we thank Prof. Marcel Just for supplying them. The other sentences were added by us.)

Instructions for Running the Experiment

To run this experiment, insert Disk 1 into your computer and enter the MEL Lab as instructed in Section 0.2. Select **Cognition** from the topic menu and **Reading Comprehension: Linking Inferences** from the specific experiment menu. Instructions on the computer screen will then explain the experiment and what keys to use for your responses. This experiment involves reading a series of sentences and then trying to decide whether one sentence contradicts any of the previous sentences. Try to read the sentences at your normal reading speed. *Materials needed*: Pencil and paper, if no printer is available, to copy down the results reported in the table at the end of the experiment.

Expected Running Time = 40 minutes

Questions

1. What is the dependent variable in this experiment?

2. What are the independent variables?

3. What are some important control variables?

4. What are your results? Is there an effect of lag? Do indirect verbs require longer integration times for the target sentences?

5. Compare your results with those of Carpenter and Just (1977, p. 124 ff.)

6. Carpenter and Just (1977, pp. 127-128) reported additional analyses of eye-movement recordings made during reading of the sentence series. Do those data shed additional light on the inference process? While this experiment did not measure eye movements, do you feel that you made more regressions for indirect verbs? What information were you seeking when you made such regressions?

Advanced Questions

1. This experiment used the time from when one sentence appeared to when the subject went on to the next sentence to measure "reading time." What other processes might be involved, other than the time to read the sentence? Note that many things could be affecting reading time on a trial-by-trial basis. Momentary inattention, lapses of memory, and the like could all affect this time. For that reason, researchers rely on averages across a number of trials. How many trials are needed for a stable average? Try randomly selecting samples of different sizes from the individual trial data. How do your results look when they are based on only two trials (or three, or four)?

If you have some sophistication in statistics, you might want to consider the issue of estimating a "true" reading time based on samples of various numbers of trials. What effect does the number of trials entering into the average have on the *standard error*? Can you use this information to make a decision about the number of trials needed for reasonable accuracy?

2. Another approach to studying reading comprehension measures reading time for each word, with the subject controlling reading time by pressing a key on a computer keyboard to have it display the next word. Daneman and Carpenter (1983) report a study on the relationship between working memory capacity and the integration of potentially ambiguous material during reading. What was their general result?

3. How might studies using reading times and/or eye-movement tracking to study reading comprehension impact on the teaching of reading? Beck and Carpenter (1986) have addressed this issue.

Extension Experiments

1. One change you could make to this experiment would be to have only a single sentence displayed at a time, thus preventing regressions to earlier sentences. What effect would this have on the reading times for target sentences following direct and indirect verbs? In this case, the subject must rely on memory for the opening sentence. Do regressions to previous sentences make reading faster? Or are you better off making inferences based on memory?

2. Convert the experiment to present words sequentially using the Rapid Serial Visual Presentation format to determine on what specific words the reading times increase.

3. How could you use reading times to determine whether different versions of a paragraph are easier to read?

References

Beck, I. L. & Carpenter, P. A. (1986). Cognitive approaches to reading: Implications for instructional practice. *American Psychologist, 41*, 1098-1105.
Carpenter, P. A. & Just, M. A. (1977). Reading comprehension as eyes see it. In M. A. Just & P. A. Carpenter (Eds.) *Cognitive Processes in Comprehension*. Hillsdale (NJ): Erlbaum.
Daneman, M. & Carpenter, P. A. (1983). Individual differences in integrating information between and within sentences. *Journal of Experimental Psychology: Learning, Memory, and Cognition, 9*, 561-584.

Reading Comprehension

Individual Data

Number of Intervening Sentences (Lag) Between Opening Sentence and Target

	0	2
Direct Verb	——	——
Indirect Verb	——	——

Cell entries are MEAN READING TIMES (msec)

Reading Comprehension: Linking Inferences

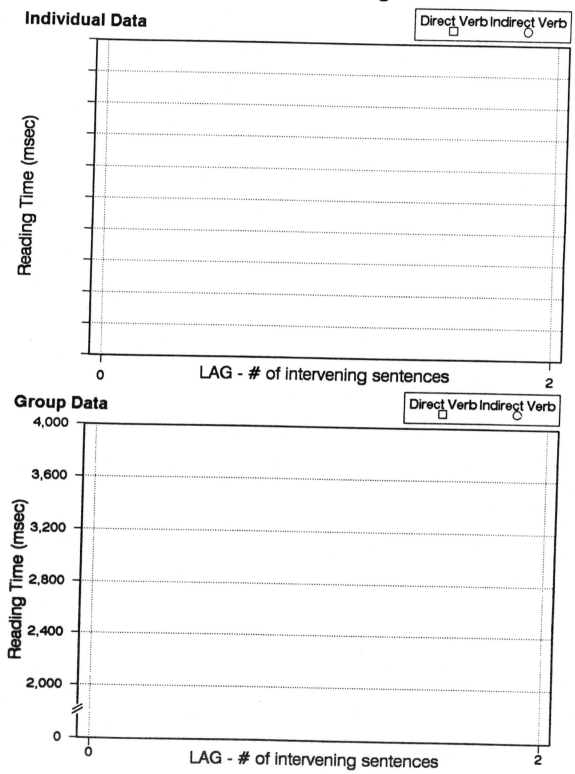

Individual Data

Direct Verb Indirect Verb
□   ○

Reading Time (msec)

0   LAG - # of intervening sentences   2

Group Data

Direct Verb Indirect Verb
□   ○

4,000

3,600

3,200

2,800

2,400

2,000

0

Reading Time (msec)

0   LAG - # of intervening sentences   2

3 Experiments in Social Psychology

Humans, like many other organisms, are social creatures. Any psychology that claims to give a general account of how we function must deal not just with how we function in isolation, but also how we function within a social context. How we make judgments about others, how we act toward others, what we remember about others, and why we judge, act, or remember are all part of social psychology.

We all must make social judgments: Is this person honest? Friendly? Hard-working? But what controls those judgments? A major area of social psychology is concerned with these questions of *social judgment*. We all must also interact with others. How does our behavior influence theirs? Should I cooperate with this person, or compete? Which will be of the most benefit to me? To them? To society? Another major issue for social psychology is *social behavior*, or our actual behavior in social settings. Of course, that behavior is partly determined by other persons' behaviors, so the situation is quite complex. Despite that complexity, social psychologists have made progress in understanding humans in their social context.

Some of the approaches of social psychology are illustrated in the exercises of this section. Many of these issues also have importance beyond the realm of psychology itself. Economics, business, political science and sociology are all disciplines concerned with the actions of individuals in social contexts, and the study of social psychology can give interesting insights into those disciplines as well.

3.1 The Prisoner's Dilemma

Abstract

"The prisoner's dilemma" is the name given to a type of competitive game in which a player tries to win points by choosing to compete or cooperate with his or her opponent. The number of points each player scores depends upon the choices they both make. If they both cooperate they both score more points than if they both compete. However, if one player competes and the other cooperates, the one who competes earns more points than the one who attempted to cooperate. This game has interested social scientists because it is akin to many real-life situations, such as the nuclear arms race, union-management negotiations, and even two friends deciding what movie to attend!

A. W. Tucker, an early pioneer in the mathematics of game theory, gave the name "prisoner's dilemma" to a certain class of games of strategy. Here is how the prisoner's dilemma was described by Luce and Raiffa (1957) in their book *Games and Decisions*:

Two suspects are taken into custody and separated. The district attorney is certain they are guilty of a specific crime, but he does not have adequate evidence to convict them at trial. He points out to each prisoner that each has two alternatives: to confess to the crime the police are sure they have done, or not to confess. If they both do not confess, then the district attorney states he will book them on some very minor trumped-up charge such as petty larceny and illegal possession of a weapon, and they will both receive a minor punishment; if they both confess they will be prosecuted, but he will recommend less than the most severe sentence; however, if one confesses and the other does not, then the confessor will receive lenient treatment for turning state's evidence whereas the latter will get "the book" slapped at him. (p. 95)

As you can see, there is a basic conflict in this situation between each individual's goals and their common rewards (or punishments). Unable to talk directly to your partner in crime, should you hold out or confess? If you know that your partner will also hold out, then clearly you should, too. But if you distrust your partner, or want to minimize your own sentence, you should probably confess.

The prisoner's dilemma game (PDG) is a way to formalize this situation, and the exercise you will do with the PDG has you play it in varying ways, to illustrate the possible outcomes. Of course, the situation described above would be of interest only to criminals and prosecutors, and this exercise would not be of much interest. But the PDG turns out to be a very good model for a great many situations of interest to social psychologists, sociologists, political scientists, biologists, and mathematicians.

Now we will develop a more formal analysis of the PDG (see Advanced Question 1 for a further development). When you play the computer version of the prisoner's dilemma, your opponent will be the computer, which will play each of several strategies. You will be shown a "payoff matrix" like the one below, which shows how many points you will win under various conditions. The actual numbers are arbitrary, but larger numbers represent larger rewards (or smaller punishments). Choice "A" is to cooperate, while choice "B" is to defect, or fail to cooperate. In the original prisoner's dilemma, cooperating would mean refusing to confess, while defecting would be to confess. For this version, you will earn "points," rather than shorter sentences, but the basic situation is otherwise the same. The numbers in parentheses are the points each player earns for a given pair of choices. The first number represents your points, and the second your opponent's. Note that you are to try to win as many points as possible.

	A	B
A	(3,3)	(0,5)
B	(5,0)	(1,1)

Your choice (rows A and B)

Note that with this payoff matrix you have two choices in each round--cooperate (A) or defect (B). What should you do? Suppose that your opponent cooperates (chooses B). Your best choice then is to defect (earning 5 points, row B, column A) rather than to cooperate (which earns only 3). On the other hand, if your opponent defects, cooperating would earn you nothing, and you would be better off if you also defect (earning 1 point). As you can see, your point earnings will depend on whether or not you can determine your opponent's strategy (and also on what that strategy is). If only one round of the game is played, you would be better off defecting, which guarantees that you win *some* points.

A more realistic version is the one you will play, where there are a number of rounds of choices in each game (this is called an *iterated* PDG). In this case, the best outcome for you would be if your opponent always cooperated, and you always defected. But it is not very realistic to expect any opponent to behave that foolishly. Nobody likes to lose all the time!

The best mutual outcome is for you and your opponent to cooperate with each other. That is, cooperation will lead to the most points won by you and your opponent together (though your individual earnings may not be as high as they could be if you sometimes defected). True mutual cooperation thus involves each person making a small sacrifice for the overall good. For this reason, the situation embodied in the PDG is sometimes called the "tragedy of the commons" (Hardin, 1968)--if some resource is held in common (such as grazing land), and each person attempts to maximize his or her own use (by grazing more cattle), then soon there will be no resources left for anyone.

Other examples of "real-world" situations that are comparable to the PDG follow. Try to consider, as you read them, how they fit the payoff matrix above.

Consider the "arms race" between the United States and the Soviet Union. If both sides decide to arm themselves the cost to each is very high. If both sides agree not to arm themselves they both benefit economically. But if one side decides not to arm and the other side does arm itself, the outcome would be a disaster for the side that failed to arm. Of course, there are many other factors affecting such decisions, such as verifiability if the two sides decide to cooperate. But in many ways this situation is parallel to the prisoner's dilemma described above--the costs or benefits to each side depend on what *both* sides do.

Another (less deadly) form of the PDG is played if you and a friend discuss where to go for dinner. Suppose you want Chinese food, while your friend has a yen for pizza. You do not like pizza and your friend does not like Chinese. If you both insist on having your way, you may end up not going out at all, and you both lose. If one of you insists on your choice and the other goes along, then one of you gets what you want, but the other person has a bad time. Finally, if you both cooperate, you may decide on some other restaurant that you *both* like. In this case, neither of you gets what you want most, but both of you get meals you like.

Bargaining between a union and the management of a company is also like an iterated PDG, in that the bargaining for a new contract involves a series of agreements over various terms of the contract. In bargaining on each term of the contract, the two sides can cooperate by settling on a mutually satisfactory compromise, or either side can insist that its bargaining position cannot be compromised. Cooperation by both sides leads to the maximum mutual benefit. Either side can increase its own "winnings" by defecting and insisting on its own terms, but there is always a risk in this case. If management always defects, the workers will likely go out on strike, while if the union always defects, it may drive the company into bankruptcy.

Axelrod (1984) describes "cooperation without friendship" that occurred between British and German soldiers in the trench warfare of WWI. Despite considerable effort by the high commands on both sides, there developed some fairly elaborate devices for avoiding killing each other, based on the fact that aggressive action led to retaliation. This "live-and-let-live" system of mutual cooperation in illustrated by a soldier's description:

> It would be child's play to shell the road behind the enemy's trenches, crowded as it must be with ration wagons and water carts, into a bloodstained wilderness....but on the whole there is silence. After all, if you prevent your enemy from drawing his rations, his remedy is simple: he will prevent you from drawing yours. (Hay, 1916, pp. 224-225, cited in Axelrod, 1984)

A simple personal case of the prisoner's dilemma game occurs whenever you buy material you could illegally copy (e.g., text books, journals, video/audio tapes, computer software). For example, with computer software, if you cooperate by purchasing the software and the manufacturer cooperates by keeping prices low, many people can afford to have programs they could not possibly afford to develop themselves. However, if too many people use pirated copies, either prices go up for the people who cooperate or the company goes out of business. The net effect is that both lose. In some of these situations society defines cooperative behavior. For example, you may legally copy a single chapter of a book for classroom use or video tape a program to view at a later time. Your opponent's choice on each round is made independently of your choice on that round. That is, the opponent does not know what your choice is on that round when its choice is made.

Method

When you begin this experiment, you will get complete instructions for playing the PDG against the computer. A payoff matrix is presented, which tells you how many points you and your "opponent" (the computer) will earn for each combination of choices. You will then make your choice, and your opponent will also make a choice according to one of four strategies. The points you each earned will then be reported. There will be four games of ten rounds each, and your goal is to earn as many points as possible. Please note that you are to try to maximize your winnings, which does not necessarily mean that you want your opponent to win fewer points.

In each game, your opponent will adopt one of four strategies. Those strategies will not be known to you in advance. You should try to determine the strategy your opponent is using, in order to maximize your points.

Instructions for Running the Experiment

To run this experiment, insert Disk 1 into the computer and enter the MEL Lab as instructed in Section 0.2. Select **Social Psychology** from the topic menu and **The Prisoner's Dilemma** from the specific experiment menu. Instructions on the computer screen will then explain the experiment and what keys to use for your responses. This experiment requires that you play several rounds of the Prisoner's Dilemma Game against the computer. Speed does not matter. Rather, you should try to get the highest score you can in each round. *Materials needed*: Pencil and paper, if no printer is available, to copy down the results reported in the table at the end of the experiment. *Things to notice*: What sort of strategies does the computer seem to be using? Were you able to devise effective strategies?

Expected Running Time = 18 minutes

Questions

1. One purpose of this exercise was to compare the success of the different strategies employed by the computer. For that comparison, what are the independent and dependent variables?

2. Which of the computer's strategies works best against the various strategies employed by the students? Against which of the computer's strategies do students win the most points?

3. Can you tell what strategies the computer employed? Describe what you thought they were. Describe the strategies you tried to employ.

4. What might be the effect on this game of being able to meet with your opponent and discuss what you should both do? Of course, in "real-world" situations such as bargaining between the U.S. and Soviet governments, such discussion is possible--but later reneging on agreements is possible as well. Insko et al. (1987) present a report of a group version of the PDG with varying possibilities for contact between the groups or between representatives of the groups.

5. What sort of strategy might you adopt to try to "signal" your willingness to cooperate, if you cannot communicate with your opponent and your opponent is initially uncooperative? Is the strategy called Tit for Tat able to do this?

6. What is the effect of not being "nice"? Compare the computer's points for Tit-for-Tat and Suspicious Tit-for-Tat.

Advanced Questions

1. The various payoffs to a player can be described as follows (Axelrod & Dion, 1988):

> R = *R*eward for mutual cooperation
> S = *S*ucker's payoff (you cooperate, your opponent defects)
> T = *T*emptation to defect
> P = *P*unishment for mutual defection

The PDG is defined by a situation where $T > R > P > S$, and $R > (S + T)/2$.

Show that the payoff matrix for the games you played (the same as in the beginning of this Chapter) fits the requirements for the PDG.

Explain why the PDG has these requirements.

2. Milinski (1987) has described experiments with three-spined stickleback fish that suggest they have evolved a Tit-for-Tat strategy for how a pair of sticklebacks approach a predator. How did he simulate cooperation and defection, and what were the results?

3. Can species evolve the ability to employ certain strategies in real-world situations that are analogous to the PDG? See Axelrod (1984) and Axelrod and Dion (1988), as well as Milinski (1987) for discussions.

4. What strategies are best? The answer depends in part on what strategies are being playing against. Axelrod (1984) and Axelrod and Dion (1988) report the results of a computer tournament pitting various strategies against each other.

5. How did you respond to the Change of Heart strategy? Did you learn to "trust" your opponent? Compare this to the problem facing the United States of how to deal with the Soviet Union: a long-time enemy is now offering

unilateral reductions in troop strengths and nuclear weapons.

6. The PDG as we have considered it so far involves only two people (or two "sides"). But many real-world problems involve competition for resources among many people, each of whom can make an individual decision. Such a situation occurs in problems of overpopulation (decision to have few or many children), pollution (decision of whether or not to pollute), and behavior in panic situations (decision of saving yourself versus helping others). What factors might influence competition and cooperation in this "N-person" PDG? See Komorita, Sweeney, and Kravitz (1980) for a discussion of the N-person PDG, as well as for references to a number of real-world dilemmas that it models (including those listed above).

7. How might your memory (or lack of memory) for the previous moves affect the play? In general, what is the effect of "noise" on the outcome of the PDG? See Axelrod and Dion (1988) for a discussion.

Extension Experiments and Topics

1. What is the role of *group* decision-making in the PDG? What is the role of *contact* between the groups? Insko et al. (1987) tested issues such as these.

2. What are the most effective strategies? Axelrod (1984) discusses several. One way to explore this issue is to play strategies of your own against the strategies programmed into the computer. See the discussion of the Social Bargaining paradigm from the Experiment Generator in Section 0.5.

3. In this workbook, we have avoided a mathematical treatment of the PDG. Interested students may want to pursue this aspect of game theory, a branch of mathematics that deals with finding optimum solutions to various kinds of games. The PDG you played is specifically called a "two-person, non-zero-sum game." A beginning treatment of game theory may be found in COMAP (1988, Chapter 11). Davis (1970, chapter 5) also provides a good non-technical introduction to the game-theory analysis of the PDG. Almost any book on the mathematics of game theory will contain a more technical discussion.

References

Axelrod, R. (1984). *The evolution of cooperation.* New York: Basic Books.

Axelrod, R. & Dion, D. (1988). The further evolution of cooperation. *Science, 242,* 1385-1389.

COMAP (1988). *For all practical purposes: Introduction to contemporary mathematics.* New York: W. H. Freeman.

Davis, M. D. (1970). *Game theory: A nontechnical introduction.* New York: Basic Books.

Hardin, G. (1968). The tragedy of the commons. *Science, 162,* 1243-1248.

Hay, I. (1916). *The first hundred thousand.* London: Wm. Blackwood.

Insko, C. A., Pinkley, R. Hoyle, R., Dalton, B., Hong, G. Slim, R., Landry, P., Holton, B., Ruffin, P., & Thibaut, J. (1987). Individual versus group discontinuity: The role of intergroup contact. *Journal of Experimental Social Psychology, 23,* 250-267.

Komorita, S. S., Sweeney, J. & Kravitz, D. (1980). Cooperative choice in the N-person dilemma situation. *Journal of Personality and Social Psychology, 38,* 504-516.

Luce, R. D. & Raiffa, H. (1957). *Games and decisions.* New York: Wiley.

Milinski, M. (1987). TIT FOR TAT in sticklebacks and the evolution of cooperation. *Nature, 325,* 433-435.

1. Did you feel that you could identify the strategy your opponent was using?

2. Were your opponent's choices usually predictable?

3. Did you feel that there were times when you could trust your opponent to cooperate?

4. Were you able to devise strategies of your own to counter your opponent's strategies?

5. Could you remember the choices made in previous rounds and use that information to help evaluate your opponent's strategy?

The Prisoner's Dilemma

Individual Data

Opponent's Strategy

	Hardball	Change of Heart	Tit-for-Tat	Suspicious Tit-for-Ta
Player:				
You	___	___	___	___
Opponent	___	___	___	___

Cell entries are POINTS EARNED

The order in which the strategies appear in this table is not necessarily the order in which they were presented in the experiment.

The Prisoner's Dilemma

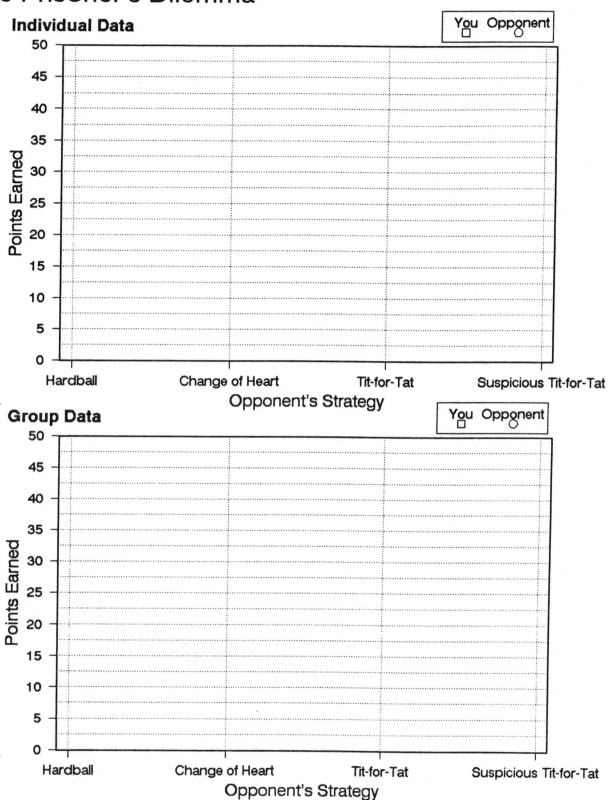

Individual Data

You □ Opponent ○

Points Earned

50 — 45 — 40 — 35 — 30 — 25 — 20 — 15 — 10 — 5 — 0

Hardball   Change of Heart   Tit-for-Tat   Suspicious Tit-for-Tat

Opponent's Strategy

Group Data

You □ Opponent ○

Points Earned

50 — 45 — 40 — 35 — 30 — 25 — 20 — 15 — 10 — 5 — 0

Hardball   Change of Heart   Tit-for-Tat   Suspicious Tit-for-Tat

Opponent's Strategy

Description of Strategies--Prisoner's Dilemma Game

In the PDG exercise, you play against the computer, which is programmed to employ one of four strategies in each game. Those strategies are described below. Please note that the order in which the strategies were presented to you was random, and so was probably *not* the same as the order in which they are discussed below.

In the computer game, choice A was to cooperate. Choice B was to compete, or in Axelrod's terms to "defect."

Tit-for-Tat

This strategy was suggested by Anatol Rapoport for a "tournament" held by Robert Axelrod that played a number of strategies against each other (Axelrod, 1984, Axelrod and Dion, 1988). This strategy turned out to be the best of those tested, and is very simple: cooperate on round one and then in later rounds do whatever your opponent did on the last round. If your opponent cooperates, you cooperate on the next round. If your opponent defects, you defect on the next round. Why is this a good strategy? "What the analysis shows is that an effective strategy is not to start defecting: never be the first to defect. But if the other side defects, be provokable. It also pays to be forgiving after you've been provoked, so as to keep the conflict as short as possible. It pays to respond promptly if someone does something you do not like" (Axelrod, quoted in COMAP, 1988, p. 223). Note that if you figured out that the computer was using this strategy, your earnings would be maximized by cooperating on all remaining trials. This strategy has been described by Axelrod (1984) as nice, provokable, and forgiving. Nice means that the strategy calls for you to always cooperate in the first round. Provokable means that a defection by your opponent is responded to by you defecting in the next round. Forgiving means that if the other player returns to cooperating, you do too.

Suspicious Tit-for-Tat

This strategy is the same as Tit-for-Tat, except that the computer defects on the first move. All the remaining rounds are played the same--make whatever choice your opponent made on the last round. The intent of this strategy is to see how your behavior is affected when the initial signal from your opponent is one of non-cooperation. Does that make it harder for you to realize the computer's strategy? In the terms used above, this strategy is provokable and forgiving, but not nice.

Hardball

"Hardball" is the name we have given to a strategy of almost total defection. In this game, the computer chose to defect in all rounds except 5 and 10. Note that the computer made its choices without regard to yours--what you did had no effect. The expectation is that this strategy will lead to relatively low points earnings for both the computer and you, because the best response to consistent defection is to reply with defection. This strategy is a modification of what Axelrod (1984) calls All D (for "always defect").

Change of Heart (or Gorby's Surprise)

We named this strategy "Change of Heart" because the computer defected on rounds 1-5, then changed to Tit-for-Tit for all the remaining rounds. The expectation is that you would take a while to learn to "trust" your opponent when the change of heart occurred, and your opponent began to cooperate.

3.2 Measures of Personality Traits

Abstract

In addition to experiments and other studies designed to discover the psychological processes that humans have in common, there are also studies designed to determine how people differ. Examples of such studies of "individual differences" include intelligence tests and personality tests. In this exercise, students complete abbreviated versions of several personality tests. While these brief versions are not generally adequate to actually test the students' responses, they do serve to show the types of items each test uses. The personality traits tested are anomy, locus of control, self-esteem, social desirability, and self-monitoring.

In most of the experiments in the MEL Lab, the purpose is to discover what aspects of psychological functioning people have in common. But, in addition to those shared attributes, people also differ in many ways. A second tradition in psychology has been to study these "individual differences" to see what they have to say about psychological functioning. This exercise on personality testing is intended to acquaint you with some examples of this approach. A common research tactic with personality tests, as well as other measures of individual differences, is to see whether the scores on the test correlate with scores on other measures of personality, as well as demographic measures such as income, ethnicity, and education.

Below are brief descriptions of the various scales which you will see illustrated, with definitions of the personality traits being measured, and some discussion of other variables with which they are correlated.

ANOMY. The anomy (pronounced AN-uh-me) scale illustrated in this exercise is the same 9-item scale used by McClosky and Schaar (1965), who conducted two large surveys in which people completed this scale, as well as a number of other scales designed to measure various social attitudes. The concept of anomy comes originally from the work of the sociologist Durkheim (1897), who described it as a condition of normlessness, or not having a feeling of sharing social norms. Durkheim saw this condition as arising from the loss of customary restraints in a capitalistic society devoted to greed and wealth. For him, anomy marked the loss of social restraints and moral limits. McClosky and Schaar have taken a somewhat different approach (and a more research-oriented one), asking what personal factors might be related to feelings of anomy. Their scale consists of items such as "With everything so uncertain these days, it is almost as if anything could happen." High scores indicate high levels of anomy, while low scores are associated with low anomy.

McClosky and Schaar report a number of relationships between other variables and anomy. Educational level was negatively related to anomy: persons with higher educational levels were more likely to score low on anomy. A scale of "mysticism," which was designed to reveal the degree to which people believe that supernatural forces affect their destiny, was strongly positively related to anomy: persons with high scores on the mysticism scale were more likely to also have high levels of anomy. "Psychological inflexibility" was also positively related to anomy, as were manifest anxiety and aggression. One rather interesting finding came from scales of agreement with extreme left- and right-wing political positions. Persons scoring high on either of these scales tended also to have high anomy scores. McClosky and Schaar discuss the degree to which anomy reflects social conditions, and the degree to which it is also determined by psychological factors.

SELF MONITORING. "Individuals differ in the extent to which they monitor (observe and control) their expressive behavior and self-presentation. Out of a concern for appropriateness, the self-monitoring individual is particularly sensitive to the expression and self-presentation of others in social situations and uses these cues as guidelines for monitoring and managing his own self-presentation and expressive behavior. In contrast, the non-self-monitoring person has little concern for the appropriateness of his presentation and expression, pays less attention to the expression of others, and monitors and controls his presentation to a lesser extent" (Snyder, 1974, p. 536).

Snyder and Simpson (1984) have further described persons high in self-monitoring as "particularly responsive to situational and interpersonal cues," while persons low in self-monitoring are "individuals whose actions typically reflect underlying attitudes, dispositions, and other personal attributes" (p. 1281). These quotes describe the sort of personality trait that Snyder attempted to measure with his 25-item scale of self-monitoring. The version used in this exercise is only 10 items in length, with those items taken from Snyder's original scale. An example of an item designed to measure self-monitoring is "I may deceive people by being friendly when I really dislike them." For this scale, high scores reflect high levels of self-monitoring. Snyder conducted several studies to offer evidence of the validity of this scale. One was based on the assumption that actors would have higher-than-usual levels of self-monitoring, since their profession requires that they adopt different roles and portray them convincingly. This turned out to be the case, with a group of professional actors scoring significantly higher in self-monitoring than a group of Stanford undergraduates. On the other hand, psychiatric patients are argued to show less variation in their responses across situations, and Snyder found that they score lower in self-monitoring on average than did his Stanford undergraduate controls. In other studies, Snyder found that persons who scored high on self-monitoring were better at expressing emotion when asked to read a passage out loud. More recently, Snyder and Simpson (1984) reported differences between high- and low-self-monitoring individuals in the patterns of their dating behavior, with persons high in self-monitoring more likely to adopt an "uncommitted" approach to dating, and persons low in self-monitoring tending toward more committed relationships.

LOCUS OF CONTROL. Rotter (1966) devised the original scale of locus of control, with the intent of measuring the degree to which persons perceive reinforcements (rewards) as being due to their own behavior (*internal* locus) or due to forces outside themselves, such as luck or fate (*external* locus). Rotter argued that persons' responses in many learning situations may depend powerfully upon the degree to which they feel that the outcome is under their control, or is controlled by fate or powerful others. In this scale, persons must choose which of two statements they agree with the most, with one statement reflecting an external and the other an internal locus of control. An example of a sentence pair is the following. "What happens to me is my own doing." vs. "Sometimes I feel that I do not have enough control over the direction my life is taking." The actual version of the LOC scale that you will complete in this exercise is an 11-item scale devised by Valecha (1972). The items are a subset of Rotter's original scale.

Rotter's work on locus of control has led to a large body of research by many individuals. In fact, the subject index of the Psychological Abstracts for 1987 has three *pages* of entries under "internal-external locus of control." For example, Kelley et al. (1986) found that persons with an external locus of control were more likely to engage in potentially self-destructive behaviors such as smoking and driving unsafely. Further, in situations where there is pressure to conform it has been found that persons with an internal locus of control are less likely to do so (Crowne & Liverant, 1963).

SOCIAL DESIRABILITY. One aspect of personality is the degree to which we tend to seek the approval of others, or avoid disapproval. Crowne and Marlowe (1964) reported studies using a scale of "social desirability" that they devised. The scale consists of 30 statements that the subject is to rate as true or false in regard to themselves. The statements were carefully chosen, however, to have two main attributes: "First, they are "good," culturally sanctioned things to say about oneself; and second, they are probably untrue of most people" (p.21). An example is, "I am always courteous, even to people who are disagreeable." Notice that while most of us would like to think that we are unfailingly courteous, in truth hardly anyone can claim that they always are. Thus, this scale is designed to determine the degree to which a person is motivated by approval, and avoids doing or saying things that may lead to disapproval. Crowne and Marlowe (1964) report a number of studies showing differences between high- and low-need-for-approval subjects. One example involved subjects having to decide which of two briefly presented cards had the most dots on it. The subject performed this experiment along with four other students who were confederates of the experimenters. On a number of trials, the confederates gave the incorrect answer. The issue was whether the actual subject would tend to agree with this choice or not. Persons with a high need for approval as measured by the scale were consistently more likely to agree (at least publicly!) with the confederates' choices.

SELF-ESTEEM. Another important individual difference between people is their degree of self-esteem. Do you think well of yourself, or do you feel like a failure? Rosenberg (1965) attempted to measure self-esteem with a simple ten-item scale, which is reproduced as part of this exercise. An example of an item from this scale is "I certainly feel useless at times." Rosenberg's main concern was self-esteem in adolescence, and he tested a large number of high-school students with his scale, to see if self-esteem is related to other variables in their lives.

Among Rosenberg's findings were that only children tended to have higher self-esteem than children with siblings (though the number of siblings made no difference). The adolescents' perceptions of how interested their parents were in them also was related to self-esteem. Adolescents with low self-esteem were also found to be less likely to participate in extra-curricular activities (though the size of the differences here was not large). When Rosenberg tested the adolescents' expectations for success in a career, he found that those high in self-esteem were more likely to expect to be successful. Research in industrial/organizational psychology has found that persons with low self-esteem are less apt to choose jobs that are suited to their needs and abilities (Korman, 1967). Other research indicates that the "vicious cycle" in which low self-esteem leads to failure, which reinforces low self-esteem, etc., can be broken by getting the person to attribute failure to the difficulty of the task, rather than to their own inadequacies (Brockner & Guare, 1983).

Concerns in testing

Two major concerns must be addressed in regard to any test, whether it is a personality scale such as those just outlined, a standardized test such as the SAT or an IQ test, or an experimental test of memory. Those concerns are the *validity* and *reliability* of the test.

Validity

Validity refers to whether a test measures what it claims to measure. As an example, suppose you devised an "intelligence" test that consisted of measuring how many sit-ups a person could do. That test would clearly be invalid--it simply isn't measuring intelligence. Often, of course, problems of validity are more subtle. For example, if an intelligence test has many items with vocabulary that you do not know, it would not be a valid test for you. Your low score would not reflect a lack of intelligence, but simply that you don't have the same vocabulary as the test maker. Unfortunately, it is difficult to measure validity. We must be content to estimate it in various ways. Three such approaches are briefly described below.

Face validity refers to a sort of common-sense approach. Counting how many sit-ups someone can do and calling it a test of intelligence lacks face validity. On the other hand, an item like "At times I think I'm no good at all" does seem to have face validity as a measure of self-esteem, because it seems clear that someone with high self-esteem would probably not agree with it, and someone with low self-esteem more likely would. While you should be concerned about face validity, it should be obvious that this is a limited approach--what seems obvious "on its face" to you may seem quite implausible to others, and there is no good way to settle the argument.

Predictive validity is another approach, concerned with how well the results of the test predict how well you will do on other measures that *should* be related. For example, an intelligence test should correlate reasonably well with school performance. Put another way, scores on an intelligence test should predict school performance fairly well if the test is valid, since how well you do in school is partly determined by intelligence. In many practical situations, however, predictive validity is quite low. Almost any time a test is used to select persons for training (such as using the SAT to select who gets into college) the apparent predictive validity is low due to *restriction of range*. Whenever we restrict access to training to only those with high scores, and only graduate those who did well during training, we have restricted the range of scores in such a way that predictive validity will be (predictably!) low, but not because our measure is invalid.

Concurrent validity refers to whether a test correlates well with other tests designed to measure the same trait. If I devise a new test for a medical problem, for example, its results should agree well with those of other tests already in use. For many psychological traits, however, we have no agreed-upon measure against which to check a new measure. Suppose scores on a new test of intelligence correlate highly with scores on another intelligence test. We can certainly conclude that they measure the same thing, so *if* the old test is measuring intelligence, the new one is, too. But we then have the problem of figuring out whether the old test is valid!

Reliability

Reliability refers to how well the test measures whatever it is measuring. If a test is reliable, it should yield consistent results. As an example, a bathroom scale is designed to measure your weight, and is probably fairly reliable. But suppose you had a five-year-old guess peoples' weights. That would almost surely be highly unreliable. Reliability turns out to be easier to measure than validity, and two approaches to measuring it are detailed below.

Test-retest reliability refers to the correlation between scores on the same test given twice. If an intelligence test is reliable, you should get about the same score each time you take it, since intelligence presumably doesn't change much across short periods of time. You can see that there can be a problem. This method of measuring reliability assumes that taking the test will not change future scores on the test. For long intelligence tests or achievement tests this is likely true, but it could be a problem for a test where you have a chance to practice before you take it again, or to look up the answers.

Split-half reliability is a way to measure reliability when test-retest reliability will not work. This method consists of calculating the correlation between one half of the test and the other half. In practice, this is often done using odd- and even-numbered items. On the SAT, for example, it is reasonable to assume that your score based on the odd-numbered items will be about the same as your score based on even-numbered items, thus indicating that the test is reliable. Split-half-reliability gets around some of the problems of test-retest reliability, but should only be used when there are a fairly large number of items on the test. (More sophisticated approaches of the same general sort include Kuder and Richardson's KR-20, or Cronbach's Alpha.)

One thing to remember about reliability and validity is that they are partly *independent*. That is, a test could be reliable but not valid, and vice versa (though any measure of validity will be reduced if reliability is low). An example would be measuring intelligence by how many sit-ups someone could do. Test-retest reliability would be high (if you can only do 10 sit-ups today, there is no reason to think you will be able to do many more or fewer two days from now), but the test would still not be a valid measure of intelligence. On the other hand, a test can be valid but not reliable. The example above, of having a five-year-old guess peoples' weights, would probably be reasonably valid, since a five-year-old understands the concept of weight, and something about how to judge it, but it would still be unreliable, since a young child would likely not be very consistent in his or her judgements.

Method

In this exercise, you will complete five brief personality tests. Two of the tests (the 9-item Anomy scale and the 10-item self-esteem scale) are presented in their complete form. The other three are abbreviated for the sake of time. The 11-item locus-of-control scale uses a subset of Rotter's original 29 items that was devised and tested by Valecha (1972). Twelve of the 33 items from Crowne and Marlowe's social-desirability scale are included, as are nine of the 25 items from Snyder's self-monitoring scale.

When your instructor reports the data, they will be scored in the following way. The "proportion correct" will indicate the proportion of items on which you indicated the trait being measured. For the Locus of Control scale, a high score indicates a highly *external* locus of control, while a low score indicates an *internal* locus. On the other scales, higher scores indicate higher degrees of the trait being measured.

MEL Lab: Student Workbook v.1.6; © *PST - Do not reproduce*

Instructions for Running the Tests of Personality Traits

To run this experiment, insert Disk 1 into the computer and enter the MEL Lab as instructed in Section 0.2. Select **Social Psychology** from the topic menu and **Measures of Personality Traits** from the specific experiment menu. Instructions on the computer screen will then explain the procedure and what keys to use for your responses. This exercise illustrates five tests of different aspects of personality. Each consists of 10-12 questions or scales. *Things to notice*: Do these tests seem to you to be measuring the traits they claim to measure?

IMPORTANT NOTE: In order to preserve anonymity, your usual subject number will *not* be used. Instead, the computer will automatically fill in the subject number '99' for everyone. You will be able to decide whether or not your wish to see the results when you finish the study. If you do not, you will still be able to view them later. Because the usual subject number is not used, the instructor will not be able to identify individual data.

Please be honest in your answers to the scale items.

Expected Running Time = 12 minutes

Viewing and Printing Your Results

You may view or print a table of your scores on each of the five scales after you have finished the study and before you run another study. See Section 0.4 for details.

Questions

1. Discuss the reliability of one test. How has that reliability been measured by researchers, or by the author(s) of the scale? Do you feel that it was reliable? That is, would you probably make the same responses again if you took the test over?

2. Discuss the validity of one test. How has validity been estimated in research on the test? Does the test appear to have good face validity? Do you feel that you could easily make yourself "look better" by giving dishonest answers?

3. Think about what each scale measures. Would you predict that scores on any of the scales would be correlated? Which ones and why? Compare your answer to the obtained correlations.

Advanced Questions

1. What are the goals of self-monitoring, according to Snyder? See p. 527. Would all of these goals be active, or might any one of them lead to high self-monitoring?

2. Are high self-monitoring and high need-for-approval (as measured by the Social Desirability Scale) the same thing? After all, persons who have a high need for approval may seek to gain that approval by conforming to others' behavior. Crowne and Liverant (1963) report such a finding. Snyder (1974, p. 528-529) argues that they are different (though obviously sometimes related) constructs.

3. What is the relationship between need for approval, and locus of control? It might be argued that a person who has an external locus of control (sees rewards as coming from external sources) may feel a greater need to seek social approval. Crowne and Liverant (1963) report findings relevant to this issue.

4. To what extent do these scales seem to reflect enduring personality traits? To what degree do they reflect a person's moment-to-moment changes in the traits? After all, I might not usually think I am a failure, but if I fail at a number of tasks in a short period of time, I might respond very differently.

5. Much of the research reported using these scales has compared persons who scored particularly high on the scale to persons scoring particularly low, and looked for other differences between them. Does this approach tell us anything about people who score nearer the mean on the scales?

References

Brockner, J. & Guare, J. (1983). Improving the performance of low self-esteem individuals: An attributional approach. *Academy of Management Journal, 26,* 642-656.

Crowne, D. P. & Liverant, S. (1963). Conformity under varying conditions of personal commitment. *Journal of Abnormal and Social Psychology, 66,* 547-555.

Crowne, D. P. & Marlowe, D. (1964). *The approval motive.* New York: John Wiley.

Durkheim, E. (1897/1951). *Suicide.* (J. A. Spalding & G. Simpson, trans.). Glencoe (IL): Free Press.

Kelly, K., Cheung, F. M., Singh, R., Becker, M. A., Rodrigues-Carillo, P., Wan, C. K., & Eberly, C. (1986). Chronic self-destructiveness and locus of control in cross-cultural perspective. *Journal of Social Psychology, 126,* 573-577.

Korman, A. (1967). Self-esteem as a moderator of the relationship between perceived abilities and vocational choice. *Journal of Applied Psychology, 51,* 484-490.

McClosky, H. & Schaar, J. H. (1965). Psychological dimensions of anomy. *American Sociological Review, 30,* 14-40.

Rosenberg, M. (1965). *Society and the adolescent self-image.* Princeton (NJ): Princeton University Press.

Rotter, J. B. (1966). Generalized expectancies for internal versus external control of reinforcement. *Psychological Monographs, 80* (Whole No. 609), 1-28.

Snyder, M. (1974). Self-monitoring of expressive behavior. *Journal of Personality and Social Psychology, 30,* 526-537.

Snyder, M. & Simpson, J. A. (1984). Self-monitoring and dating relationships. *Journal of Personality and Social Psychology, 47,* 1281-1291.

Valecha, G. K. (1972). Construct validation of internal-external locus of control as measured by an abbreviated 11-item IE scale. Unpublished doctoral dissertation, The Ohio State University.

Personality Test

Individual Data

The percent of responses indicating the trait are shown below for each of the five scales.

Anomy scale = _____
(high scores indicate high levels of anomy)

Abbreviated Locus of Control scale = _____
(high scores indicate an external locus of control)

Self-Esteem scale = _____
(high scores indicate high self-esteem)

Social Desirability scale = _____
(high scores indicate high levels of motivation for approval)

Self-Monitoring scale= _____
(high scores indicate high levels of self-monitoring)

3.3 Impression Formation

Abstract

An important aspect of social psychology is how we form impressions of other people, based on limited knowledge about them. Asch (1946) performed an experiment that is basic to this subject, and that experiment is replicated in this exercise. Asch had subjects read a brief set of terms describing a hypothetical person, then tested people's impressions of that person by having them rate the person on a number of dimensions. What he found was that some descriptors are very powerful in determining our impressions of other people.

When you meet a new person, how do you form an impression of them? That is, what things about them might influence how you perceive them? In this exercise, you will repeat a famous experiment done some years ago by Solomon Asch (1946). In that experiment (there were actually several versions of it), Asch had subjects listen to a series of adjectives (personality traits) describing a person. The subjects were then asked to write a character sketch of what they thought that person was like. In addition to the character sketch, Asch had his subjects complete check-lists of opposing traits (such as "sociable-unsociable"), indicating which of the two terms was most likely to be true of the person described. Asch found striking differences in ratings given by two groups of subjects when the description of the person they were to rate differed in only one trait. Asch called such traits "central," because he viewed them as especially important for impression formation. Some other traits that were tested yielded very little difference in impressions, and Asch called these "peripheral" characteristics.

Psychologists have long been interested in how we come to know other persons, but a major problem for studying this sort of question was how to approach it experimentally. One important aspect of Asch's work was that he was able to study impression formation experimentally and *quantitatively*. That is, he was able to make repeatable measurements about the effect of various descriptors on judgements of personality, and was able to show that such judgements could be manipulated systematically.

One question that might seem obvious is whether the results of experiments like Asch's really apply to every-day types of judgements. After all, Asch's subjects were asked to write character sketches and choose traits based on a brief description of a *hypothetical* person. Would the same result occur if the description was followed by actually meeting the person described? Kelley (1950) performed just such an experiment. Students in a class read a brief career and character sketch of a visiting lecturer. The lecturer then led a class discussion for 20 minutes. Subjects were then asked to rate the lecturer on a number of scales (some of which were the same as Asch's). The results were strikingly similar to Asch's, and confirmed that his results were not just the result of the abstract setting in which the ratings were made. Moreover, student subjects given descriptions that were expected to lead to a favorable impression were also somewhat more likely to interact with the lecturer by joining the class discussion.

While Asch's research dealt with impression formation, social psychologists have also studied other aspects of how we come to know other people, such as person memory, or memory for information about the target person (e.g. Belmore & Hubbard, 1987). Several aspects of research on impression formation are presented in the Advanced Questions section below.

Method

This exercise provides a replication of Asch's Experiment 1. Subjects are shown a list of adjectives describing personality traits (such as "determined" and "practical"). After reviewing those traits, the subjects are asked to choose which of a pair of adjectives is most likely to be true of the person described. Because the subject must choose one of the two terms, this is called a "forced-choice" rating. Eighteen adjective pairs are rated in this way.

Subjects are assigned by the computer to one of two groups, differing only in the list of personality traits they are shown at the beginning.

Instructions for Running the Experiment

To run this experiment, insert Disk 1 into the computer and enter the MEL Lab as instructed in Section 0.2. Select **Social Psychology** from the topic menu and **Impression Formation** from the specific experiment menu. Instructions on the computer screen will then explain the experiment and what keys to use for your responses. *Materials needed*: None.

Expected Running Time = 5 minutes

Questions

1. What is the dependent variable?

2. What is the independent variable?

3. What are some important control variables?

4. What are the results? Which of the 18 pairs of adjectives on the check-list shows differences between the two groups?

5. Do your results agree with those of Asch (1946)? See p. 263, Table 2, for a report of the percent of subjects choosing each term.

6. What is the purpose of Asch's Experiment 2? Why is this an important control experiment? What were his results?

Advanced Questions

1. One difficulty for interpreting Asch's results was that he classified traits as "central" or "peripheral" depending on the outcome of the check-list ratings. The "warm-cold" trait pair yielded large differences, and hence was described as central to impression formation. In another experiment, he presented lists of descriptors differing only in describing the person as "polite" versus "blunt." This pair made little difference in the ratings, and hence was described as peripheral. But is there any way to predict *in advance* which traits are central and which are peripheral? Wischner (1960) tackled this problem. How was he able to make such predictions?

2. How do the goals that you bring to bear in social situations influence your perception of other people and your memory for information about them? When you meet someone and form an impression and memories of them, does it matter whether you expect to have to work closely with the person? See Devine, Sedikides, and Fuhrman (1989) for a discussion and some experimental evidence.

3. Suppose that you hear a description of someone you expect to meet later, and you form an impression based on that description. Suppose further that you later are told that part of the description was incorrect. What influence does that have on your impression? Does it matter whether the information you are told to disregard was favorable or unfavorable? Wyer and Budesheim (1987) report several experiments on these issues.

4. Descriptions of a person can vary in many ways. Among these are *morally*-related descriptors (such as honest/dishonest), and *ability*-related descriptors (such as intelligent/stupid). Do we treat these types of descriptors

differently in forming impressions of persons? Skowronski and Carlston (1987) suggest that we do, and in some interesting ways.

Extension Experiments

1. One control experiment that Asch performed (his Experiment 2) was designed to test whether the "warm-cold" distinction affected the overall impression of personality, or acted independently of other descriptors. This version of the experiment simply omitted the words "warm" and "cold" from the descriptors, but added them to the check-list.

2. What other traits might be "central"? A simple extension of the experiment you have done is to manipulate other pairs of adjectives. Wishner (1960) discusses predicting which traits are central, and which peripheral. Another interesting approach is to use descriptors of *behaviors* ("Returned a wallet he found to its owner"), rather than personality traits (honest/dishonest). See Skowronski and Carlston (1987) for examples. Another approach might be to change the other descriptors used. Would the "warm-cold" distinction make the same difference if the other personality traits described were different?

References

Asch, S. E. (1946). Forming impressions of personality. *Journal of Abnormal and Social Psychology, 41*, 258-290.

Belmore, S. M. & Hubbard, M. L. (1987). The role of advance expectancies in person memory. *Journal of Personality and Social Psychology, 53*, 61-70.

Devine, P. G., Sedikides, C., Fuhrman, R. W. (1989). Goals in social information processing: The case of anticipated interaction. *Journal of Personality and Social Psychology, 56*, 680-690.

Kelley, H. H. (1950). The warm-cold variable in first impressions of persons. *Journal of Personality, 18*, 431-439.

Skowronski, J. J. & Carlston, D. E. (1987). Social judgement and social memory: The role of cue diagnositicity in negativity, positivity, and extremity biases. *Journal of Personality and Social Psychology, 52*, 689-699.

Wishner, J. (1960). Reanalysis of "Impressions of Personality." *Psychological Review, 67*, 96-112.

Wyer, R. S., Jr., & Budesheim, T. L. (1987). Person memory and judgements: The impact of information that one is told to disregard. *Journal of Personality and Social Psychology, 53*, 14-29.

Thought Questions

1.   Was the description that you wrote of the person generally positive or generally negative?

4 Experiments in Human Factors

Human Factors is the application of our knowledge of human abilities (memory, motor skills, attention, etc.) to the design of machines and tools for human use. Consideration of the experimental psychology of human behavior can aid in the design of many types of equipment--nuclear power plant control rooms, aircraft instrumentation, computer work stations and software, and even such everyday things as our office telephone systems. Human Factors developed as a discipline during World War II. Aircraft manufacturers found that doing research on how to arrange knobs and dials in cockpits could greatly reduce both accidents and training time. In the 1970's Human Factors studied human-computer interaction to address such questions as what layout is best for computer keyboards and what types of "menus" work best for users of computer programs.

Consider the last time you had trouble operating some machine, such as a complex photo-copying machine. What should the manufacturer have considered about Human Factors in good design? The memory, learning and problem-solving abilities of humans should certainly be considered in relation to how the machine works and what humans must do to operate it. But the world is full of machines and other things that are hard to learn and hard to operate. Sometimes that may be inevitable, but in too many instances, it is due to a lack of consideration of Human Factors.

Human Factors, in the use of information about human abilities in the design of systems for human use, is illustrated in the exercise that follows.

While the MEL Lab currently has only a single experiment directly testing Human Factors applications, many of the experiments in Perception and Cognition serve as part of the knowledge base for human factors. Basic studies of attention, memory, problem-solving, signal detection, and many other areas have contributed to the development of Human Factors.

4.1 Human Factors in Telephone Systems

Abstract

Human Factors is the application of our knowledge of human abilities (memory, motor skills, attention, etc.) to the design of machines and tools for human use. Consideration of the experimental psychology of human behavior can aid in the design of many types of equipment--nuclear power plant control rooms, aircraft instrumentation, computer work stations and software, and even such everyday things as our office telephone systems. In this exercise, two different office telephone systems are simulated, and the ease and accuracy of use is measured. The first system is designed to parallel the System 85™ developed by AT&T and currently in use in many businesses and universities. The second is a system developed by undergraduate psychology students at the University of Pittsburgh, applying our experimental knowledge of mnemonics to the problems of transferring calls, setting up conference calls, and the like. In addition to demonstrating the need for human factors consideration in design, the exercise illustrates the use of questionnaire data from a survey of subjects' impressions of the systems.

An important application of psychology is designing better human-machine interfaces. Whenever a new machine is built for humans to use (e.g., phones, photo-copying machines, video-tape recorders, computer word processors, pilot cockpits, nuclear power plants, space stations) it is critical that humans learn to operate that complex system quickly and reliably. *Human Factors* is the study and application of psychological research to humans working with man-made systems. You have learned to use many machines and have probably seen examples of good and bad human factors designs. For example, the standard touch-tone buttons of a phone are easy to read and are spaced so that there are few times you press the wrong key due to movement errors. In addition, when each key is pressed, you get good auditory feedback (i.e., a unique tone) as well as tactile feedback (i.e., you feel pressure when you start to push and a clear stop when the key is at the end of its travel). The following lab examines Human Factors applications to the design of such a system, and was based on extensive previous research on keyboard configurations and ease and accuracy of entry of telephone numbers.

Many systems are designed with little regard to human factors considerations. This occurs as a result of a lack of expertise, as well as a lack of time and care. Many nuclear power plant control rooms illustrate poor human factors design. They were often designed with hundreds of neatly arranged knobs with small labels. This was done because the control rooms looked neater and were slightly cheaper to build. The problem is that in a stressful situation an operator might turn the wrong knob and cause a serious accident (see McCormick, 1976). In some power plants operators have even try to overcome this poor design by placing unique stimuli next to critical knobs to reduce the chance of such errors. While this might help make the controls more discriminable, and thus reduce error, it should be clear that the best solution would be to design the system properly to begin with. In contrast, knobs in a cockpit have different shapes and colors providing discriminable and redundant cues (label, location, shape, and color) so critical functions (e.g., lowering landing gear versus turning off engines) are less likely to be triggered by mistake.

Consider the last time you had trouble operating some machine, such as a complex photo-copying machine. What should the manufacturer have considered about human factors in good design? The memory, learning and problem-solving abilities of humans should certainly be considered in relation to how the machine works and what humans must do to operate it.

In this exercise you will evaluate two alternative methods of designing a phone system to enable the person to execute special functions (e.g., send and transfer calls and arrange conference calls). The first system is designed to parallel the System 85™ developed by AT&T and currently in use in many businesses and universities. The second was designed by undergraduate psychology students incorporating mnemonic memory techniques to simplify learning. We will refer to the two conditions as the *digit condition* and the *mnemonic condition*. In the digit condition each function is specified by a single digit. For example, to pick up a call ringing in the area you type "=-9". In the mnemonic condition, each function is designated by a letter code that provides a mnemonic aid for that memory cue for that function. For example, to pick up a call ringing in the area you press "=P".

The learning literature suggests that mnemonics can aid learning and hence the mnemonic condition should be better. With a mnemonic approach you try to give the learner a simple rule to use as a cue to retrieve the desired information (see also section 2.9). In the phone case you want to associate the proper key presses with the action the subject thinks about when doing the experiment. An easy rule would be to press the first letter of the word describing the function. The letters are already printed on the phone push buttons. All that you would have learn is the proper names for the functions. They you recall the function, find the letter, and press the key. The major functions are Hold, Transfer, Forward, Pick-up, and Conference call. To execute the function you would press a special function key, the "*" on the regular phone and the letter key (e.g., for Transfer press "*T" and then the number you are transferring to).

If you were gambling the fortunes of a billion dollar company on marketing a new phone system for business, would you: a) use the digit condition, b) use the mnemonic condition, or c) run a ten hour experiment to find out which is better?

Method

In this experiment, subjects operate two different simulated telephone systems, and must learn five different functions for each in turn, including call forwarding, adding a person to a conference call, transferring a call, placing a caller on hold, and picking up a call ringing the in area. One system is based on the AT&T System 85™ (with minor changes to adapt to a computer keyboard rather than a push-tone phone). The other was developed by students in an undergraduate laboratory course in research methods, and was based on well-known mnemonic principles. In this experiment we will use the top row of numbers and the "-" and "=" as an alternative to the number keypad. The - and = keys represent special keys such as the * and # keys on the phone keypad. The top row of number keys on the keyboard are used. Simply cut out the phone template, at the end of this section, and lay it above the number keys so you know what letter matches each digit. *It is important that you put the template on before running the experiment*; otherwise, this becomes an unreasonable test of the system. Since phones already come with the numbers printed on them, it is important that a comparable memory aid is provided. This experiment does not use the numeric keypad on the right of the keyboard since it is arranged in a different order than the phone keypad and the keys do not come with the letters printed on them. The order in which the two systems are learned and tested is counterbalanced across subjects. After a brief period of learning and practice on each system, the subjects will perform the various functions over 25 test trials. At the end of the experiment, a questionnaire will be presented, asking about ease of learning and use of the systems.

Instructions for Running the Experiment

To run this experiment, insert Disk 1 into the computer and enter the MEL Lab as instructed in Section 0.2. Select **Human Factors** from the topic menu and **Human Factors in Telephone Systems** from the specific experiment menu. Instructions on the computer screen will then explain the experiment and what keys to use for your responses. Speed of responding does not matter. Rather, you should try to be as accurate as possible. A template is printed at the end of this chapter, and you should cut out that template. Instructions will be given on how to use that template. *Materials needed*: Pencil and paper, if no printer is available, to copy down the results reported in the table at the end of the experiment.

Expected Running Time = 25 minutes

Questions

1. What are the dependent variables in this experiment?

2. What is the independent variable?

3. What are some important control variables? Describe the counterbalancing used in this experiment.

4. What are the results? Is one system faster and/or more accurate than the other? Do subjects show a clear preference for one system over the other? If so, is that congruent with their performance?

5. What is it about mnemonics that makes it easier to learn systems that use them? What characterizes a good mnemonic?

6. Describe a system that you have had trouble learning to use and design a brief study to explore alternative designs for such a system.

7. *External validity* refers to whether experimental results can safely be generalized to the "real world." Certain aspects of the experiment you have completed are rather artificial. Consider problems of external validity relating to the choice of subjects, type of instruction, amount of training, and lack of requiring the person to talk to someone on the phone while making the responses.

Advanced Questions

1. How might having job aids available (such as cards listing the special functions) affect performance?

2. How much money might the better system save a large university relative to the poorer system? Assume that the university has 2000 employees that regularly use the phone system 250 days per year and that they would use an average of 5 special functions (as illustrated in this experiment) per day. Also assume that every failed phone action (e.g., failed transfer of the call) costs the university $1.00. Make a projection based on the relative differences in accuracy at the end of training in your lab's data. How much would be saved by using the better system?

3. Reanalyze the data, including the order of learning the two systems as a second independent variable. Do the data suggest an asymmetry of transfer? If so, what implications does this have for the validity of this experiment?

4. Discuss the advantages and disadvantages of the experimental approach to human factors design.

5. Real-world tasks often take weeks to learn. How does this complicate interpreting research results?

Extension Experiments

1. Compare the effects of job aids (such as reference cards) to learn the digit system. What would be the benefits of pictorial, verbal, and combined reference cards?

2. How would you test reading and proof reading efficiency for text presented on a computer screen versus printed on paper (see Gould, 1968)?

3. Microwave ovens can be programmed either by entering the time directly (e.g., push 3-2-1 for 3:21) or by

pressing the units (press minutes three times, tens of seconds twice and seconds once). Which is better? Which would be better for the blind (assuming tones are sounded whenever a button is pressed)?

References

Card, S. K., Moran, T. P., & Newell, A. (Eds.) (1983). *The psychology of human-computer interaction.* Hillsdale, NJ: Erlbaum.

Deininger, R. L. (1960). Human factors studies of the design and use of push-button telephone keysets. *Bell System Technical Journal, 39*, 995-1012.

Gould, J. (1968). Visual factors in the design of computer-controlled CRT displays. *Human Factors, 10*, 359-376.

McCormick, E. J. (1976). *Human factors in engineering and design.* New York: McGraw-Hill.

Human Factors in Telephone Systems

Individual Data

Please Note: The order in which the phone systems are presented is counterbalanced across subjects. Therefore, the order in which you learned the systems may not correspond with the order in which they are listed on the table and plot.

	Phone System	
	System A AT&T System 85	System B Mnemonic System
Accuracy	____	____
Response Time	____	____

Cell entries are MEAN PERCENT CORRECT and MEAN CORRECT RESPONSE TIME (sec)

Human Factors in Telephone Systems

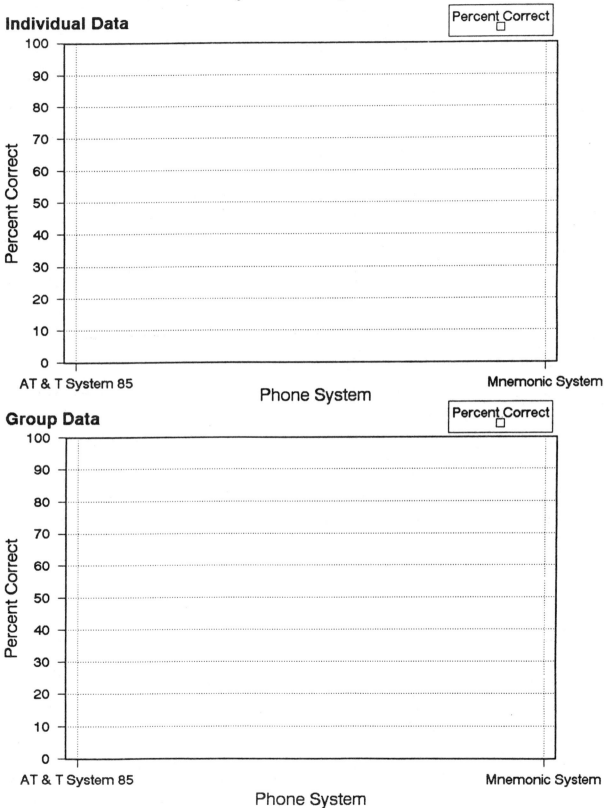

Individual Data

Percent Correct

Percent Correct

100
90
80
70
60
50
40
30
20
10
0

AT & T System 85   Mnemonic System

Phone System

Group Data

Percent Correct

Percent Correct

100
90
80
70
60
50
40
30
20
10
0

AT & T System 85   Mnemonic System

Phone System

Before running the Human Factors Telephone Systems experiment, cut out the template below and place it above the number keys on your keyboard. Use the "1" and "=" keys to line up the template's "1" and "=" symbols.

Cut along this dotted line.

	ABC	DEF	GHI	JKL	MNO	PRS	TUV	WXY		
1	2	3	4	5	6	7	8	9	0	-	=

5 Appendix: Other Information

This appendix contains some more detailed considerations of two types of research--reaction-time experiments and surveys or questionnaires.

5.1 Reaction Time Procedures

Abstract

Reaction time (RT) is the time from when a stimulus appears until a subject responds to it. RT has become a widely-used dependent variable for research on cognition, perception, and other aspects of psychology. In this exercise, the basics of RT research are outlined, including blocking versus randomization, within- versus between-subject designs, number of choices, the probability of a stimulus, and the location of the stimulus. Three experiments illustrate various aspects of RT research.

Reaction time (RT) is a standard measure in cognitive and perceptual psychology. This is reflected in the fact that many of the exercises in the MEL Lab use RT as a dependent variable. The concern for many of these exercises is how various independent variables affect RT--that is, how RT is changed when we deliberately manipulate the stimuli in some way. But RT is also affected by many variables in which we are not directly interested. These are called *control variables*. Control variables are those things (other than the independent variables deliberately being manipulated) that might affect the dependent variable in an experiment and therefore must be controlled in some way so that they do not influence the outcome.

This exercise is designed to acquaint you with some of the many control variables affecting RT. In addition, this exercise will also be concerned with the stability of RT across trials, and the issue of how many trials should be averaged in order to determine the "true" RT for a given condition of an experiment, as well as a number of other issues in RT research. Three experiments are included in this exercise, designed to illustrate the operation of several control variables.

Following a definition of RT, we present a discussion of the events that occur in a typical RT experiment. Next, we discuss a number of factors that can affect RT, and which must be considered in designing experiments employing RT as a dependent variable.

RT defined. For most research in psychology, RT is defined as *the time from the onset of a stimulus to the time the subject responds*. For the purposes of these exercises, this is the time from stimulus onset until a key is pressed indicating a response. It is important for comparing the results of different experiments to realize that RT as defined above may vary with the type of response required. For example, imagine the following simple experiment. The subjects are to indicate which of two letters was seen on the computer screen. The independent variable is clarity: the stimulus was either clearly seen or masked by visual "noise" cluttering the screen. Obviously, subjects would be faster at recognizing a clear letter than a masked one. But suppose further that we did two versions of this experiment, differing only in how the subjects respond to indicate which letter was seen. In one version, they must press the '1' and '2' keys on the computer keyboard to indicate which letter appeared. In the other version of this experiment, they must press a lever to the left or right to indicate which target letter they saw. Overall RT might well be longer in the case of the lever-press, because the mechanical resistance is higher, or because the distance to be moved is farther, or because different muscles are employed in the two types of responses. In this case, we would have to be very cautious about comparing the results of the two experiments. Differences in the obtained RT's might be due solely to mechanical factors, and not reflect any differences of interest. For this reason, we must be careful in comparing the outcomes of experiments using different responses. Whether we used a relatively fast key-press or a relatively slow lever-press will affect *overall* RT, but in either case the response to the masked letter would be slower than the response to the unmasked letter. In comparing experiments, then, the crucial issue is whether the same *pattern* of RT's is seen, rather than whether overall RT differed.

While we have defined RT as the time from stimulus onset to a response, RT is sometimes defined in other ways. In much research in kinesiology, for example, RT is defined in relation to the onset of a muscle potential (electromyographic signal), while the time from that first electrical activity in the muscle to when the response movement itself is completed is called Motor Time. *Because RT is sometimes defined differently, and because it can depend on the nature of the response apparatus, it is important in RT research that the definition of RT and the nature of the response be made explicit, and reported in the Procedures section of the research report.*

RT is also sometimes classified as *simple RT* or *choice RT*. In simple RT, a subject makes one response to a single stimulus. This requires only a judgement about the presence of a stimulus, and does not involve a decision about the nature of the stimulus. When more than one type of stimulus can occur, and the subject must indicate the stimulus type by his or her choice of responses, we are studying choice RT. In this exercise, and throughout the MEL Lab, "RT" means *choice* RT unless noted otherwise.

RT Experiments--General Considerations

In developing the general considerations for RT research, we examine issues concerning the events that take place on each *trial*, how *blocks* of trials may differ, and finally how these combine to form the *experiment* as a whole.

What happens on each trial?

Typically, RT experiments consist of one or more series (blocks) of trials. While the specific stimulus may vary from trial to trial, certain aspects of the experiment are usually the same on each trial. There is often a *fixation* mark of some kind, to let the subject know where he or she should be looking when the trial starts. *Initiation* of a trial may be under the subject's control, allowing the subject to begin a trial whenever he or she is ready. Alternatively, initiation of a trial may be automatic, controlled by the experimenter or computer. In this case, a *warning* signal is typically given, to allow the subject to get ready for the trial. (Sometimes the appearance of the fixation mark acts as the warning. Sometimes a tone or other signal is used.) After a trial is initiated (by the subject or automatically), there is usually a brief delay before the stimulus appears. This delay is called the *foreperiod*, and may vary from trial to trial or be fixed (unvarying). (The foreperiod is usually fixed for choice RT tasks.)

At the end of the foreperiod the stimulus is presented. In many experiments there is only a single event making up the overall stimulus. In others, there may be distractor elements displayed on the screen. In either event, timing of the reaction begins when the *critical stimulus* is displayed. The critical stimulus refers to the element in the display that determines the appropriate reaction (i.e. which key to press). The *stimulus duration* (how long it remains in view) will largely be controlled by the nature of the stimulus display. For example, if eye movements during the stimulus presentation could affect the experiment, a very brief (say, 100 msec) presentation is often used, since it takes some time after the stimulus appears for an eye movement to begin. If the stimulus duration is so short that the subject gets only a glance at the stimulus, the display is described as a *data-limited* display.

Another issue for defining a trial is that of how long to give the subject to respond. In most of the experiments in the MEL Lab, you must respond with a key-press within some limited time. The choice of that time depends on the sorts of RT's expected, with the time allowed being set so as to encompass any legitimate trials. If the task is an easy one, with RT on most trials being less than 500 msec, the time allowed for a response may be relatively brief--2 seconds or so. If no response occurs in that time period, the trial is counted as an omission.

Many harder tasks, however, have typical RT's of 1-2 seconds. In this case, the time allowed for a response should be increased accordingly.

Feedback about accuracy and/or RT is usually given following a response. Feedback about accuracy is usually provided, telling subjects whether they were right or wrong in their choice of a response. It should be noted, though, that subjects are generally aware of having made an incorrect response. The accuracy feedback emphasizes the importance of correct responding. Because the usual RT instructions emphasize speed of reactions, RT feedback is important, since it lets subjects monitor their own performance.

Other terminology. The *inter-trial interval* (ITI) is the time from the end of one trial to the beginning of the next. If the subjects control initiation of the next trial, they also control the ITI. When it is important to control ITI, trial initiation must be controlled by the computer or experimenter.

In some experiments, there may be more than just a single stimulus. For example, if subjects must judge whether two letters they see are the same or different, they might see one letter and then see the second some short time later. That delay before the second stimulus is the *inter-stimulus interval* (ISI). The ISI is time from the onset of the first stimulus to the onset of the second. Another term for this is *stimulus onset asynchrony*, or SOA.

What happens in a block of trials?

The entire series of trials making up an experiment is usually divided into *blocks* of trials. That division may simply reflect time constraints. In a long experiment, we want to be sure that subjects take occasional pauses, so we may break the entire series into shorter blocks, with rest pauses between them. More importantly, the division of the experiment into blocks may be an integral part of the experiment itself. The rest of this section treats that situation.

Blocked versus random presentation. Suppose there are two or more different sorts of trials being presented in an experiment (comprising two or more levels of each independent variable). A question to consider is whether these different sorts of trials should be presented together in each block with the two types alternating in *random* order, or whether the series of trials should be *blocked*, with all trials of one type presented, followed by all trials of the other.

Suppose that we ran two experiments in which subjects must respond by pressing the correct key to indicate either which of four letters is present (four-choice RT), or which of only 2 letters is present (two-choice RT). The two experiments differ only in whether the two types of trials (two-and four-choice) occur *randomly* (within a single block), or are *blocked*, with all of the two-choice trials occurring together, and all of the four-choice trials occurring together.

The typical outcome of such experiments is graphed in Figure 5.1.1. Note that both experiments show that four-choice RT is longer than two-choice RT, which is just as expected. But the difference between two- and four-choice RT is considerably larger for blocked presentation than for random presentation. That is, *the results of the experiment depend (in part) on the choice of blocked versus random presentation of the stimulus types.* Why should this be so? In this experiment, the explanation seems to be that random presentation leads the subjects to sometimes ignore whether the trial is two- or four-choice. That is, the subjects seeing the stimuli in random order may treat many of the two-choice trials as if the were four-choice. That raises the mean RT for two-choice responses, while having no effect on four-choice responses.

In general, then, the choice of random or blocked presentation must depend on whether subjects given random ordering of trials will adopt different strategies than those given blocked order. In the case of the experiment above, subjects in the random-order experiment seem to have often adopted the strategy of ignoring whether there

Figure 5.1.1 Typical outcome of an experiment comparing two and four-choice RT using blocked and random presentation

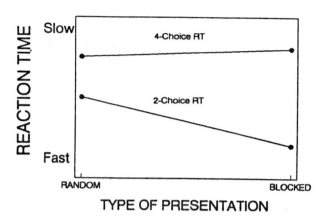

were two choices or four, and treating many two-choice trials as if they were four-choice trials. Thus, the blocked version gives us the better estimate of the actual time required for two or four choices.

When blocked presentation is used, the issue of *counterbalancing* of treatment orders is raised. In the blocked version of the two- versus four-choice experiment (two levels of one independent variable), half of the subjects did the two-choice trials first, while half did the four-choice trials first. This counterbalancing is designed to remove (or at least balance) any effects of carry-over from one block of trials to the next.

Certain control variables are almost always controlled by counterbalancing. One is the mapping of stimuli to responses. If we were interested in comparing the speed of reactions to the targets 'S' and 'H' in the two-choice version of the experiment above, we would need to have half of the subjects respond by pressing the '1' key for S and the '2' key for H. Half would respond in the opposite way, pressing the '2' key for S. This controls for any possible difference in RT due to the different responses themselves, and is necessary because some muscular actions take longer than others.

If we were not actually comparing responses to 'S' and 'H,' but instead averaged these trials together, this counterbalancing may not be necessary. In other experiments, however, it can be absolutely crucial. In the exercise on "Perceptual Matching" (Section 1.4), for example, subjects must indicate that two stimuli are the same by pressing one key, or that they are different by pressing another. Since one aspect of that experiment is to compare "same" and "different" responses, it is important to counterbalance the mapping of the response keys to same and different stimuli. Otherwise, we might find a difference between "same" and "different" responses and conclude that the differences in the stimuli caused that difference, when it was really just due to a lack of proper counterbalancing. (Alternatively, a failure to counterbalance might lead to a finding of no difference, when there really was one.)

What happens within the whole experiment?

An experiment is composed of one or more blocks of trials. If the experiment is particularly long, it may be broken down into *sessions* of one or more blocks each. In that case, counterbalancing of blocks across sessions may also be required. An experiment most often begins with *instructions* about the nature of the experiment, and some *practice* trials. When the experiment is concluded, some form of *debriefing* is often used to show the subject the purpose of the experiment and to permit questions about it. Instructions, practice, and debriefing are considered separately below.

MEL Lab: Student Workbook v.1.6; © *PST - Do not reproduce*

Instructions. The purpose of the instructions in any experiment is to let the subject know what will be happening and what the correct responses are. In RT research, instructions should also emphasize that subjects are to respond as quickly as possible while still remaining accurate. "Accurate" is typically considered 10% or fewer errors, though this would also depend on the specific experiment.

In long experiments it is also advisable to instruct subjects that they should take occasional breaks, to rest their eyes. If trials are initiated by the subjects, these breaks are under the subjects' control. Otherwise, it is a good idea to "build in" breaks by having blocks of trials that are fairly short (e.g., 5-10 minutes). Occasional breaks avoid having the subjects just staring at the screen and pressing keys like zombies. This means that subjects are less error-prone, and also that RT is less subject to added variability due to eye strain, mental fatigue, and the like.

Practice. Most experiments ask people to do unfamiliar tasks, and require them to indicate their responses by pressing keys that have no previous association with the stimulus. If asked to press the '1' key if an H appears and the '2' key if an S appears, subjects must first learn to associate 1 with H and 2 with S. At first, subjects will be very slow and error-prone in their responses, simply because they have to carefully think about which key to press after they identify the target letter. After a while, subjects no longer have to think about which key to press, and their responses become faster and more accurate (see Section 2.13 above on Automaticity). For this reason, we usually give considerable practice on the task before actually beginning to collect data. For the exercises in the MEL Lab, we typically give only about 10 practice trials, due to time limitations. Note, however, that most research gives far more practice. The effect of this practice is to reduce the variability of RT during the experiment itself.

In a short experiment, completed in a single session, one block of practice trials is usually all that is needed. If the experiment extends over several sessions, a brief block of practice trials is usually given at the beginning of each session and the first session is often treated as a practice. If the type of stimulus display or responses change from block to block, it might also be necessary to have practice before each block of trials.

Debriefing. When an experiment is over, it is usual to debrief the subject. The debriefing typically is a simple matter of telling the subject what pattern of RT's you expect to find and why. That is, the debriefing is used to explain to the subject what the experiment was about. Subjects may also be shown their individual results. A second reason for a debriefing is to get comments from the subjects about their own experience. While such comments may not be part of the data proper, they can sometimes reveal the use of strategies that the experimenter had not considered, or may even point up flaws in the design. Remember that subjects have spent some of their time during the experiment trying to figure out "what is going on." In doing so, they may notice things about the experiment that the experimenter never noticed--including problems.

How many trials?

Why not just have the subject respond once to each type of display, and take that single RT as the "score" for that condition? This would certainly be faster, since few trials would be needed. The problem with using this procedure, however, is that it ignores the large variability in RT that is due to factors other than the independent variables. RT varies from trial to trial, *even if the stimulus does not*. That variability comes from momentary changes in attention, among other things. Note that we cannot pay attention evenly and uniformly for any length of time. Even when you are listening to a fascinating lecture, you will find your attention wandering from time to time. The same thing happens in RT experiments, when the subject sits doing trial after trial. Occasionally, subjects will start a trial when their attention is not focussed on the task. When this happens, a very long RT usually results. Long RT's due to inattentiveness would be expected to occur about equally often for all stimulus types, so averaging a few such trials with many others creates no problem.

Another way to look at the problem of number of trials per condition is to realize that the RT on each trial provides an estimate of that subject's "true" RT for that condition. Each individual estimate is not very reliable, for the reasons given above. We therefore combine a number of estimates (RT's on many trials), to provide a better (more reliable) estimate of "true" RT. If you have had a statistics course, you will have been introduced to the notion of a *confidence interval*. Recall that the confidence interval estimate of the population mean becomes more and more precise as the sample size increases. Similarly, our estimate of true RT becomes better and better as sample size increases--though in this instance, sample size refers to the number of trials per subject, rather than the number of subjects. By employing the formula for the confidence interval, you could determine the number of trials needed to have a certain level of accuracy. For most purposes, however, such precision is unnecessary. In practice, 15-30 trials per condition per subject seem to provide a satisfactory result. This is enough trials that a few aberrant trials will have little effect on the mean RT for that condition. In the exercises in the MEL Lab there are sometimes fewer trials than this, because some limitations were required to complete the exercise in part of a single class period. In actual research, on the other hand, time limitations are less of a problem, and far greater power is obtained when each subject's RT for each condition is based on a larger number of trials.

Between- versus within-subjects designs.

Another issue of importance to RT experiments is that of whether the independent variables should be manipulated between subjects or within subjects. *Between-subjects* variables are ones where different subjects are tested at each level of the variable. For our example of two- versus four-choice RT, that would mean that subjects do *either* the two-choice version *or* the four-choice version, but not both. *Within-subjects* variables are those where each subject is tested at each level of the variable. For our example, this would mean that each subject does *both* two-*and* four-choice trials (either in random or blocked order).

Which method is preferred? Suppose we wanted to determine the effect of alcohol on RT's to a simple stimulus, and we have 20 subjects available. We could randomly assign 10 subjects to perform the task drunk and 10 to perform it sober, then compare those mean RT's. This would be a between-subjects design. But why not test each subject both sober and drunk? That way we have 20 subjects in each condition. This would be a within-subjects design. (Of course, we would want to counterbalance the order, and test some subjects sober and then drunk, and others drunk and then sober.) It should be clear that an analysis based on 20 subjects per group is more powerful than one based on only 10 subjects per group. (Note that the type of statistical analysis would change slightly, since a within-subjects design violates the assumption of independent samples. In this case, comparing two means, we would use the *t*-test for independent samples with the between-subject design, and the *t*-test for dependent ("correlated", "matched-pairs") samples with the within-subject design.)

The main thing to note about the example above is that a within-subjects design is clearly better. But there are severe limitations to its use as well. A within-subjects design works fine in this example because if we test subjects drunk, then test them sober a few days later, we can be fairly sure that the only systematic difference in them is in whether or not they are sober. Similarly, when comparing RT to two versus four stimuli, we can be fairly sure that making a choice between two stimuli does not have a later effect on making a choice between four stimuli (or vice-versa)--at least if we have blocked the trials. But in many situations we cannot make the assumption that there is no carry-over from one condition to another. For example, if we wanted to compare RT to naming meaningless shapes following two different types of training we would have to use a between-subjects design, because if we have a subject learn something by one method we cannot then "erase" that learning. If they performed faster following the second round of learning, is it because that method of learning is better? Or is the difference simply due to the *added* learning? Another situation in which we are forced to employ a between-subjects design is when the variable is "attached" to the person, and cannot be experimentally manipulated. Variables of this kind include sex, race or ethnic background, and religion. Also when experiments take many hours per subject, it may be easier to run many subjects in parallel for only a few hours than to run a few subjects for many weeks.

In general, then, within-subjects designs are to be preferred *if* we can reasonably assume that there are no carry-over effects of one level of an independent variable on performance at other levels of that independent variable. If we cannot make that assumption, we must employ a between-subjects design.

There are also some experiments that employ *both* within- and between-subjects independent variables. These are usually referred to as *mixed* designs. For example, suppose in the two- versus four-choice RT experiment that we wanted to compare the patterns of RT's for males and females. Our two independent variables would be number of choices and sex. Number of choices (two vs four) would be a within-subjects variable, for the reasons outlined above. But sex (male vs. female) would be a between-subjects variable, since no subject could be in both groups.

Other considerations in RT research.

A number of other factors that must be considered in designing research employing RT as a dependent variable are discussed below. Wickens (1984, Chapter 9) provides a more detailed account of most of these same issues.

Speed-accuracy trade-off. In research employing RT as the dependent variable, we are usually interested in showing that RT *differs* for different levels of the IV(s). A serious problem can arise, however, if the conditions associated with faster RT also have higher error rates. Such a condition is called a *speed-accuracy trade-off*, because the subjects may be trading accuracy for speed. That is, they may be faster on those trials because they are pushing themselves for speed, but ignoring the higher error rate that often goes with that effort. Consider the comparison of RT's for subjects when tested drunk and when tested sober. Suppose the mean RT was 450 msec, whether they subjects were sober or drunk. Could we conclude that alcohol had no effect on RT? If the error rate was the same for both conditions we could. But suppose further that an examination of error rates found only 5% errors when subjects were sober, but 30% errors when they were drunk. In this case, it looks as if the difference in RT is uninterpretable since subjects were responding too quickly (and hence inaccurately) when they were drunk.

Fortunately, in most RT research we do *not* encounter speed-accuracy trade-offs. In fact, most of the time the fastest conditions will have the *lowest* error rates, while the longest RT's will come in conditions with the highest error rates. In this case, difficult stimuli lead to both slow and sloppy responding. In any case, it is a wise practice to examine error rates for evidence of speed-accuracy trade-offs. To avoid this problem, instructions to the subjects usually stress that they must be as fast as they can in each condition but *without sacrificing accuracy*. That is, the error rates should be uniformly low for all conditions.

Stimulus-response compatibility. In most RT research, the connection between the stimulus and the response is arbitrary. We can have the subject press '<' for an S and '>' for an H or '>' for an S and '<' for an H--the mapping of stimulus to response is arbitrary. But occasionally the mapping is not arbitrary. Consider the same experiment, but using L and R as stimuli, instead of S and H. If you had to press '<' for an R and '>' for an L, for example, you might be both slower and more error-prone than otherwise, because of the association of L with "left" and R with "right." Making a "left" response to an R might well produce some response competition, resulting in a slowing of RT. Basically, any time a stimulus implies a certain direction of response (such as L and R implying left and right responses), there are potential problems of S-R compatibility. Stimulus-response compatibility is one of the issues addressed in the experiment Reaction Time Procedures: Retinal Locus.

Probability of a stimulus. In most of the experiments in the MEL Lab, and indeed in much research with RT as a dependent variable, we present each type of stimulus equally often. In this way, we eliminate guessing by the subject, since each stimulus is equally likely on each trial. Sometimes, however, we may present one stimulus more often than another, and this can have major effects on RT (and error rate). In general, the commoner stimulus is responded to more quickly and more accurately. Why is this so? Suppose that in the experiment on recognizing S and H we presented an H 80% of the time, and an S 20%. Subjects would quickly realize this, and would *expect* an H most of the time. On any trial, if the target *is* an H, there is likely to be a fast response. But if the target is an S, the subjects must overcome their expectancy, and their preparedness, for H. The result is a slow response, and a high probability of error.

Because of these considerations, it is best to always have the different trial types equally likely whenever randomization is used. Unequal stimulus probabilities are best avoided unless they form part of the research itself. The effects of unequal stimulus probabilities are illustrated in the experiment Reaction Time Procedures: Stimulus Probabilities. In that experiment, you will complete three blocks of trials. In one, the S and H occur equally often. In another, the S occurs 80% of the time, while in another the H occurs 80% of the time.

Number of different responses. As illustrated in the experiment Reaction Time Procedures: Number of Choices, RT increases as the number of possible responses increases. This relationship has long been known, and was quantified in the early 1950's, when Hick and Hyman, working independently, each noted that RT increases linearly with the logarithm (base 2) of the number of alternatives. What that means in effect is that additional alternatives will increase RT, but the effect of that increase is smaller as the number of responses becomes larger. This effect is not usually of much concern, but must be kept in mind when comparing the results of several experiments--if they used different numbers of response alternatives, the RT's cannot be directly compared.

Intensity and contrast. At least for low levels of illumination, the more intense the stimulus, the faster the RT. Once the stimulus reaches an intensity where it is clearly visible, however, further increases will have little effect. Similarly, increasing contrast (the difference in intensity between the stimulus and the background) will decrease RT, up to a point where the stimulus is clearly visible. Either low intensity or low contrast would produce a data-limited display.

One common problem in controlling intensity and contrast is *ambient light* (the light present in the room). A display that may seem very weak under ordinary room lighting may seem quite bright when room lights are off and windows covered. Because the conditions under which you conduct the exercises in the MEL Lab are likely to be less than ideal, we have tried to avoid experiments that would be greatly affected by ambient light. In experiments employing brief, data-limited stimulus displays (such as the measure of the duration of the icon in Section 1.2), it is important that ambient light be carefully controlled.

In addition to lowering apparent intensity and contrast, ambient light may result in glare or reflections on the display screen of the computer. In this case, lights must be shielded or the computer moved to prevent such interference.

The location of the stimulus can have a powerful effect on both RT and error rates. One experiment that accompanies this exercise illustrates this effect by asking subjects to indicate which of two letters occurred on each trial. Subjects are told to look directly at a fixation mark (+) before starting each trial. The stimulus letter then appears to either the left or right of the fixation, and either close to it or farther away. The brief, data limited (50 msec) stimulus duration was chosen so that eye movements do not play a role. (While you may indeed look toward the stimulus, the time needed to begin an eye movement after the stimulus appears is long enough that the stimulus will be gone before you can re-fixate your eyes on it.) The typical outcome of this experiment is that RT increases (along with error rates) as the stimulus moves from *foveal vision* (straight ahead) to *peripheral vision*. This effect is illustrated in the experiment Reaction Time Procedures: Retinal Locus.

The point of this experiment is that *retinal locus* (where on the retina the image of the stimulus falls) must be controlled by randomization or counterbalancing if the stimuli are not all presented in the same location. If one type of stimulus is presented in the fovea, and another in the periphery, differences in RT might occur (or fail to occur), but they could be due to differences in the location of the stimuli, rather than to differences in the stimuli themselves. Note the location of the subject's head relative to the screen must also be controlled. This is often done by use of a chin rest or viewing hood to keep the subject's head relatively stable.

Method

Three separate experiments accompany this chapter, each designed to illustrate a different point. Because each takes only about 15 minutes, you might want to complete them all.

Reaction Time Procedures: Number of Choices

This experiment employs a simple letter-identification task. Four letters (Q, J, S, and H) are responded to by pressing one of four response keys with the index and middle fingers of the two hands. Each subject completes three blocks of trials. One block consists of 20 trials of two-choice RT. For this block, only Q and J appear as targets. A second block is the same, except that only S and H appear as targets. The third block consists of 40 trials of four-choice RT, with all four letters appearing as targets. The comparison of interest is between the mean RT for the four-choice trials and the mean RT for the two-choice trials (averaged across both blocks).

Reaction Time Procedures: Stimulus Probabilities

This experiment uses three blocks of trials of a two-choice letter-identification task (indicate whether the target letter is a Q or a J). The three blocks of 40 trials each differ only in the probability of each target. In one block, the target letters are equally likely. In another block, 80% of the trials have a Q as the target, while 20% have J as the target. The third block simply reverses the probabilities to 80% for J and 20% for Q. The comparison of interest is between RT's for each target as the probability of each is manipulated. Also note that error rates may be increased, as well as RT, when a target is relatively rare.

Reaction Time Procedures: Retinal Locus

The purpose of this experiment is to illustrate the changes in RT that occur as a target moves further from foveal vision. Again, two-choice letter-identification is the task, with the two target letters equally probable. Targets occur in one of six positions: one, five, or ten spaces to right and left of the central fixation. The targets are again Q and J, with each appearing equally often in each of the six possible positions. One focus of this experiment is whether RT increases as the targets appear further from straight ahead. (Since each target letter appears to both left and right of the fixation, the subject's best strategy is to look directly at the fixation.) Note that in this experiment, the stimulus letter only appears for 50 milliseconds. This fast presentation rate was used to prevent eye movements from playing a significant role in bringing the target into focus. With a presentation this brief, any eye movement will probably not begin until after the stimulus has already left the screen.

In this experiment, we have deliberately *not* counterbalanced the direction of the responses: Q is always responded to by pressing the period key (.), while J is always responded to by pressing the slash (/) key. Because of this mapping of stimulus to response, a Q appearing to the left of the fixation is responded to by pressing the left-most response key, while when a Q appears to the right of fixation, the correct response is still toward the left. The opposite holds, of course, for the response to J. One thing to examine in the data for this experiment is whether responses for a given target letter are slower when the response is made on the "opposite side" from where the target appeared.

Instructions for Running the Experiments

To run these experiments, insert Disk 1 in drive A: and type **EXPERIMENT**. Select **Appendix/Other** from the topic menu and the specific **Reaction Time Procedure** (as outlined above in the Method section) from the specific experiment menu. Instructions on the computer screen will then explain the experiment and what keys to use for your responses. You may complete each of the three versions of this experiment, as detailed above. Because these studies employ reaction time as the dependent variable, you should try to respond as quickly as possible while still keeping errors to a minimum. *Materials needed*: Pencil and paper, if no printer is available, to copy down the results reported in the table at the end of the experiment.

Expected Running Time = 18 minutes each

Questions

1. What are the independent and dependent variables for the experiments you performed for this exercise?

2. Describe the control variables involved in these experiments. Which variables are controlled by randomization? Which are controlled by counterbalancing?

3. Examine the error rates for the different conditions of one of the experiments. Is there any indication of a speed-accuracy trade-off? What indicates that such a trade-off did (or did not) occur?

4. (For Number of Choices) What is the effect of having to choose from among four choices instead of only two? If there is an effect, why might it occur?

5. (For Stimulus Probabilities) What is the effect of changing the probabilities of the stimuli? Does RT change? Do error rates change? When one target appears only 20% of the time, do you have more errors?

6. (For Retinal Locus) Does the location of the stimulus matter for reaction time? For error rates? Is there an effect of stimulus compatibility?

Advanced Questions

1. Why would it be important to *vary* the foreperiod in an experiment measuring simple RT (i.e., RT to a *single* stimulus, not involving a choice of responses)?

2. For the data from Reaction Time Procedures: Number of Choices (two- versus four-choice RT with blocked presentation), compute the dependent-samples t-test comparing the mean RT's across subjects for two- and four-choice responses two ways. For the first test, use the RT's averaged in the usual manner. That is, the two scores for each subject are their mean RT's based on 40 trials each in the two- and four-choice conditions. For the second test, simply use the first trial of each type as that subject's score for that condition. Which test is more powerful (leads to the larger value of t)?

3. Compare the power of within- and between-subjects designs in this manner. For the data from the experiment on Number of Choices, compute the dependent-samples t-test comparing the mean RT's for two- and four-choices responses. Note that this is a within-subjects design. Next, divide the subjects who performed that experiment into two groups (either randomly, or using odd- versus even-numbered subjects). For one group, assume that they did *only* the two-choice task, and for the other group, assume that they did only the four-choice task. This will result in a between-subjects design. Compare the mean RT's for two- and four-choice responses using the independent-samples t-test. What is the effect on the value of t? On the degrees of freedom?

4. As noted above, RT increases with both the number of choices *and* the probability of each target. Discuss how these are both expressed in the same unit of measurement in an information-theory approach to RT. (See Wickens, 1984, Chapter 9.)

Extension Experiments

1. Wickens (1984, Chapter 9) discusses many variables affecting RT, and many of these could easily be programmed using the MEL Lab experiment editor.

References

Wickens, C. D. (1984). *Engineering psychology and human performance*. Columbus, OH: Charles E. Merrill.

RT: Number of Choices

Individual Data

Reaction Time Procedures
RT as a Function of the Number of Choices

	Number of Choices	
	2	4
Reaction Time	——	——
Accuracy	——	——

Cell entries are MEAN CORRECT REACTION TIME (msec) and MEAN PERCENT CORRECT

RT: Number of Choices

Individual Data

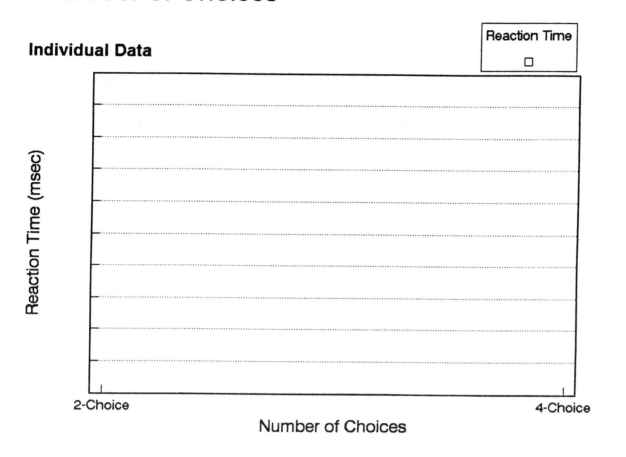

Reaction Time
☐

Reaction Time (msec)

2-Choice   4-Choice

Number of Choices

RT: Stimulus Probabilities

Individual Data

Reaction Time Procedures
RT as a Function of the Probability of a Stimulu

Probability of Each Stimulus

Target	Q=0.80/J=0.20		Q=0.50/J=0.50		Q=0.20/J=0.80	
	Q	J	Q	J	Q	J
Reaction Time	_____	_____	_____	_____	_____	_____
Accuracy	_____	_____	_____	_____	_____	_____

Cell entries are MEAN CORRECT REACTION TIME (msec) and MEAN PERCENT CORRECT

RT: Stimulus Probabilities

Individual Data

Target = Q Target = J
□   ○

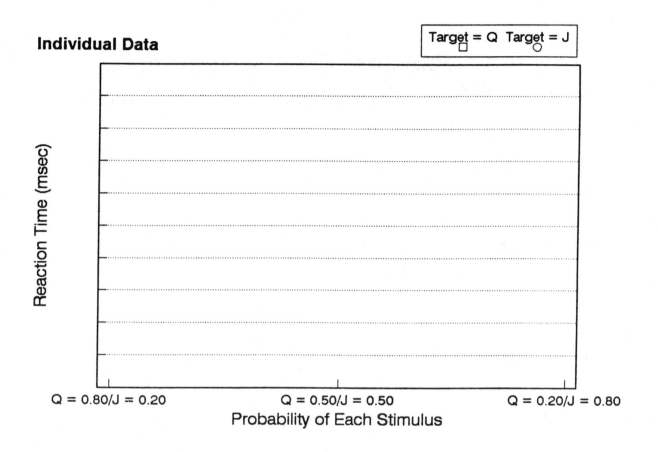

Reaction Time (msec)

Q = 0.80/J = 0.20   Q = 0.50/J = 0.50   Q = 0.20/J = 0.80
Probability of Each Stimulus

RT: Retinal Locus

Individual Data

Reaction Time Procedures
RT as a Function of Retinal Locus

Direction of Target From Center

	Left			Right		
Number of Spaces	1	5	10	1	5	10
Reaction Time	_____	_____	_____	_____	_____	_____
Accuracy	_____	_____	_____	_____	_____	_____

Cell entries are MEAN CORRECT REACTION TIME (msec) and MEAN PERCENT CORRECT

MEL Lab: Student Workbook v.1.6; © PST - Do not reproduce

RT: Retinal Locus

Individual Data

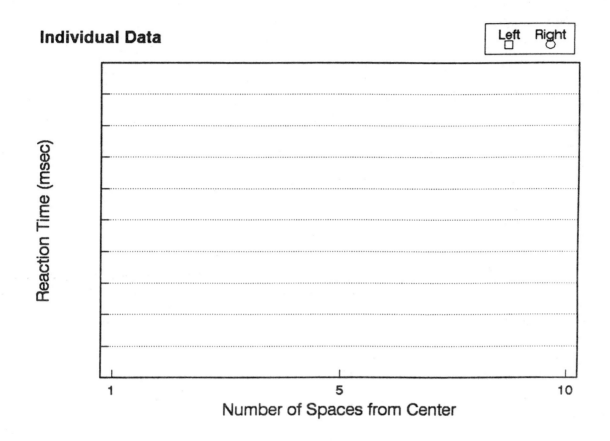

Left	Right
□	○

Reaction Time (msec)

1   5   10

Number of Spaces from Center

5.2 Surveys and Questionnaires

While much of MEL Lab is concerned with experimental research, many researchers in psychology also rely on questionnaires of various kinds to explore both individual differences (for example, scales to measure personality traits) and social-psychological problems such as attitudes towards various social issues. Of course, surveys and questionnaires are also used by sociologists and public-opinion pollsters for studying similar issues. In this appendix we present some basic information about surveys and questionnaires, including their construction and analysis, and issues of sampling. In addition, details are given for creating your own questionnaires using MEL. This brief presentation makes no claim to treat the topic of survey research in more than an introductory manner, and the student is advised to consult one (or several) of the many textbooks on survey research for more details. The reference list at the end of this chapter lists several books that may be helpful.

We begin with some suggestions for surveys that you might want to carry out. Next, we address a number of issues of item construction, sampling, and data analysis. Finally, we detail the use of MEL Lab's Survey program to construct your own survey.

Suggestions for Surveys

A problem confronting the student who is interested in carrying out a survey as a class assignment or project is to identify a topic for the survey, an appropriate population from which to sample, and a means of sampling. Herewith are two suggestions. In the section below on *sampling* we give a detailed discussion of how you might sample from (a) students on your campus and (b) citizens in your community.

Replicating a published poll

One good approach is to find a public opinion poll of some kind and then administer that same poll (or some questions from it) to a new sample taken from your community or from students at your college. An excellent source for poll results are the journals *Public Opinion* and *Public Opinion Quarterly*. Many of their articles are devoted to discussing the results of all kinds of polls. Another source is the *General Social Survey* (see Davis & Smith, 1985). If you can find a poll that was based on a national sample of college students, you could do an interesting comparison of your campus to the national figures.

Several recent polls have questioned undergraduates concerning their knowledge of world events, geography, history, etc., and have usually found a rather low level of knowledge. It might be interesting to replicate such a poll, especially if you think your school will do very well. Of course, one limitation of such polls is that they don't usually *compare* the undergraduates to another sample (say, of college-educated adults). This limitation means that you can really draw few conclusions. Are students really less well-prepared than they used to be? You should consider, if you undertake this kind of poll, how you can sample from a relevant control group. While the faculty at your school are hardly representative of the whole adult population, they are handy. And a comparison of students to faculty might prove interesting, whether the survey is based on knowledge, attitude, or belief.

Making your own poll

If you choose to write your own poll, instead of replicating an existing one, you may find that the most convenient populations from which to sample are students at your college or university and citizens of the city where you live. Possible topic areas include subjects of current interest to students or the community, such as crime on campus, the quality of dorm life and cafeteria food, attitudes toward city government, preferences in an upcoming local election, opinions about local public schools, and many others. Try to choose a topic about which people are likely to have an interest. This not only makes it easier to get people to respond, but also means that the responses will be less haphazard than if you ask for opinions on something about which your respondents know little and care nothing.

Ethical Considerations

Before discussing the construction of surveys and issues of sampling, we need to address some ethical problems that can easily arise, especially when sampling from students on your campus.

Informed consent to participate is a necessary part of *any* research using human subjects. Surveys do not have a major problem in this regard, since it is difficult to force people to take a poll against their will. The mere fact that they agree to participate establishes informed consent, since they know precisely what question they are answering--no deception is possible. But problems can arise. **Do not use fraternity or sorority pledge classes as respondents.** If you are in a fraternity or sorority, this might seem like an easy way to get some subjects. However, such persons will likely not feel that they can refuse a request from a fraternity brother or sorority sister to participate. If that is the case (and note that you probably will have no way to tell), then informed consent has *not* been obtained. (In addition to the ethical problem, this group would hardly constitute a representative sample of college students.)

Confidentiality is another potential problem. Respondents have an absolute right to assume that their individual responses will *not* be made public or used against them. Be sure that the survey data are recorded in such a manner that individual respondents cannot be identified later. This is best accomplished by simply not recording the respondents names. If you do keep a temporary list of names, destroy it as soon as it is no longer needed. Remember that **you** have the responsibility to maintain confidentiality. This is not an abstract principle: **do not discuss a respondent's individual answers with *anyone*** in a manner that will identify the respondent. That includes your friends, other students with whom you are working on the survey, as well as the instructor. (Of course, you might have a respondent ask you about various items at a later time. In that case, they are revealing their responses, and you have no ethical problem.)

Revealing how a fellow student responded may seem innocuous, and in many cases it is hard to see how any harm could come. But keep in mind that violating confidentiality may make it harder for you to get additional respondents, or may make future surveys by other classes impossible.

Construction of Questionnaires

The construction of good surveys or questionnaires is not an easy task. Our own biases and hidden assumptions can shape the items in ways that seriously affect the responses. We hope that the following discussion can aid you in avoiding some pitfalls. Unfortunately, there are no rules that guarantee success. There is one rule that can at least help you avoid some mistakes: *Always pretest the survey items.* The most careful researcher may sometimes write a bad item. By having a number of people critique the items before they are used you may at least manage to eliminate ones that are clearly inadequate.

General considerations

One of the immediate difficulties faced in writing a survey or questionnaire concerns the problem of defining and measuring the concepts in which you are interested. To illustrate: suppose that you want to survey students at your college or university concerning their attitudes toward religion. You could just ask them to rate their attitude as positive or negative. But clearly this leaves a lot to be desired, since attitudes about religion could vary in the *degree* to which they are positive or negative. You could instead ask subjects to give a rating of their attitude along a scale with several points, such as strongly positive, positive, neutral, negative, and strongly negative. But even this may not do so well, since it fails to define "religion." Some persons may feel negatively toward "organized" religion but still feel that religious belief plays a very positive role in their lives. "Religion" may mean vastly different things to different people, so that they are, in effect, answering different questions! In addition, a single item testing this attitude may not serve as well as a series of items designed to reflect various different aspects of religion: How often do you attend church? Are you a member of a church? Do you believe that religion is a force for good in the world? (Of course, the use of multiple items attempting to assess the same basic construct then leads to the difficulty of whether or how to combine those items into an overall score of "attitude toward religion.")

The point here is not that *religion* is hard to define, and attitudes toward it hard to measure, but that most social constructs, and the terms used to describe them, are ambiguous. But too often we believe that we "know" what a term, like religion, means. This belief may not pose a problem if the respondents to the survey share that meaning, but we cannot assume that they do.

Content of items

Survey items usually address one of three content areas: facts, beliefs, and feelings or attitudes.

Items dealing with facts are perhaps the easiest to write: Do you contribute to the United Way? Do you use the public library? Do you use Brand X? This class of items can usually be made clear and unambiguous, but may still lead to problems if asking about past behavior. Limitations of memory and availability of the information must be taken into account. A pretest should identify any items that respondents might misinterpret.

Items dealing with beliefs would include such things as: Does the United Way spend your contribution on the most important community needs? Does the public library have the types of books you enjoy reading? Does Brand X get your clothes cleaner than your previous brand? Availability of information is again important. If a pretest indicates that most respondents do not know anything about the content area, then you may want to revise or omit the item, since people will often respond even when they have no knowledge, leading to very "noisy" data.

Feelings and attitudes can also be assessed with surveys, using items such as: How do you feel about the United Way? Do you approve of the way the President is handling his job? Do you enjoy doing laundry? Survey items designed to elicit information about feelings and attitudes may often be more difficult to construct than those simply asking for information, because they are more likely to be ambiguous and to depend on context. The same person who admires the President's handling of domestic issues may be disturbed by his foreign policy, for example. In that case, their answer to a question about approval of the President's handling of his job may depend on which context (foreign or domestic) is most readily recalled or most recently in the news.

Types of items

A number of types of items are available for use on surveys. These can take the form of questions ("Do you know anyone who has used illegal drugs?") or statements ("I believe that the death penalty is a deterrent to crime") with which the respondent must indicate a degree of agreement. You should not feel that you are restricted to only a single type of item; a combination is often used. Suit the item to the information you are trying to gain. No single type is best for all purposes.

In addition to choosing the forms of the items, you must also choose the form of the answers. Answers can be indicated in an *open-ended* or *closed-ended* fashion. In the former, no limit is put on the choice of answers, while in the latter the respondent must choose from the available responses. Open-ended questions have the advantage of not forcing the responses into a preconceived "mold," but have the serious disadvantage of often being difficult to analyze, especially if the respondent gives long answers. Closed-ended questions have the advantage of ease of scoring, but you must be sure that the alternatives offered cover all relevant categories. The following particularly bad example was actually used on a survey. Respondents were asked to indicate their religion, with alternatives of "Protestant," "Catholic," "Hindu," "Moslem," or "None." Not only are many religions (Judaism, Buddhism, etc.) omitted entirely, but no "Other" category is offered. Are Buddhism and atheism really the same thing? To make matters even worse, many Christians do not regard themselves as either Catholic or Protestant. These include members of the Greek and Russian Orthodox churches, Mormons, and many evangelicals, as well as others.

Responses to questions and statements are often measured along a scale. One example is the Likert scale, which consists of a series of graded responses indicating degree of agreement with a statement, such as strongly agree, agree, neutral, disagree, strongly disagree. Scales usually have from 5 to 9 response categories with which to indicate strength of agreement. Of course, the scale could also be labelled to indicate degree of approval/disapproval, belief/disbelief, or some other dimension. The number of response categories to permit should be neither to large nor too small. With fewer than five categories a problem will arise because respondents tend to avoid the most extreme response categories. At the other extreme, nine categories is about as many as respondents can reliably discriminate.

Pitfalls

No list of problems that can arise in items can be exhaustive, but a few can be pointed out.

Clarity. Items should be readily understood. Do not assume that the respondent will know the latest jargon about governmental (or other) matters. An item like "Do you support increased funding for SDI research?" may well lead to a blank stare instead of an answer, unless the respondent is familiar with the program. Respondents may feel obliged to provide an answer, or not want to appear ignorant, and give a meaningless answer to what is (to them, and therefore in fact) a meaningless question.

Items are sometimes unclear because they really ask two questions at once. Suppose respondents are asked to rate their agreement with the following statement: "Military spending is too high, and the money could better be used to clean up the environment." If they say they agree, just what are they agreeing to? One could surely favor reducing military spending without necessarily wanting the government to spend the money on something else! It would be better to first ask about military spending and then ask those who favor reducing it the additional question of how the savings should be used.

Length. Most respondents will expect to be able to read and understand an item quickly. Long items may not be read thoroughly, leading to responses that are not truly indicative of the respondent's views. There is often a trade-off between length and clarity, and the researcher must weigh that balance. Pre-testing can help identify items that are either unclear or too long.

Negative items. Avoid these; they may be misunderstood or misread. Asking respondents to rate their agreement with "The death penalty is a deterrent to crime" will cause fewer misunderstandings than the same rating of agreement with "The death penalty is not a deterrent to crime." If the respondent overlooks the "not" in the statement, he or she may well give the opposite answer from what was intended.

"Biased" items. There are many kinds of bias that can creep into questions, and they cannot all be detailed here. The main point, though, is to avoid wording questions in ways that might make certain types of answers unacceptable. Imagine a question like this: "Do you agree with Adolph Hitler's view that communism will ultimately fail?" Even an ardent anti-communist might not want to appear to be associating himself with Hitler. A positive bias can occur as well, in an item such as "The President has warned that we face a growing trade deficit and recommends increased tariffs. Do you agree that increased tariffs are the best solution?" A respondent who has no real opinion of his or her own may reply "Yes" simply based on the president's endorsement.

"Personal" questions. Try to provide alternatives that make it easy for the respondent to reply. For example, it is best not to simply ask people to report their income. Many will feel this is highly intrusive. Asking them instead to indicate which range of income they fall in will often work much better. "Do you earn a. less than

$10,000 per year? b. between $10,000 and $20,000," etc. is less likely to make the respondent ill-at-ease. Additionally, you should avoid starting a survey with personal questions. Save them for later, when the respondent has relaxed a little and gotten used to the types of questions you are asking.

Ordering of questions

The ordering of the questions within a survey may also affect the outcome. Imagine, for example, a survey that has a series of questions about the respondent's perception of drug use in the community, followed by a question like "What is the greatest problem facing America today?" You should not be surprised if they rate drug use as one of the worst problems, since you just spent a few minutes bringing it to their attention. The same question asked of the same person in a more neutral context might well elicit a different answer.

Sampling

Populations and samples

The principle purpose of most surveys is *not* to find out what the specific respondents interviewed feel about an issue, but rather to use their answers to try to estimate how the whole community, state, or nation feels. In other words, we use our *sample* to try to estimate something about the whole *population*. A population consists of everyone of the type being studied. That might mean all adults, all likely voters, all students at your college or university, all citizens of the United States, or all of whatever group you are interested in. If you want to know how the citizens of your city feel about some recent political event you could, of course, simply ask them all. You could then say with precision that (at least on a certain date), say, 74.2% opposed a bond issue for new schools, while 11.6% favored it, with the rest having not made up their minds. Here, the population is all voters in the town, but clearly you cannot reasonably expect to interview every single one of them, unless you live in a very small town! A major issue for survey research, then, is how to restrict yourself to a small enough number of interviews that you can get the job done, but still have the results apply to the whole population. To do this, you must select a sample of voters in the community. If you are careful in your selection, you can then make reasonable (though not perfect) predictions, based on your sample, about what percent of the whole population have a certain opinion.

Sample selection

In selecting a sample from a population, the single most important issue is whether the sample is *representative* of the population. If it is not, then the whole survey is simply a waste of time. A number of approaches can be taken for sampling, but the most common is some variety of *random* sampling. The basic idea behind random sampling is to select members of the population in such a manner that each member has the same probability of being in the sample. If this is done, then the proportions of different groups in the sample should be about the same as their proportions in the population. Several problems arise, however. In a large population, it may be nearly impossible in practice to randomly select individual people. In addition, random samples can vary in their characteristics from those of the population. While this does not happen often, it can happen. Several modifications of "simple" random sampling have been developed, and a few are outlined here. Following that, there is a brief discussion of how to choose randomly among a set of elements.

Stratified random sampling. An approach used by most public opinion polls is to select respondents randomly, but with a constraint--namely, that the proportions of different types of respondents must fit the proportions of the population. Thus, if African-Americans make up 12% of the national population, they should make up 12% of the sample, and so on for other groups. The variables (ethnicity, in this example) that define the strata should be ones that are likely to affect the outcome of the survey, and you then select persons within a stratum randomly. The strata to choose will depend on the type of population and the type of survey. For example, national opinion polls at election time often stratify on sex, race, religion, party preference, age, and region of the country, since each of these is known to be related to voting patterns in national elections. For other populations and other issues, very different strata might be chosen. For a stratified random sample of students at your college or university, for example, you might stratify on year in school, grade point average, and major. The main thing to remember is that a stratified random sample will result in certain variables (the strata) being guaranteed to be represented in the sample in the same proportions as in the population.

Clustering represents another modification of simple random sampling. Suppose that you wanted to collect a state-wide sample of high-school students. Getting a list of all high-school students in the state and then randomly selecting from that list would be an arduous task, to say the least. A way to reduce the problem to manageable size would be to first take a random sample of high schools, and then get a random sample of students within each school. The randomly chosen schools from which the randomly chosen samples came are thus the "clusters" for our sample.

Clustering also offers a solution to a problem encountered in telephone surveys. If you randomly sample from the listing of numbers in the telephone book you will be missing some of the 10-25% of households that have unlisted numbers. Randomly generated telephone numbers are a way around this, but at any time as many as 80% of the possible numbers within a given prefix are not in use, resulting in a great deal of wasted time. A way to avoid this is to call a single number within each cluster of 100 numbers (such as 424-6300 to 424-6399). If it is not a number in use, then eliminate that cluster (e.g., 6300-6399) from further calling, since most of the rest of those numbers will also be unused. If the number is in use, then interview that person and keep calling numbers in that cluster until some pre-set number is reached (say 5 responses), then begin looking for another cluster. This is likely to reduce the number of calls to non-working numbers to only 50% or so (high, but not as high as 80%), and will include a random sample of unlisted numbers.

Other techniques. Other techniques of sampling are available, and books on survey research will detail them. One we will note briefly here is to combine stratification with clustering. In the example above of selecting a sample of high-school students by first selecting a sample of high schools, you might want to also impose stratification, selecting rural, small town, and big city high schools in proper proportion to the population, and then randomly selecting your clusters of high schools from within each stratum. You might also then stratify within each selected cluster (school), so that males and females, and different classes, are represented in the correct proportions. You would then randomly sample individuals within each stratum (sex, class).

How *not* to sample. A word of caution is needed about one method *not* to use in selecting a sample. You have doubtless seen "reader's polls" conducted by popular magazines, television shows, and newspaper columnists, who ask their readers to call a "900" number or to fill out a card and send it in. The results are then tabulated and presented as meaningful information about the general population. **Do not be fooled.** At the absolute best, these samples are representative only of the readers of that magazine or column. They are usually not even that good, however, since the sample was *self-selected*: only people who really wanted to responded. If the survey concerns anything at all controversial (say, opinions on abortion) the sample is probably only representative of people who read that magazine and have a strong opinion on the issue. People who do not have a firm opinion, and people who do not have an extreme opinion, are far less likely to respond to such a poll. The result is that such "unscientific" polls are uninterpretable. (Of course, self-selection may operate in a random sample, since not everyone will be willing to complete the survey. But unless respondents with one particular view are far more likely than others to refuse to complete a survey, there should be little systematic bias, and people with extreme views will almost certainly not predominate.) Note, no matter how strong or large the self-selected group's opinion is (e.g., of ten thousand surveyed 90% agree), it can *not* be assumed to provide a useful estimate of a larger unselected population.

Sample size

How large does a sample need to be? The easy answer is "As large as possible." But please keep in mind that **the size of a sample can never be large enough if the sample is not representative.**

The selection of the sample size is rather complex, and beyond the scope of this workbook (see the references (especially Kalton, 1983), or other books on survey methodology). The general approach, however, involves the notion of a *confidence interval*, which you may have encountered in a statistics course. You have probably heard the results of opinion polls on the news, reporting the percentage of people who favor or oppose some view or candidate. That discussion usually contains a statement something like "This poll has a margin of error of plus or minus three percentage points." They are reporting the 95% confidence interval for that proportion. A 95% confidence interval means that if 45% of the respondents in the *sample* favored candidate X, we can be 95% certain that the true percentage in the *population* was between 42% and 48% (45% plus or minus 3%). (That is, we can assume that if we repeated the poll 100 times, the sample proportion favoring candidate X would be between 42 and 48% in 95 or more of those 100 samples.) The general approach to determining sample size is to turn that on its head. Instead of asking what the confidence interval is, given your sample size, you can choose how accurate you want the sample to be (within 3%, 1%, 10%, or whatever) and then find the sample size that will yield that level of accuracy when estimating a population proportion from a sample proportion.

You should keep in mind that you do not need as large a sample if you are not interested in comparing sub-groups of the sample. If you want, for example, to compare the proportions of males and females favoring a candidate, or holding a given view, then a larger sample size will be needed than if you are only interested in determining what proportion of the general population holds that view.

Sampling from Your School or Community

Students at your school and citizens of your community make good populations from which to sample for a class project. Several considerations in such sampling are given below.

Sampling randomly. Selection of a random sample from your school can be done fairly easily, since most schools publish a campus directory. (A few students may have asked to be omitted from that directory, but they should be few enough to cause no problems.) One scheme would be to randomly select a page number (using a table of random numbers or computer-generated random numbers), then randomly select an entry on that page. Simply continue this until you have enough names on your list, then contact each of those persons and ask them to complete the survey (by phone, by mail, or in face-to-face interviews).

A random sample of either people or households in your community may be a bit more difficult. If you plan to do a mail survey, check to see whether a city directory is published that would list all addresses. For a telephone survey you could use the local telephone directory, the city directory, or random numbers added to the three-digit prefixes used locally. (See the discussion above concerning telephone survey sampling.)

Stratification. If you use a stratified random sample, the choice of the strata will depend in part on the nature of the survey. Some general considerations for sampling from students at your school might include the following. Stratify on sex of the respondent, matching your sample to the proportions of males and females at your school. Stratify on whether a person is a member of a fraternity or sorority, with independents and "greeks" represented in your sample in the same proportions as in the population of all students. Stratify on class standing (freshman, sophomore, etc.), again matching your sample to the proportions in the population (usually far more freshmen than seniors). You might also choose to stratify on the basis of college (Liberal Arts, Engineering, Business, etc.) or major (or both). The registrar at your school can provide you with a breakdown of how many students are in each college or major.

If your population of interest is the community, you will face somewhat different problems. Stratification by sex is relatively easy. You certainly want to avoid having your sample be unrepresentative in regard to "socio-economic status," but this is difficult to determine without extensive questioning that many respondents will find invasive. A good strategy to adopt would be to stratify on location within the community. If you use a map, you can keep track of the locations of the households surveyed, and can then be sure that all sections of the community are represented. This should lead to reasonably good representation of wealth, ethnicity, and other factors.

Writing Your Own Surveys using MEL Lab

Your instructor has files that you may use to create your own questionnaires. Your instructor may hand out instructions on how to make MEL Questionnaires. However, before creating a computerized questionnaire, consider whether a computerized survey is the right approach. A survey conducted on the computer has the advantage of automatically entering the data for later analysis (either using the SANALYZE program that your instructor has or using other statistical packages), but it has some drawbacks as well. One is simply that you have to have a computer! Many times it is either impractical or impossible to bring the respondents to the computer, or the computer to them. (You might not want to carry it door-to-door.) Using the Survey program for your own computerized survey will be most practical if you are only using a small sample, or for a telephone survey. If you have a telephone and a computer you could fairly easily sample from your town or college, using the Survey program to present the questions for you to read to the respondent, and then allowing you to enter the respondents' answers immediately.

You can create your own computerized questionnaires by basically editing the text of the questions. Your instructor has a sample questionnaire experiment you can run and instructions on how to: add questions; specify the type of questions (e.g., multiple choice, bi-polar, fill-in and matching); modify the text for the instructions, question, alternatives and answer; and analyze the questionnaire data.

References

Babbie, E. (1973). *Survey Research Methods.* Belmont (Calif.): Wadsworth.

Bradburn, N. & Sudman, S. (1989). *Polls and Surveys: Understanding What They Tell Us.* San Francisco: Jossey-Bass.

Davis, J. & Smith, T. (1985). *General Social Surveys, 1972-1985: Cumulative Codebook.* Chicago: National Opinion Research Center.

Gallup, G. (1978). *The Gallup Poll: Public Opinion, 1972-1977.* Wilmington (Delaware): Scholarly Resources.

Gallup, G. (1979 to present). *The Gallup Poll.* Wilmington (Delaware): Scholarly Resources. (Annual volumes.)

Kalton, G. (1983). *Introduction to Survey Sampling.* Sage University Paper series on Quantitative Applications in the Social Sciences, Number 07-035. Beverly Hills (Calif.): Sage Publications.

Sudman, S. & Bradburn, N. (1982). *Asking Questions: A Practical Guide to Questionnaire Design.* San Francisco: Jossey-Bass.